2/16/

TO NATIONAL FUND -

THANKS FOR LOADING
THE BATTLE TO
INSURE THERE IS
NO SECOND TERM!

SECOND TERM

A NOVEL OF
AMERICA IN THE LAST DAYS

JOHN PRICE

Christian House Publishing, Inc.

SECOND TERM

A NOVEL OF AMERICA IN THE LAST DAYS

Copyright © 2012 by John Price

www.SECONDTERM.com

www.ENDOFAMERICABOOK.com

Library of Congress Control Number – 2011916857

Price, John
SECOND TERM
A Novel of America in the Last Days

ISBN-13: 978-0-9840771-4-4 (Kindle)

Printed in the United States of America

Published Books by the Author

AMERICA AT THE CROSSROADS

Repentance or Repression

Christian House Publishing, Inc. 1976

AMERICA AT THE CROSSROADS

Tyndale House, 1979

THE END OF AMERICA

2nd Edition, 2011

(Available in print form on Amazon and e-version on Kindle)

SECOND TERM

A Novel of America in the Last Days

Second Term is Book One of a trilogy of novels arising from events that may well occur in the second term of an American President.

The *Second Term* series is based on Biblical prophecy, written by five Prophets, in both the Old and New Testament. The prophetic verses reveal the future of a rich, influential and powerful end times nation.

The Following Are Facts

Borgholm, Sweden

On July 20, 2003 Pastor Ake Green stepped into the pulpit of his church in Borgholm and delivered a sermon. Because of what he said he was arrested, convicted and sentenced to time in jail. His sermon was an analysis of what the Bible says about sexual relations outside of marriage. He cited scripture in support of his message that God created marriage to be between a man and a woman.

Pastor Green was charged with violating a new 2002 Swedish hate speech law under which "express(ing) disrespect for a group of people" is a crime punishable by a jail sentence of either two or four years. Just before its passage, Swedish Prime Minister Goran Persson told the Swedish Parliament, the Riksgaden, that under the new hate speech law Swedish pastors and priests "would not be permitted to preach from the pulpit that homosexuality was unnatural".

The District Court in 2004 found Pastor Green guilty and sentenced him to a month in prison. The Prosecutor then requested six months as the sentence. His conviction was appealed to the Court of Appeals (Hovratt) where Pastor Green's attorney argued that his client's religious rights had been violated. In February, 2005 the Court of Appeals overturned the conviction which was then appealed by the Prosecutor to the Swedish Supreme Court.

The Supreme Court ruled that Pastor Green was guilty of violating Sweden's hate speech law. But it felt that his conviction would not be upheld by a European Court reviewing the case as it could possibly violate the European Convention on Human Rights. His conviction remains on the books.

Port Arthur, Australia

On April 28, 1996 Martin Bryant killed two persons whom he believed had cheated his father. He then drove to Port Arthur, a tourist attraction historic site, where he killed 35 shopkeepers and tourists, including twelve persons in fifteen seconds. 20 others were wounded. Bryant was a seriously disturbed psychopath. Educators and others had warned of his propensity to violence in the past. He pled guilty to all counts and was sentenced to 35 life sentences.

Australia had just elected a new Prime Minister, John Howard, who made the shootings into a national crusade to ban private ownership of guns, which was widespread. Saying that he "hated guns", that "ordinary citizens should not have weapons" and that he didn't want Australia to follow the "American example" of gun ownership, he convinced the States to adopt laws banning most private gun ownership. Public sentiment that swelled after the Port Arthur shootings overwhelmed the arguments of gun owners. Private gun ownership was prohibited (with very limited sports and hunting exceptions), with the laws requiring that guns be turned in to the government by their owners. They were paid as they turned in their guns, in that the national Constitution required that the Australian government could not take property without just compensation.

Gun ownership is only allowed for pest control, hunting, target shooting or collecting. Self-defense was not, and is not today, a valid basis for a permit to own a firearm. Each firearm is registered to the licensed owner by a traceable serial number. Australians cite the shootings at Port Arthur, located on Tasmania, a State of Australia, as the catalyst that led the nation to abolish the right of a private citizen to own a firearm.

What Follows is Fiction. Or is it?

DEDICATION

SECOND TERM

chronicles the divisive national debate over the

Lawrence McAlister Hate Speech

and Hate Weapons Elimination Bill,

which took place during the President's Second Term.

Inserted in this chronicle, where appropriate, is the personal

narrative of his involvement in the national argument

over eliminating hate speech and the right to own firearms

written by John Madison,

one of the leading opponents of the McAlister Bill.

This series is dedicated to John Madison and to all of the

modern day American patriots mentioned in this series who

fought to uphold Americans' right to free speech and religion

and to keep and bear arms

under the First and Second Amendments to the

Constitution of the United States of America,

while in that struggle,

placing in peril and frequently sacrificing,

their lives, their fortunes and their sacred honor.

AMENDMENT ONE

TO THE CONSTITUTION

OF THE UNITED STATES OF AMERICA

Congress shall make no law respecting an establishment of religion,

or prohibiting the free exercise thereof;

or abridging the freedom of speech, or of the press;

or the right of the people peaceably to assemble, and to petition the

Government for a redress of grievances.

AMENDMENT TWO

TO THE CONSTITUTION

OF THE UNITED STATES OF AMERICA

A well regulated militia,

being necessary to the security of a free state,

the right of the people to keep and bear arms

shall not be infringed.

(The Bill of Rights was adopted on December 15, 1791)

I.

America Debates 113-S.1 The Lawrence McAlister Hate Speech and Hate Weapons Elimination Bill

ONE

Dallas, Texas

"POTUS is down! OH, NO!...Repeat, the President....is down!"

"Appears to be an upper front shot...bleeding...he's behind the podium ...on the platform.....Protocol SkyHook. STAT! ....Full perimeter. STAT, STAT."

With these frantically shouted words Secret Service Agent Stephen Quinn was only confirming what hundreds of thousands of day viewers could see with their own eyes – the President had been shot and was down.

Normally, viewership of a day time Presidential speech outside of DC would not be large, but this was no normal day. The elections were just eleven days away, and this President was behind in virtually all of the polls, except for CBS, which gave him a lead so thin that the poll's margin of error dwarfed the purported lead. Clearly, the question of the re-election of this President was in doubt. That is, his re-election was in doubt before the bullet sliced through his right shoulder.

The major news outlets led their initial reports of a shooting of the President by reminding their audiences that the site of the shooting was the same city in which John F. Kennedy was slain – Dallas, Texas. No one could know, of course, this soon after the trigger was squeezed how this President would fare. Was it a fatal shot? Was he merely wounded and would survive as did President Reagan? As in any act of violence of this nature, the crowds of supporters in City Hall Plaza panicked, running away from the open area of the Plaza as quickly as possible. Within seconds, the

Secret Service, following well-rehearsed plans, had covered the President's body, followed by carrying him swiftly off the back of the stage erected for the speech in the Plaza, and to an ambulance, always kept nearby for just such a purpose. President Bush, 42, noted that as long as he could see the ambulance tasked to carry him, and he wasn't in it, he was ok.

News coverage being what it is in the age of satellites and the internet, tens of millions, and then, billions, of residents of the world soon heard the news from Dallas, holding their collective breath for what would inevitably follow – either the good news of the President's diagnosed likely survival of the assassination attempt, or instead, the tragic news that he had succumbed to the malevolent plans of his assailant, or assailants.

Within ten minutes of the shot being fired, CNN set a new timing record in concluding that the act appeared to be that "of a lone gunman", though no one had any idea who the shooter was, or even where the shot came from. Federal investigators, however, narrowed the location of the shot to a one inch circular hole cut in a vacant office window in a building a block and a half distant from the campaign event platform, so far away that it had not been felt necessary for the building to be secured prior to the event. Forensics experts concluded that the shooter had to have been a highly skilled, well-trained sniper to make the shot, given the distance and angles.

Early suggestions of a "lone gunman," though, were quickly discarded as news began to break of the simultaneous fatal shooting of the Director of the Bureau of Alcohol, Tobacco, Firearms and Explosives, Lawrence McAlister, as he was enjoying a late lunch at the Rive

4

Guache, a favorite restaurant of well paid lobbyists and administration insiders, located not far from the White House. The ATF Director died at his restaurant dining table, from a hand gun shot to the back of his head, slumping forward into his dessert, within just minutes of the time that the President was struck 900 miles away in Texas. The news from Dallas was so overwhelming, though, that it was almost an hour before the networks began to cover the second shooting. Even federal law enforcement authorities, understandably preoccupied with Dallas, didn't receive word about the murder of a federal official in a DC restaurant until a flash message was conveyed through the Federal Bureau of Investigation's secure alert system.

Just as the second airplane's striking the second World Trade Center Tower instantly changed everyone's perception from a tragic accident to a damnable terrorist attack, the news from DC of the slaying of a high ranking federal official, at about the same time as the shooting of the nation's CEO, had the same effect. News of the second shooting led officials to instantaneously conclude that the government of the United States was under attack. The various federal agencies charged with law enforcement responsibilities alerted their key employees to the potential of a widespread assault on federal officials. The Vice President, Cabinet officers, Congressional leaders and Supreme Court Justices were all taken to pre-arranged secure locations. Employees of the ATF were sent home following receipt of word that their Director had been slain, to protect them should any attempt be in progress to bomb the ATF offices on New York Avenue in DC. With the second shooting of a federal official, it was clear that the events required the government to shift into full crisis mode. Official Washington, DC does crisis mode well.

The startling news from Dallas and DC, as compelling as it was, ratcheted up even further in the midst of the evening's news coverage of the two shootings, as talking heads on all media outlets read directly from the AP instant news feed. Chris Walters of Fox News covered the breaking news:

"....and so, as we have been extensively reporting, the President has survived, thankfully, this dastardly, might I say also cowardly, attack today. The bullet passed through his body and apparently just below his right shoulder joint, and just above his right lung. His was a classic 'through and through' shot, according to medical experts. One doctor at Parkland Hospital, which is where President Kennedy was pronounced dead in 1963, as you will recall, said that of all of the places to receive and survive a torso bullet wound, the President's entry site was the best, from a survivability viewpoint. Americans are united in being thankful for that. Here is a segment from the news conference late today from Parkland. Dr. Chap......wait...yes.

"I'm sorry, I've just been told in my ear piece by my news director that the AP is issuing an emergency news flash. No, it's apparently not about the President, who remains in stable condition, thankfully. But, there has been *another shooting,* I repeat, a *third shooting,* all on this incredibly alarming day. A thus far unidentified United States Senator has been admitted to a hospital in South Carolina, no details on which hospital, reportedly, and....this, according to the AP, and I quote, 'the unidentified Senator is suffering from a gunshot wound...apparently in critical condition...but still alive'.

"We've been reporting on the murder here in DC earlier today of the Director of the ATF, the Bureau of Alcohol,

6

Tobacco, Firearms and Explosives, Lawrence McAlister. We have been careful to warn our viewers not to draw any early conclusions about these two earlier reported attacks on federal officials. They most likely are related. They *could* be related, particularly because of their timing, but frankly, we don't have any official, at any level, who is willing to go on the record and say that they are related.

"That, though is likely going to change, and change very soon, I would think in light of this AP news flash....and now, yes,...here's an update coming in from the AP....the Senator had evidently been shot much earlier in the day, but was only discovered, in a nearly expired condition, about an hour and a half ago....apparently by a family member...they're saying a nephew of the Senator...who found the Senator in his boat house in South Carolina....and he was unconscious....let's see here...suffering from a quote significant loss of blood unquote. No word here on the nature or extent of the Senator's wounds.

"Nobody likes to speculate, of course, but with this reference to the boat house, and to the South Carolina hospital, I'm being told by our news staff here at Fox that the victim here is almost certainly Senator Blivens, that is, it appears that it is....uh....highly....likely that the victim is U.S. Senator James R. Blivens. The Senator is one of the President's loyal supporters, and one of the more liberal Senators, though he's from a southern State. He bucked the trend of conservatives elected from Southern States, because his father had been an icon in the Senate for seven terms.

"This shooting report is obviously somewhat different from the 2010 attempted assassination on Congresswoman Gabrielle Giffords in Arizona, as her shooter was caught, fortunately, at the scene of the shooting at a town hall meeting at a mall in Tucson. As you know, she survived, some would say almost miraculously, a bullet in her brain, though a federal judge and five others were killed.

"All of this today comes near the end of a violent campaign season, as has been widely reported. Since the national party conventions there have been several incidents where persons have been injured in protests and demonstrations. Most of them appear to have been organized in favor of or against the President. Some, however, were against a few of the more controversial candidates for Congress, on both sides of the aisle. Unfortunately, it's been a difficult, historically quite violent and bloody, campaign. And as the campaign winds up, now these three tragic shootings.

"While we await further news on the shooting in South Carolina, I would just like to comment about what I'm beginning to hear from our friendly competitors on cable and beginning to read on some of the blogs. Just as in the Arizona shooting where journalists and some bloggers immediately jumped to conclusions, unwarranted as it turned out, and speculated that the shooter was a 'right winger', I am starting to hear, actually increasingly now, that these two earlier reported shootings were the acts of right wingers, or the militia or tea party folks. I would suggest that everybody in my profession just hold on, be patient and let the federal agencies, and the state authorities, do their jobs. We don't need any witch hunts at this point in time. We've got enough troubles, obviously, without pointing fingers, or assessing blame....this early.... and....without all the facts. Enough said. Now let's take a quick break and we'll be back to try and sort all this out for you." Walter's unsolicited advice was ignored by most American media.

8

TWO

Washington, DC

American political history records several "October Surprises", two of the most notable being the filing of legal charges against a Reagan aide days before the Presidential election, and the last minute revelation of DUI charges against President Bush 43, almost costing him his election. Some Gore loyalists still maintained that it did. But only the most calloused politician would suggest that the attempted murder of two elected federal officials, and the killing of a third, was a form of a 'political dirty trick'. No media reported any such suspicions raised by any source on the record.

Except for a few isolated and limited exceptions, from the far fringes of both the left and right wings of the political spectrum, no one seriously suggested anything except the obvious – a conspiracy to assassinate the President and other high federal officials had come close to succeeding.

Presidential historians were called into television and radio outlets to put the conspiracy into perspective. "No, Charles, except for the Lincoln Conspiracy, all other attempts to assassinate American Presidents, whether successful or not, were by single gunmen", replied Historian Dorene Goodwink to her network interviewer the morning after the shootings were labeled by many in the mainstream national media as the "Guns Against Government Conspiracy".

"But, what about the JFK assassination, there are still many who think that Lee Harvey Oswald didn't act alone?"

"There'll always be conspiracy theorists who question every suspicious act, Charlie. However, let's look at a true, actual conspiracy of men, and it appears, also women, who got together to accomplish one primary objective – to decapitate the federal government by killing its President and certain members of the President's Cabinet. That, historically, was a confirmed joint action, a conspiracy, to violate the law through murderous acts."

"I take it you see similarities with yesterday's three shootings, here in DC, as well as in Texas and South Carolina?"

"On its face there was a conspiracy yesterday to kill, with guns, high federal officials. Fortunately, our President is doing better than expected, we all understand, and he is expected, his staff is reported as saying, that he may be back on the campaign trail before election day. Unfortunately, Senator James R. Blevins is still in critical condition, and it's not known if he will survive his wounds. And, of course, the Director of the ATF, Lawrence McAlister, has passed. I express my condolences to his family."

"Dorene, except for the obvious fact that all three were shot at about the same time, roughly, on the same day, why do you conclude, to use your words, that there was a conspiracy, on its face?"

"Secretary of State William Seward, was attacked, and nearly killed, but for his neck brace that spared him from his assailant's knife stabs, in his home the very same night as Lincoln was shot at Ford's Theater. The conspirators' plans to kill Vice President Andrew Johnson and General Grant fell apart at the last minute. The conspirators were convicted and hung for working together to kill officials of the government. Plus, and this is quite important in light of what happened yesterday, they acted together for a common

10

political purpose. The Confederate States had lost the war, with surrender by General Lee just five days before. These conspirators were trying to throw the government into turmoil and confusion, thus hoping to lead Confederate soldiers to continue fighting. They tried to change the government, and history, through violence, using weapons of violence and hate, guns and bullets."

"So, how is that like yesterday's shootings?"

"Simple, really. Just answer these questions. Who hates this President? Who's made it their publicly stated goal to try and prevent his re-election? Who's organized in every State and every city of any size to defeat the President? Who hates the ATF and its efforts to prevent the proliferation of guns in this country? Who hates Senator Blevins, arguably the most liberal member of the U.S. Senate?"

"Now, to be fair, Dorene, just because a large group of right wingers wants to defeat the President at the polls doesn't automatically mean they want to take his life, isn't that true."

"I've made my statement, Charlie. This is a right wing, gun-toting straight up conspiracy, and the three bullets that were fired by guns held by these gun-loving radicals are clear evidence of what I'm saying, and what the early polls this morning are showing – that most Americans think that it's obviously the tea party, self-styled patriot wing nuts that tried to pull this off. They're the ones that were trying to change America, and change its elected and appointed leaders through the barrel of a gun. We can't let that happen. What a sad day for America".

"Well, thanks, Dorene, for your time today and your passionate and informed analysis. Any final words?"

"Only this. My study of history tells me that it's now finally time to correct that clumsily written, ambiguous, and we learn, again, that exceedingly dangerous Second Amendment. There should be no right to own hate guns particularly when those weapons are used to try to change governments. Australia has banned private ownership of guns, America needs to do the same thing. Let's ban the right to own weapons of hate – and do it now, before even more good people are killed. In addition, though this may be more controversial, we need to re-examine how this country has allowed all manner of hateful speech, and violent words, to lead to more shootings....and, to....well....to just more hate. The hate has to stop. We must curtail hateful speakers and stop their violent words."

"But, Dorene, don't we have a problem with the two U.S. Supreme Court decisions in 2008, the D.C. vs. Heller case, and in 2010 in the McDonald vs. Chicago decision? Those two cases interpreted the Second Amendment as applying to individual gun ownership and applied the Amendment to the states. Right?"

"Charlie, both of those cases were decided 5-4. Just one vote made the difference. With the President's recent appointment, and the Senate's confirmation, of Justice Sheila Newton to the high Court, the ball game has changed. Changed dramatically. Justice Newton is a known progressive, I would even use the term liberal. She replaced Justice Kennedy, a Reagan appointee, who had been a swing vote on many cases. Kennedy did vote with the majority in both pro-gun cases. Though Justice Kennedy was 76 years old, he had told friends that he would stay on the Court through the President's first term. But, as we know, health reasons led to his resignation in April this year, and to Justice Newton's appointment."

"Dorene, how do you see all of that working in the growing public demand to ban guns in this country after these horrific shootings of three federal officials?"

Dorene looked deep into the camera's lens and uttered words that would be quoted for many months to come. "Charlie, if the Congress has the guts to pass a bill outlawing private ownership of guns, I think it would be quickly upheld in a test case by the Supreme Court. I'm saying that the Court would reverse itself, as it's done in the past. It looks like it could be 5 to 4 *against the gunners*, Charlie, and that's a very good thing. It's time to change the law."

"Well, folks, noted Presidential Historian Goodwink has sounded the alarm. Is anyone in the White House, or in the Congress, listening?"

As it turned out, people at both ends of Pennsylvania Avenue were well ahead of the renowned Presidential historian.

THREE

Washington, DC – GWU Hospital

No one in the national media could recall any news conference even remotely like this one. When the White House Press Office sent the initial e-mail notice, some in the media were openly skeptical of its source, but it was certainly authentic. It read:

WHITE HOUSE PRESS OFFICE MEDIA EVENT ADVISORY

At 1730 hours, tomorrow, Thursday, November 1st, the President will meet with pool reporters (confirm last week's listing for your outlet's inclusion) at George Washington University Hospital, 900 23rd Street NW. Check in with the SS Agent in Charge at the Main Entry to be escorted to the President's Suite. The President will be joined by Congressional Leaders (list not confirmed at this juncture), along with Mrs. Blevins and ATF Director McAlister's widow.

No questions will be taken, nor any answered, on any campaign issues, including polls. All statements made and questions addressed will deal with new legislation that will be proposed and announced at the M.E. Network TV limited to one camera per outlet/same for newsprint. Questions? Contact Janice as usual. 202-555-1212 x1257

The University Hospital's Presidential Suite certainly lived up to its name in terms of its decor, but its over-all size limited the number of people who could squeeze into its confines, thus curtailing the media personalities who could attend. This had the effect of bruising some egos, understandably so, given recent events and the historic news-making nature of this prime time media event in a hospital with a wounded President. The closest the media had gotten to President Reagan was his wave from his hospital window. By the time of the media event, the executives of the major media had reached an agreement to rely on pool coverage, with most placing their national anchors either at desks to be set up in the lobby of the Hospital or outside, if the weather cooperated. It was anticipated that possibly as many Americans could watch this media event as had watched the moon landing or the launching of the Kuwaiti war.

The pool picture of the President, on an I.V. and a pulse monitor, setting upright in his hospital bed, surrounded by his family and Congressional leaders, made page one of newspapers not only in the U.S., but in most of the world. There had never been a Presidential photograph quite like it, a fact confirmed by Historian Goodwink later that night in network color coverage of the historical event.

What took pool reporters by surprise was what the President didn't say, which was to say, he said nothing. The First Lady graciously thanked the media for coming, thanked the Secret Service for protecting her husband and thanked the medical staff at Parkland and now at GWU for their excellent medical care. She then explained that the President would not be making public comments at this media event, because, she said, the President's doctors had advised, because he was on pain killing medication, he should not make public comments.

Political strategists for the President's opponents also thought that the President was right not to speak, or at least was smart not to do so. The media event turned out to be adversarial in nature, but the ominous words spoken were

16

by others, not from the candidate who was facing the voters in just four days. The President's sole visible contribution was a wide, winsome smile when a pool reporter at the end of the media event shouted out, "How're you feelin' Mr. President?" The hospitalized President responded by raising a single thumb up with his left hand, carefully keeping his bandaged right shoulder and arm under his hospital covers. Click. Click. Photo Op Number Two.

Thus, the opposition's campaign professionals concluded, the President got the best of both worlds. He gained additional sympathy as the surviving intended victim of a Presidential assassination attempt, plus, he was able to send a message to the party faithful, and those in key electoral blue states, but with words spoken by others, not by the candidate. They were his words, but he didn't have to say them.

The First Lady led the attack, with a few well-chosen, rehearsed, words. "My dear husband is here today, and alive today.......because a bullet missed its target – his heart. His heart is as compassionate as America's heart – which in the last few days has cried out to solve this national peril that we all face. Anyone of us could be killed, taken down at any stage of life, by a bullet fired from a weapon of hate.....a gun. I know that my husband will want to work with the Congress that the people will choose to elect next Tuesday to insure that weapons of hate are weapons of the past. He has asked these leaders of our nation's Congress to be with him today, as we move towards that goal. Continuing to fix our nation's economy that was broken when he took office will remain a major goal, but ridding our nation of hate weapons, and eliminating the hate speech that inflames our nation, will be his *priority goals* for passage by Congress in the upcoming session of Congress. The President will thus prioritize along with gun control the control of this nation's increasing hate speech, as the two so frequently go hand-in-hand.

"Finally, I just want to say that my husband and his doctors had originally hoped that he would be well enough to finish the last few days of the campaign out amongst the voters, the Americans that we all so truly love, but sadly, he needs his rest and time to recover, so that he can continue to be our President, if the voters agree, to serve in his second term. I just want to add ....whoever tried to keep my husband from serving his .... whoever did this horrible thing....whom many in the media are speculating must be from the radical right....though we don't know yet, of course....must be caught and prosecuted to the full extent of the law. May God bless America and its voters as they decide next Tuesday the future direction and fate of our great nation."

Even the most jaded journalist in the room found that they had moist eyes as the First Lady spoke. The White House's overnight polls showed that Americans supported the President's non-involvement in the balance of the campaign before the election, with over 66% supporting the President's decision not to campaign and not to speak until he was fully healed.

The First Lady then introduced the Senate's Majority Leader, Senator Harold Reese and the House Minority Leader, former Speaker Nadia Pelham, who then spoke briefly, as they also issued a prepared statement to the media:

JOINT STATEMENT

OFFICE OF THE SENATE MAJORITY LEADER

OFFICE OF THE HOUSE MINORITY LEADER

Senator Reese and Representative Pelham join in assuring Americans that the nation's long nightmare of gun violence and death will soon come to an end. To achieve this essential outcome, we will join together with the Administration to draft a bill to be considered by the new Congress in January to address our nation's hopeless addiction to guns, and also to put teeth in the Shepard/Byrd Hate Crimes Prevention Act. Hate weapons and hate speech must be curtailed, even eliminated in most cases, if we are to survive as a free people. We will name this new law after the brave fallen Director of the ATF, Lawrence McAlister, taken from us too soon by an act of hate and violence. The sponsors of the bill, to be announced next Thursday, November 8th, have agreed to denominate the legislation, to be introduced as 113 – S.-1, the *Lawrence McAlister Hate Speech and Hate Weapons Elimination Act*. We look forward to its swift and fair consideration by the new Congress, as well as its early passage and adoption into law. We are both committed to expediting the scheduling of hearings and mark ups consistent with the urgency of this critical legislation. The hate-mongers among us have gone too far this time, as

they will soon learn. This nation will deprive
the haters, by law, of their weapons of hate and
curtail their hateful words. Our American way of
life deserves no less.

FOUR

New York City, NY

Election Night

Chip Meadors, the MSBCN talking head, who once famously told viewers that whenever he heard the President speak he got an electric charge up his leg, could hardly contain himself. Voting booths in Indiana, traditionally the first State in the nation to conclude voting, had only been closed for two minutes when Meadors made his cable network's official call:

"Yes,... yes,... indeedy, its now *official, it's official,* based on overwhelming results of exit polls in the Hoosier State, MSBCN is calling Indiana for the President. Indiana will be solidly blue. That's a HUGE win for the President, folks, as Indiana hasn't voted for a Democrat for President for several decades. And, that means that we can....just a minute,...oh, really. OK. Well, I'm being told that...actually, that a Democratic candidate for President carried Indiana four years ago....Can you double check that, Tom? I don't...OK, well, you have the stats in front of you, and I don't, but, in any case, it's still a *major* win for the President. If he continues this trend, and, yeah I know it's only a one State trend at this point, but if he keeps it up, he will be handily re-elected to a second term. That should encourage a lot of Americans, frankly, like yours truly, who have been pacing the floor today, all of us worried about how the voting would turn out. The next states to close their polls will close them in one hour and we'll know a lot more then."

The mood up the street in New York City at the Fox News studios was slightly less ebullient. Shane Harrison, not smiling, nor apparently feeling any electric shocks up his leg, turned his attention to camera two:

"Folks, I've covered elections and election campaigns for 12 years and I've never seen the public opinion polls right before election day take such a decided shift in favor of a candidate. The Bush drunk driving story made a six point difference, but according to Zogby, CNN, CBS, the Wall Street Journal, just about all the polls, the President went from an average of 4.8 points down before October 26th to last night's final polling showing him up by a full 6 points. That's an almost 11 point shift, and it's almost unheard of in American politics. That many people don't normally change their minds about voting in such a short time. Over time, over many weeks or months, maybe, but not in only eleven days."

Grenda Sandora, obviously less upset with the polling results than her co-host of Fox Election Night Coverage, wasted no time in challenging his comments. "Shane, you may be right about the size of the shift in voter sentiment, but you're staring at the trees and missing the forest, so to speak. What living being on this planet doubted that the President would win today, and win really big? For crying out loud, Shane, he was shot, and could have been killed, in what everybody now knows was a conspiracy, though how wide spread we still don't know. All in an aborted attempt to take down this government and this Administration, by violence, in what the President's supporters, and most of the media, are calling the Guns Against Government Conspiracy. How could any fair-minded American voter look at those pictures of the President and his lovely wife, the First Lady, from Walter Reed Hospital and not be moved to tears? I knew the election was over, not when I heard he was shot and survived, but when I saw him in that hospital bed with his body bandaged up....it still makes me....tear up...Shane...say....something...please."

"Look, Grenda, we all have compassion for the man and for his family. Nobody that I know favors the use of violence, certainly not like we saw last week, but my only point is....well, my....I just hate to see elections as important as this one settled and decided because of a single event, even as horrible as the attempted assassination clearly was. We face staggering levels of national debt, a looming overhaul of our nation's health care system, widespread civil unrest, a declining dollar, possible food shortages...and here we are for the last few days and all anybody could talk about in the national media was the crazed acts of unknown persons, who no matter what their unhinged motivation, did this nation no good. They may have dealt the country a potentially fatal blow by re-electing the President to a second term. These shooters, whoever they may be, must be caught, charged, given a fair trial and either executed like Timothy McVeigh, or at least imprisoned for life."

Every major media outlet soon called the election for the President, most agreeing that control of the Senate would remain with the President's party, and that the next Speaker of the House would be former Speaker Nadia Pelham, by a hefty margin of newly elected Democrat Representatives. The other 49 states split 34 for the President and 15 for his opponent. The states were mostly western states, including Texas, in which gun advocates, tea party and patriot groups appeared to have their greatest electoral strength. The electoral college final count was even more lop-sided, 378 for the President and 160 for his Republican opponent.

FIVE

Sandusky, Ohio

Dr. Adam Nation never expected to be a politician. He had frequently declared how much he detested politicians, from all political parties. Thus, it came as quite a surprise when Dr. Adam Nation agreed to run for Congress as a Tea Party backed candidate from the 9th District of Ohio, traditionally a Democrat District. Dr. Nation was a respected forty-six year old OBGYN who had developed firm political beliefs about how government should function. He was fed up with seeing his patients' retirement funds chewed up by a federal government that couldn't seem to control its spending, but which was unable to encourage job growth, choosing instead to incur trillions of dollars of new debt. He became the consensus choice by Tea Party activists to run for Congress from his District. When the votes were counted he had bested the two candidates from the Democrat and Republican parties, and joined nearly sixty others like him in the new U.S. House of Representatives. The Tea Party Members organized within the Republican Party and voted for the new Republican Speaker to replace Democrat Speaker Nadia Pelham. But, lest anyone take their votes for granted, they formed their own Tea Party Caucus in the House. Washington, DC had taken notice that they had arrived and that politics in America had changed.

Congressman Nation wasted no time in establishing himself as a leader in the U.S. House. Political media profiles routinely described him as ruggedly handsome, frequently referring to his 'muscular Marine build'. Unlike most of his classmates in medical school, who went into lucrative medical practices after medical school, Dr. Nation joined the Marines and served his country as a medical doctor, frequently in combat zones. At five foot ten inches he didn't tower over his colleagues, but his engaging personality led them to enjoy his company. A principled conservative, he had promised himself, his wife, his college aged children and the voters of his district one major promise. He assured them that "I'm going to change Washington, I will not allow Washington to change me." Like all Americans, he had frequently watched the newly *elected* eventually become the new *establishment*, and then become the new *embarrassment*. He was committed to not letting it happen to himself. He decided this after a talk he had soon after his election with a former Congressman who had lived through all three stages. The Congressman had served in the House as a conservative Republican, risen to a leadership position and then resigned in shame. He first reached out to Adam Nation within days after Nation's surprise upset election. He drove to Ohio to meet with the Congressman-elect.

"Thanks for meeting with me, Congressman. I certainly know how busy you are as you wind up your practice and head to DC soon. I asked to see you because I think I may be able to be of some help as you take on your new duties."

"Congressman, first of all, I'm not a Congressman yet, as you know, so just call me Adam. There are lots of people, I'm finding, who want to tell me how to take on my new duties. But, I'll admit I was intrigued by your message, I think it said I might want to talk to a fallen leader before I make the same mistakes you made. That got my attention. Congressman, I appreciate your driving over to see me."

"Adam, I'm no longer a Congressman, so just call me Mike. It's my privilege to drive over and tell you what I'm about to tell you. If somebody had done this for me, I'd probably still be in Congress. If you have a few minutes, let me share what I've learned about the arrogance of power."

"Mike, I've got all the time you need. I respected you when you were in Congress, and I thought you did the right thing when you resigned, after.... your....your...."

"Don't mince words. I resigned after my adultery was revealed, I'm sorry to say. But, we'll come back to that. Let's start with the basics. People who get elected to high public office, I'm not talking about the township council here, find an interesting thing occurs as soon as they win....they immediately begin to receive praise, even adulation, from other people. It's apparently a human failing that when we are around people that we think are important, we act differently towards them than we would if we thought they weren't important. I can't explain it, but I've witnessed it first hand, personally, and watched it affect my colleagues. One day, you're candidate Adam Nation, nice guy, normal sort of fellow. The next day, after you are elected to Congress, all of a sudden, you've become a super human. People don't call you Adam, or even Doctor, they call you Congressman, or United States Representative, or the Distinguished Gentleman from Ohio. You are now SOMEBODY.

"At first, you'll get a little chuckle out of it. Of all people, you know you haven't changed one bit. You're still the same guy you were last week. But, and here's the problem, over time, after months, and then after years, even after several years, of being idolized, and praised, and honored, and pampered....inside of yourself....you start to believe it. You begin to agree with your fawning staff who, after all, owe their jobs to you. You begin to agree with the respectful news media, who always address you by your title. You notice that most of your constituents, the voters in your

Congressional district, treat you like somebody who can bring them a better life. Most of them make it clear to you that they think you can just vote and jobs appear and grants of federal money appear and wars are won. A few, of course, won't like you, or your votes, but over time, you learn to tune those people out. You ignore them, they obviously don't know how great you are, you will quietly tell yourself. A new way of thinking sets in. With some, I've noticed that it happens almost as soon as they're elected. But, with most, it takes time. If you're a believer, it takes longer, because you know that you're still mortal. I'll come back to that.

"Adam, because 90% of all Members of Congress who seek re-election are re-elected, after two or three, maybe four re-elections, you will be tempted to become arrogant. I'm not talking about Louis XV- look down your nose - off with their heads kind of arrogance. I'm talking about arrogance in your gut. The word arrogance comes from the Latin root word arrogatus, to arrogate, or to assume something for yourself that isn't really yours. The dictionary defines it as 'to claim unwarrantably or presumptuously'. I'm not trying to lecture here, Adam, my point is this. When you are an important person for a while you begin to arrogate to yourself something that you don't have the right to claim. If you are in power, you begin to think that you actually are the source of power, and it changes how you think."

"Congressmen *have* power. What am I missing here?"

"Scripture says that all power belongs to God. He loans it, on occasion, to mere mortals, but it's His. If a judge starts thinking that he is the source of justice, or a banker thinks he is the source of economic resources, or a doctor thinks that he is the source of healing, then they arrogate to themselves what is not theirs. They become arrogant. It may not show on the outside, but inside, they begin to arrogantly think they can get away with what others who don't have what they have, could never get away with doing. You'll be able to raise a million dollars for your re-election. Lots of folks will donate to you if you're in office, many because they want something. Snap your fingers, arrange some fund-raisers and many thousands of dollars end up on your desk. You won't have to do even one pelvic exam and your bank accounts will overflow with money. It's amazing how much money comes in. Money sure affects how people think.

"And here's where I'm headed with this. One day, and it could be any given day, you'll be in your office and a cute new staff member will brush your arm as she hands you some papers, looks into your baby blues and gives you a big smile and a come-hither look. You're not a teen ager any more, but you'll start to feel like one. Your blood will race. You'll think what if, or maybe. But....self-control will kick in. You'll remember your dear wife, and your vows, and your constituents and your faith. And the temptation will pass.

"That is, until the next time it happens, and maybe the cute staffer is a little more forward this time, and maybe it's out of the office at some event. She lets you know how much she admires you. She gushes about how you should be a Senator, or maybe even President someday. You go through your list of why you can't break your wedding vows, again, but, and *this* is when it happens, you begin to tell yourself – 'Self, you deserve this; you can get away with it; you're a powerful, important Congressman. Nobody'll know. Look at how hard you work. Can't hurt anybody, really. Just some recreation to relax some.'

"It can't be that easy to fall that far...."

29

"Adam, believe me, it's incredibly easy to fall. I knew everything I had ever done, all I had ever worked for, all the pro-family, conservative stands I had taken were on the line, my family, my job, it was all right there and I did it anyway. As you can see, I'm no Cary Grant by any means, I'm less than normal height and balding, so looks have nothing to do with it. The devil is like a roaring lion seeking whom he can devour. I knew he was tempting me. My arrogance of power led me to think I could get away with it, because I was so important. Well, I wasn't and I'm not. Only by the grace of God did Melanie stay with me, but it's still very difficult on her, and our marriage was damaged, to say the least. My main regret is what I did to sully the name of my Lord.

"One other point. The arrogance of power can take you down in other areas besides sexual sin. You were elected because you believe in certain principles. I've personally witnessed my fellow Members of Congress stray. Not from their wives, but from their principles. You can fall away from why you came here simply because a lobbyist who bundled several thousand dollars in campaign contributions asks you to cast a simple little vote on an amendment here or there. You look at what you're about to do, you know it's not consistent with your core beliefs, but then you go through the same self-delusion I just outlined for physical sins. You arrogantly tell yourself that nobody will notice; it's a small issue, anyway; I should get more credit for all I'm doing to fight the fight; compared to what I've seen other conservatives swallow it's no big deal. You get the idea."

Congressman-elect Adam Nation could not have known at the time of his meeting how important his twenty minutes with a fallen Congressman would prove to be in his life, and for the nation.

SIX

Campaign Website Blog Entry by John Madison –
Entered November 7th

It was the worst day of my life. No....not just <u>the worst day</u>. Election day, November 6th, was <u>the absolute worst day</u> of my life. I know. I know. 'You can't win them all' and all that rot, but this election loss was catastrophic in nature, as it led to a whole series of legal and personal assaults about which I will shortly write. It wasn't a catastrophe because I was defeated as a candidate on the ballot. I wasn't running for office. No such luck. It was a full blown disaster for me because I managed the campaign in Texas against the candidate who won. Who was that winning candidate? Only just the incumbent President of the United States, who knew well who I was and who was reportedly not at all amused by my efforts in the hard-fought campaign to deny him a second term.

I'm getting a little ahead of myself. I've never kept what used to be called a journal, but after what happened last month, and my big mug being flashed on television screens all over the country, I decided I'd better keep a chronicle of what happened by blogging on my campaign website. I'm writing down what happened because my study of history as a student at Texas A&M tells me that the winners write the history books, and therefore, the truth is usually lost. I don't want that to happen this time.

Oh, yeah, my name is John Madison, and I am the founder and State Co-Chairman of the Lone Star Tea Party, one of several Tea Party and patriot organizations that had sprung up in our State over the four years between the President's first and, it makes my heart, and my fingers,

31

hurt to type these words, his <u>second</u> election to the White House. Even though it poses a danger to me to do so, I've decided to record the true inside story of what happened to me, our supporters and volunteers, and most importantly to our country, beginning after that fateful election day, yesterday, November 6th. I'm recording, now, of course, mainly what happened <u>after</u> the election, for an obvious reason, I'm writing this after the election. Plus, any American with a pulse knows what happened in the campaign. How the media slanted campaign coverage; how the incumbent's political party and big city henchmen effectively eviscerated the President's Republican opponent and his impressive running mate; how the labor unions (you know, the ones to which the administration handed over ownership of General Motors) and the public sector unions (the ones who had earlier declared war in Wisconsin against the taxpayers) managed to insure that the blue states stayed blue, and the red states didn't total enough electoral votes; and how the streets were filled with Occupy mobs setting fires and generally causing mayhem and dissension. The tragic, and stupid, shootings just days before the election, of course, guaranteed that we couldn't possibly win and the incumbent couldn't conceivably lose the campaign for control of the White House. We don't need to recall that disaster of a campaign. It hurts too much to remember, anyway.

Oh, yeah, how did the term 'Tea Party' come to apply to political efforts to throw out the Congress and to try to prevent a second term for the President? Everyone knows that the original term began with the dumping of tea in Boston Harbor in 1773, as an organized protest against British taxes on imported tea. OK, maybe not everybody knows this background. If you 'studied' U.S. history in a public school, they may have left out that little factoid. More recently, in 2007, the term 'Tea Party' was updated to apply to several angry voters in a large mid-western city who organized to protest grossly excessive property taxes, and who dumped tea bags in a city canal. Americans for Tax Reform in DC noticed the protest, gave the group an award, and the rest, as they say, is history. In 2009, Rick Santelli, a CNBC business reporter engaged in an on air rant from the floor of the Chicago Mercantile Exchange, calling for a "tea party" by traders throwing worthless derivatives into the Chicago River. His rant went viral as more Americans woke up to the mortgage mess being perpetuated by the federal government.

In Texas, admittedly a long way from Boston Harbor, we liked the phrase, and along with several groups, we adopted it into our formal name. We might as well have painted red-ringed targets on our backs, though, as we have since learned that all of our data files were downloaded by federal agents. What really stings is that when we initiated legal action because of the unauthorized downloading of our membership and donor files, the official response was to claim that it was all legal under the Patriot Act. I don't need to say anything about how offensive that argument was.

Campaign Blog Entry for November 12th

Well, I've been less than diligent in updating my page. I'm obviously not going to be a daily blogger. I just don't have the time. Why you ask? I've had such a hectic schedule this year that my time at our local exercise center was severely curtailed. As a result, I know I could stand to lose a couple lb's from my six foot four bod. During the campaign I ate way too much fast food during my many trips across Texas trying to persuade voters to come out and vote to throw the

President out of office. Plus, I have a real job that requires my time as an executive in the insurance industry.

I haven't been delayed in blogging daily because of time spent with our kids, who are all grown and raising their own families, so I have no excuse of time consumed by soccer games or ballet practices. My dear wife, Debbie, made sure that I had plenty of time to work on campaign needs, and still spend time with her, as the love of my life. Debbie, many of you know, is blond, petite and has a bubbly personality. As my wife and the mother of our two children, Jack and Katie, she's the best thing that ever happened to me. Jack is now a pastor over in Dallas and Katie is working overseas in commercial interior design. No, my delay since my last blog hasn't been for family reasons. I've been swamped because of the media attention my Austin speech attacking the President is still getting. I'm getting a lot of calls about the anti-gun and anti-free speech bill that we hear is being drafted by the White House.

As I said earlier, I think it's important to record the facts about what the newly elected federal Administration did to those of us who opposed them. I don't know why, really, they were so upset. We fought a good, honest and clean fight in our efforts to sway Texas voters against the incumbent President. But, it's already pretty obvious from the President's actions <u>since</u> the election that he doesn't see it that way. But, we've now learned that there is such a thing as a "<u>sore winner</u>", sorry to say. Really, how does it happen that an officer of a mid-sized insurance company from Tyler, Texas could pose a threat to the Republic? When did I become <u>an enemy of the state</u>? I am clearly being targeted because I led the effort in Texas to replace the occupant of the Oval Office. Funny thing is that before this year's campaign and election I had nothing to do with politics. I was a died-in-the-wool conservative, but I left it up to others to do something about the decline and possible fall of my beloved nation. I finally realized that our very survival as a free country was on the line if we just sat back and allowed the incumbent another four years.

Today's announcement that the President has agreed in principle with a bill to eliminate private gun ownership and to quote curtail unquote hate speech makes me alternately sick at my stomach, and mad as...well, this is being read online, so, I'll just write that I'm torn up inside over what is happening in DC over our right to speak freely and to own weapons of defense. The newly re-elected Administration has now reiterated the First Lady's George Washington University Hospital statement made right before the election that in his second term the President will get Congress to "re-interpret" the black letters written centuries ago on parchment paper. This fulfills his agenda for America, which differs radically from those aged words.

Blog made on November 29th

(Friday after Thanksgiving)

The politicians I know tell me that the Friday after Thanksgiving and any day between Christmas and New Years is the best time to sneak around and release news that you want most people to miss, especially if the details are a bit messy, or controversial. The Administration apparently decided that the best time to publicly release the details of its efforts to "re-interpret" a part of the U.S. Constitution would be while folks were occupied with the holidays. So it was that the text of the bill to re-write the First and Second Amendments was distributed by the White House Press

Office to the third string media staff who couldn't get out of working on the day that most Americans enjoyed off work. To say that their analysis of the bill was not extensive would be charitable.

What the White House Press Office and Senator Blevins' office released at the same time the text of the bill, labeled as 113-S.-1. It was to be introduced in the Congress, in the new session beginning in January, to rid the nation of privately-owned guns and shut down what was labeled as hate speech. I suspected that the Administration would have Jim Blevins act as the lead sponsor of the bill. The Senator is one of the most liberal in the U.S. Senate, even though he's from conservative South Carolina. I've noticed that happens frequently, like Senator Reese coming from Nevada. Senator Blevins was in critical condition after his shooting, but last week he had recovered sufficiently to return to the Capitol and lead the fight, from his wheelchair, for his historic Constitution-changing bill. The Senator looks like he was type cast by Hollywood for his role. Heavy-jowled....just plain heavy....balding, blustering, the Senator lays his South Carolina accent on pretty heavy when it suits his interests. With his seniority in the Senate, he was the perfect choice to lead the fight to pass the McAlister Bill, besides his October 26th shooting, needless to say.

This bill is so important that I've included on my website the full text of what they released today. *[Note: The full text of the McAlister Bill may be reviewed at www.secondtermbook.com.]* This is history in the making. It's important to understand the assault on the First and Second Amendments that Senator Blevins and his several co-sponsors, joined by Speaker Pelham, and the President, of course, are proposing to become the law of the land. It's not

1200 pages like the healthcare reform bill. In fact, being just a few pages, there are no obvious loopholes or areas of lack of clarity. 113-S.-1 states it as clearly as it can be stated - you can't own a gun, as all firearms are defined as "Hate Weapons". If you get caught owning a gun, after the 180 day redemption period for gun owners to turn in their firearms (in exchange for a few hundred bucks), you will be charged with a class C felony and then spend your next 10 years in a federal prison. How about that for clarity? There is only one exception for hunting, but it's very limited. Quite offensive is the part of the bill that rewards Americans who turn in their friends, family and neighbors who may have held onto their guns.

In addition, any person who utters or writes words considered to be hate speech by the federal censors, excuse me, by a new federal Hate Speech Review Panel that the new law, if it passes, would create, can be imprisoned, also for 10 years. That's clear enough, also. The text of the bill was apparently leaked today by its sponsors. Only time will tell if enough people of this country will recognize the danger of taking away our rights under the First and Second Amendments and defeat this assault on our Constitutional rights. We've already started organizing in this part of Texas to fight, and hopefully defeat, this dangerous bill. I have to be honest, and say that it doesn't look all that good at this early stage to defeat the bill. Bad laws get passed, and bad laws adopted, almost always during a crisis. The shootings have poisoned the atmosphere to speak out in support of owning guns, and opened the door to corking people, legally, for speaking their mind. We're doing research on how a shooting crisis in other countries led to abolishing private ownership and how some nations have shut off free speech. More on that as we learn more.

SEVEN

Private Living Quarters – White House
Washington, DC

The Federal Communications Commission, generally referred to as the FCC, consists of five members, all appointed by the President and confirmed by the U.S. Senate. The Commission has wide-ranging legal authority over the nation's airwaves, including, television, radio, cable, satellite and the internet. The Chairman of the FCC, Chadwick Cummins, was a long-time friend of the President, having worked as media and legal advisor in each of his campaigns. He didn't show up officially as media advisor in the Presidential campaign this time, as he had been serving as FCC Chairman since shortly after the President's First Inauguration. Chairman Cummins was loyal to a fault to his good friend in the White House. The President and Chadwick, had through the years watched together, enjoying Buds and Brats, nearly every NFL game by their favorite team, the Bears. The President knew that if he needed anything, anything at all, from the FCC Chairman, that Chadwick could be counted on to gladly comply.

The Commission, by law, could have no more than three of its five members from one political party. The Chairman and the two Democratic Party members were all that were needed to adopt binding rules and regulations, as a majority controlled all proceedings of the FCC. Now that the McAlister Bill was pending before Congress, the President was ready to call on Chairman Cummins to do his some advance planning for its implementation after the adoption of the bill, assuming that the bill passed and became law. Chairman Cummins was more than ready to be of assistance to his friend.

The two FCC regulations that would rock the nation several months later started as just ideas kicked around during the half time of the Bears versus Saints game in the private living quarters on the top floor of the White House. "Chad, what would you think....what would the majority of the FCC think....about applying McAlister, if it passes, to Rush and the other radio yappers? I have to admit they get on my nerves. Most of the time. A lot of what they say could be construed as hate speech, don't you think?"

"Let me work on it. We're both assuming you've got the votes to get McAlister through the House. Before McAlister, there would probably have been little hope. But....if it becomes law, we may have a way to shut these guys up, or at least seriously slow them down. As I recall, McAlister's anti-hate speech section prohibits hate speech and negative attacks on public officials. Most people are tired of all the negativity in political commercials."

"Yeah, I saw a focus group analysis in the campaign that showed that most viewers of political TV ads are fed up with one politician attacking his or her opponent, with lurid, nasty commercials."

"Blevins tells me that he thinks he will have enough support to include the ban on negative attacks on public officials. It *ought* to be popular with the public officials who can just vote to protect themselves from being criticized. The ban won't apply to candidates for office, just public officials, so it would be another incumbent protection provision in the law. But, assuming Congress passes McAlister, do you still feel that the Supremes will uphold it?"

"It's a bit of a hurdle, but with Sheila on the Court, we should be 5-4 to uphold the new law. Before Sheila, there wouldn't have been much chance, given that negatively attacking a public official is the essence of free speech. I used to teach that. Justice Hugo Black in the famous New York Times vs. Sullivan case wrote that, let's see if I can remember his statement, I taught it enough times, I should recall it by heart. He said, *'An unconditional right to say what one pleases about public affairs is what I consider to be the minimum guarantee of the First Amendment."* But, that was then, and this is now. Justice Newton will come through, and McAlister will be the law of the land. Bless her little rainbow colored heart."

"I always liked Sheila, she's gonna' be a dependable vote on the Court for years, decades even. Pass me over those pretzels, please."

"Sheila's presence on the Court is exactly why I think your Commission can do what needs to be done to shut down the nuts on talk radio and all of their hate talk. Come up with something, with some teeth. The Court'll back you up, 5-4, which is all we ever need. By the way, you know, Chad, this is the same room in the White House where George W choked on a pretzel, also watching football in fact, so be careful."

"I will, thanks. Wouldn't look good for the FCC Chairman to choke to death in the Executive Mansion. Think what the conspiracy theorists would do with that....As I said, I'll get to work on it. We've got some very smart lawyers now in the Office of FCC Counsel who can draft up something that will pass muster with Sheila and her four soul-mates. We'll be ready once McAlister is passed by Congress, signed by you and affirmed by the Supreme Court. While we're at it, how about we also do something about all the hate that's spewed across the internet on any given day? I've seen a ton of nasty stuff accusing you of about everything a person could be accused of. There needs to be some control on all that vitriol and poison that spews across the publicly-regulated internet. Autoresponders have been limiting content regarding stock advice for some time now. We should extend the concept to all politically objectionable content. Those wires and airwaves are owned by the public, you know, not the wingnuts. Let's extend our control over the internet, even more than some of the recent legislation doing so. There's too much political negativity on the net."

"Agreed, but you'll have to be careful. When China shut down some internet communications, they caught a lot of heat. You need to couch it in terms of not only just enforcing McAlister, but also protecting Americans from hate material. Anybody who's ever used the internet knows how looney it can get, so we may have less push back than you might think. Maybe we can get our Euro buddies to put on some content restrictions on their internet servers at the same time."

"I've gotten to know some of those guys over the last few years. I'll make some calls."

"Do that. Let me know what your legal geeks come up with. Oh, man....look at that!....You *know* that was pass interference....How could that ref not call....? He had his arm hooked....that was a homer call, for sure."

EIGHT

Campaign Website Blog for December 5th

If I could hit the rewind button on my life, I would go back to October 22nd and the speech I made to the National Rifle Association chapter in Austin. The NRA campaign rally just happened to be scheduled four days before the October 26th shootings in DC, Dallas and South Carolina. I suggested in my little talk that the President was planning to 'take away our guns', if he were to be re-elected to a second term, and, of course, I urged that he be soundly defeated, so that we could 'keep our guns'. How could I have known? Needless to say, after the shootings, the news clip of my Austin speech, or at least about 12 seconds of it, was a regular part of just about every frantic news special on the so-called 'Guns Against Government Conspiracy', and there were many such journalistic endeavors over the weeks after October 26th. As I said, I might as well have painted a big red target on my chest, as I became the Texas conservative that the liberals, the media, and particularly the Administration, loved to hate in the gun and speech bill debate that ensued and accelerated after the shootings. Needless to say, I've lost a lot of sleep.

That intensive national debate didn't take long after the election to start in earnest. From immediately after the President's re-election on November 6th until 113-S.-1 was officially introduced seven weeks later on January 1st, there was no secret that the returning Administration would use every power available to it to regulate speech and ban guns in America. The only unknown was what the new law would do to those Americans who didn't want to give up their weapons of protection. The hate speech provisions in the Bill received some critical public comment, but did not seem to attract the same interest as the antigun provision. Most of the media generally ignored the hate speech prohibition, which surprised me, since it posed a threat to freedom of the press. But the rumor was that the White House had quietly promised mainstream media CEOs that the law would never be used on the media, just on supposed right wing radicals, like me.

Our various tea party, patriot and gun rights organizations in Texas wasted no time after the election in organizing ourselves to fight the adoption of the bill that had been promised by the Administration to be its number one legislative priority in the new Congress. We had known since the President's hospital news conference that it would be filed, and worse yet, we had sound reason to fear that, unless we could arouse Americans to the looming danger of such a bill, that it would likely be enacted into law, given the nation's anti-gun climate and the voting strength the President now enjoyed, again, in both Houses of Congress. We didn't know at first what the Administration's bill would include. The White House Press Secretary assured reporters two days after their election victory that the bill would "include carrots and sticks".

We soon learned that the 'carrots' part of the bill was a variation of the old 'cash for clunkers' program that caused many Americans to turn in their older automobiles in exchange for cash payments from the federal government. Some federal genius must have decided that if it worked for old cars, how about old guns? This gave Americans very little credit for discerning the difference between wheels to travel and a weapon to protect one's life and family. We hoped that very few gun-owning Americans would give up their defense against death and mayhem for only five hundred dollars, or

44

in the case of a rifle or shotgun, only seven hundred dollars. But, if the bill that ended up passing included financial incentives, given the depressed state of the economy and widespread unemployment, we knew that only time would tell how many Americans out of work, and in need of cash, would end up turning in their guns, motivated by the payment.

What was not leaked until the text of the bill was released was what the President's Press Secretary meant by 'sticks' to be included in the anti-gun bill to insure compliance? A <u>felony</u> charge and conviction, with a <u>ten year prison term,</u> certainly qualified as a 'stick', if not a whole bag of sticks. The New York Times exulted that:

Finally, America will get over its sick love affair with deadly weapons. Most thinking Americans, particularly in crime-impacted cities, and the blue states on the two coasts, will step up, voluntarily do the right thing and turn in their guns. Undoubtedly, though the turning over of guns will be motivated in some parts of the country only by the proposed time in prison, a stiff enough sentence that no American should willingly want to endure, just to pack heat.

Once the nation had learned what the bill actually included, the battle lines that had been forming and loosely coalescing hardened into battle formation. The friends, supporters, associates and sycophants of the Administration were, of course, united in supporting 113 S.-1. No one was surprised by their intensity and fervor, at all levels, in organizing their members, and their family members, to push the Congress to pass the bill. Likewise, the conservative, tea party, patriot associations, and many Christian organizations, organized to exert their members and families' maximum pressure on their members of

Congress. No surprise there, either. The frantic recruiting efforts by both sides, though, centered on organizations and leaders of private associations that had not historically been aligned on either side of the gun debate, or had no prior history of interest in freedom of the press or speech issues.

Both sides instinctively knew that the final outcome came down not to what Congress did, but instead to what a handful of blue dog Democrats and liberal Republicans in both Houses, a total of less than eighty Members, would do when the determining votes were cast. The vote on the health care reform debate provided the outline for victory for the White House, in that a bill not particularly favored by most Americas, nevertheless, became the law of the land, even though by only one vote in the U.S. House of Representatives. Political pundits in the days after the McAlister Bill was released speculated that the odds slightly favored the passage of the bill, primarily because of the healthcare reform outcome.

Senator Blevins let it be known soon after the bill was made public that he intended to put the opponents of his bill on the defensive, announcing in his initial news conference how he intended to do it. Seated in his wheelchair in the imposing Senate Caucus Room on the 3rd floor of the Russell Senate Office Building, the only available room that was big enough to hold the media they knew would come out to cover the unveiling of the Bill, the Senator fired the first shot, and an impressively large shot it was. I've memorialized here the important part of what he said:

"Now that I've covered in some detail the specific provisions of 113-S.-1, let's talk a little inside political baseball, so to speak. I'm more than mindful of the intensive efforts by the gun lobby, and their misguided supporters,

because my office has been besieged by their dirty tricks, including robo-calls 24/7 to try and keep my Senate office phones from functioning. But, my friends, this is not my first legislative war. I will soon convene hearings of my Committee in this very same august and historic room, which was the site of the investigation into the sinking of the Titanic, the Army-McCarthy Hearings, as well as the Joe Valachi Mafia Hearings, and the Watergate Hearings.

"We will, of course, hear from the many supporters of my Bill to make America gun free and safe. But, just as importantly, I will be subpoenaing, not just inviting to testify, the opponents of this sensible Bill. I want to make them come out in the open, out from the shadows so to speak, and tell Americans, under the bright lights of media coverage, how they could possibly oppose a Bill to make Americans safer from gun violence. They've been sneakin' around, lobbyin' their Senators and Representatives behind closed doors, I want them out in the open, where we can all hear what they have to say. Let's look them in the eye and force these gun-lusting, right wing, bullies to say in public what we know they've been whispering privately. I'm lookin' forward to it, I'll tell you that. The wounds that I suffered in the 'Guns Against Government Conspiracy' will be worth it if we can pass this Bill and stop all the shootin'."

Senator Blevins' news conference hadn't been over two minutes before my office phones in Tyler started ringing off the hook. Somebody on Blevin's staff had leaked that I was among those being subpoenaed to testify in his Committee Hearings, starting in ten days. Great. So, John, I asked myself when I got these calls, who ya' gonna call? An obvious answer - my friend and attorney, Chuck Webster, who as it turned out, was more nervous than I was about this turn of events.

NINE

Tyler, Texas

"John Madison, how long have I known you?"

"What kind of a question is that, Chuck?" Whenever the two sparred over any topic, they both knew that John would bring up their standing grade school girlfriend joke. "You're my best friend, and you've been my best friend since I stole Patty Pierson away from you in the 5th Grade of Tyler Elementary. You've never forgiven me, have you? This is all about Patty, again, isn't it?"

"If you hadn't married Patty, later, I would have never forgiven you, but in light of the circumstances, I about had to forgive you. No, goofy, this is about how you are about to get yourself indicted, for various federal crimes and misdemeanors, if you're not *very careful*. You obviously have no clue how seriously the President, and his newly re-united Senate buddy, Jim Blevins, take the campaign speech you made in Austin just days before the shootings."

Chuck Webster was a few years younger than John Madison, but they had developed a close relationship, as Webster had helped his friend negotiate through the labyrinth of insurance industry rules and regulations. His top of his Tyler high school class standing, paved the way, along with his impressive LSAT results, to his admission to an Ivy League law school. After graduation he turned down lucrative New York and DC offers, returning instead to Texas. He wanted to raise his family in a family environment, and near his parents. Chuck Webster and his wife had decided early in their marriage that they wanted to bear all of the children that God sent them, without any restrictions or impediments. As a result, they had been blessed with ten children, ranging in age from twelve years to eighteen months. Chuck liked to joke that he would be practicing law until he was in a nursing home, just to get all of his kids through college. John and Debbie Madison, whose grandchildren lived some distance from them, loved to spend time with Chuck's brood, whom they referred to as their Tyler grandkids.

"Chuck, I understand the concept. A pro-gun Texas conservative gives a speech suggesting that if the President were to be re-elected he'll try and outlaw gun ownership. That wasn't a revolutionary thought, after all. When the President ran four years earlier a lot of people quietly suggested that's what he would do. Otherwise, why did all the gun dealers sell out of ammunition back then?"

"Quietly is the key word. No major conservative leader went so public four years ago. Low profile was the approach. But, not this time. *Right Wing Pro-Gun, Tea Party Leader John Madison* uses his campaign megaphone and fires a salvo, if you'll excuse the expression, at the President just days before he's shot by a lunatic. Wonderful timing, John."

"So? What ever happened to the First Amendment? I can't speak my mind, in a civil way, without the sky falling in on me? Plus, I would point out the obvious in all this – the President *is trying to take away our guns,* just as I said he would. Doesn't that inconvenient fact give me some cover?"

"See, John, that's what I'm talking about. You're in denial. The First Amendment? You really think these guys give a fig for the Constitution? They're re-defining the First Amendment in Blevin's anti-free speech, anti-gun ownership bill he introduced. This is the same President who promised

50

to fundamentally transform America. How do you fundamentally transform a country without altering its founding documents?"

"OK, I hear you, but the Second Amendment's right to keep and bear arms is written in our nation's DNA. I was just trying to warn the voters, using my First Amendment rights, I might add, that his second term posed a distinct danger to gun rights. So, now I should worry about getting indicted for just speaking out, in a campaign?"

Chuck Webster shifted uncomfortably in his leather lawyers' chair. It was obvious to him that his friend was headed for deep legal problems, and in spite of all of his lawyerly skills, he would not be able to head off the oncoming onslaught. He concluded that the best approach to help his friend and client was to give him the scary truth of what he was facing.

"John, buddy, here's how it's going to go. You're going to be served very soon with a U.S. Senate subpoena from Blevin's Committee on the Judiciary. You might have had more of a shot at true justice, ironically, if Senator Reese had assigned the Bill to the Committee on Homeland Security and Governmental Affairs. The problem with the Judiciary Committee is that it's packed with the Senate's most liberal, doctrinaire haters of all conservative causes and people. You'll only have a handful of days to prepare. You'll face the grilling of your life from Senator Blevins and his Committee members and Staff. They'll paint you as the instigator, at the very least, of the shootings. You'll try and defend yourself, but you are very likely to say things that will expose you to indictment. They'll indict you, not only for what you say at the Committee Hearing, but every word you uttered in the campaign will be scrutinized for 'hate speech'. They'll push the trial to a quick date. They'll convict you. You'll be watching the world from a federal facility hundreds of mile from your family. And that's the best case scenario. Now, do I have your attention, John?

"That's not going to happen."

"Why? Because you're going to listen to your lawyer, and best friend, and take the Fifth Amendment, refusing to utter words that can be used against you, to indict you?"

"Chuck, I know you mean well. I know you're scary smart in the law. I know that you have my best interests at heart and that you are probably giving me really good advice. But..."

"But?"

"But, I'm not going to refuse to answer questions by asserting my Fifth Amendment rights. That's like waving a red flag. *'Hey, look at me – I'm guilty of the crimes you're asking about – which is why I'm taking the Fifth!'* No way, Chuck, I'm not doing it."

"You don't get it. The Fifth Amendment to the Constitution was written to protect you from the ambush that Blevins and his Committee are arranging for you. It's the only way you can protect yourself from being indicted for your own words. I know it looks bad to take the Fifth, because you look like you're hiding something, but it looks a lot worse to go to prison, when you might have been able to avoid it."

"Chuck, I would agree with you and I would probably take the Fifth if the only danger to me was what I might say in front of Blevins' witch-hunting Committee. But, as you just said, and we both know, I gave over 30 speeches in the campaign, to gun groups, tea party and patriot meetings, even to a handful of Republican county Lincoln-Reagan Dinners. Most were recorded, and several videotaped. I'm stuck with what I said in those speeches. If they want to accuse me of violating the federal Hate Crimes Act, they'll figure out a way to do it, no matter what I say before the Committee."

"No doubt, John. I'm just trying to minimize the charges. One of their historical tricks in DC is to charge people they are pursuing with lying to Congress, based on a portion of the criminal code that makes it a felony to give a materially false statement or representation to the nation's lawmakers. Who do you think decides what constitutes a materially false statement? You guessed it, my friend."

"Well, then, Chuck, your job, as you sit next to me at the witness table, is to make sure that I don't lie to Congress.

"How do you propose, exactly, that I accomplish that task? I can't take back your words once they exit your pie hole."

"If I come even close to an untruth, kick my ankle, elbow my ribs or just write *indictable statement* on your legal pad. However you nudge me, I'll get the message, and try to undig my way out of the hole. But, I'm not....not...going to plead the Fifth. Frankly, Chuck, I'd rather get indicted for federal crimes than to tell the nation at the hearing that I refuse to answer questions about the shootings, and make it look like I was involved, even though I knew absolutely nothing about the shootings before the shots were fired."

"Well stated, John, but you may just get your wish. You won't look guilty – but you may find yourself guilty, anyway."

TEN

Washington, DC – Russell Senate Office Building

"Would the witness please stand and be sworn?"

With these time-honored words directed to John Madison, United States Senator James R. Blevins commenced what Washington loved best, the blood sport of reputation assassination by way of Congressional hearings. This Committee hearing, as Senator Blevins had previously announced, was being held the next day after Congress convened on January 8th in the historic Senate Caucus Room on the third floor of the Russell Senate Office Building, one of three buildings occupied by Senators for their Senatorial offices. The United States Senate Committee on the Judiciary, one of twenty standing Committees, consisted of ten Democrats and eight Republicans.

None of the eighteen Committee members were smiling. All knew that the mainstream media had decided to extensively cover the hearing, most airing the testimony live. It was political high drama show time. John Madison stood from behind the glass-topped witness table, on which were a bevy of microphones all pointed towards him, and raised his right hand. He swore to tell the truth, the whole truth and nothing but the truth, but added "so help me God" at the end, even though the oath as given to him omitted those four words, and had not included them for several years.

Senator Blevins, in his purposely emphasized low country South Carolinian accent, made it clear he was not amused. "Fine, Mr. Madison, y'all want to add y'alls' own words to our o-fficial oath, that's just fine. Ya may need all the help you can get from your version of God before this proceedin' has concluded. I see ya got ya lawyer here today. Care to introduce ya man?"

"Certainly, Senator, Members of the Committee, I'm joined today by my attorney and lifelong friend, Chuck Webster. He's a graduate of Har...."

"That'll be enough, Mr. Madison. He's identified for the record, we are not in need of his resume. Let's move ahead, now. Mr. Madison, before we take y'all's testimony, the several Members of this U-nited States Senate Committee on the Judiciary are granted the opportunity to make openin' statements. Mine, suh, will be brief and to the point.

"I don't believe that individual citizens should ever have the right to own anythin' that can be used, suh, to kill folks. I believed this before some dang fool right winger shot me on October 26th, but I'm even more of that belief and persuasion now, of course. I know all about what y'all scream about when it comes to any restrictions on ya precious guns, ya *fire*-arms. *The Second Amendment. The Second Amendment.* It's ya mantra, ya holy grail.

"In these here hearings we all gonna' look real close at your holy grail words, study 'em real close up like. America's gonna' see that the Second Amendment don't even come close to sayin' what y'all been sayin' that it says. We gonna' have a number of expert academic legal scholars to testify that the Second Amendment don't mean what it says....that is, it don't mean what it seems to say...., uh, it don't mean what it seems like it means....oh, well, you get my idea here. The scholars are gonna' tell us, I understand, that this Congress can clear up the con-fusion in the Amendment real well, by just passin' the McAlister Hate Weapons Elimination Bill. And, also, my bill will put some teeth in the Hate Crimes

Act, to prohibit hateful speech that leads to violence. Simple as that. I promised this'd be short. Uh....Let's see here. Uh, yes, I recognize the ranking member for his openin' statement, the distinguished gentle-man from Idaho, Senator Remington."

Senator Sam Remington had served in the U.S. Senate longer than all but two other Senators. In his several years of service in the Senate he had become known as a man who did not suffer fools gladly. He had long ago decided that Senator Blevins from South Carolina was, as he had said privately, 'all blow, and no go'. Senator Remington had voted on nearly every bill of importance directly opposite the votes cast by Senator Blevins. Since the senior Senator from Idaho was a rancher and hunter, he was less than enthusiastic about Senator Blevins' bill to take away his right to own and possess the several firearms he maintained at his ranch. It was widely known that for decades he had hosted in his office a weekly Tuesday night poker game for his western Senate colleagues.

As ranking member of the Committee on the Judiciary, Senator Remington was in a position to become Chairman, should control of the Senate revert to the Republican Party. Unfortunately for Senator Remington, control did not vest in the Republican Party after the election. A bit salty, Senator Remington had said that being the Committee's ranking member was about like being Vice President, but without all the fun funerals to attend. He knew that his brief opening statement wouldn't be long remembered, but that it could help set the tone for the hearings on the McAlister Bill, though the outcome of which Senate hearings there did not appear to be much doubt.

"Chairman Blevins, distinguished members of the Committee on the Judiciary, my remarks will also be limited. We all know why we are here. We all know that the McAlister Bill is designed and crafted to be an end-run around the U.S. Constitution. The majority may have the votes to pass this bill, but they don't have the votes to do it the right way, the legal way, the honest way. They don't have enough support in the country to amend the Constitution and take away the right to keep and bear arms, nor enough votes to legally take away the right of free speech, even if its controversial speech. If they didn't have the occupant of the White House and if they didn't have what may well be a majority of the Court that sets across the plaza from us, we wouldn't be here today. They wouldn't try to statutorily amend our nation's founding document, except for one man at 1600 and one new Justice across the plaza. Wouldn't happen.

"But, in my years working on this hill I've learned that you play the cards you're dealt. So, Mr. Chairman, members of the Committee, let's play this high stakes game out. Let's see if you've got enough votes in the House. It's clear McAlister will pass this body. We know that the President will sign the bill into law, if you've got the votes in the House. How will the new Justice across the plaza vote? Flip those cards up and let's see if Americans can continue to speak freely, and continue to keep and bears arms, or, alternatively, if we're going to lose those precious rights. Deal 'em, Mr. Chairman, deal 'em."

The other members of the Committee on the Judiciary delivered their opening statements, alternating between Democrat and Republican members. There were no surprises, as the Members had declared well before the hearings where they stood on the McAlister Bill, and how they intended to vote. At the conclusion of the opening statements, Chairman Blevins declared a short recess, which actually was brief, as everybody in the vast hearing room was anxious for the blood sport to begin. It was time to watch the Committee grill the Witness.

Senator Blevins wheeled back to his position and loudly banged his gavel, calling the hearing back in session, "Mr. Madison, suh, my staff's report on ya, Mr. Madison, and the information provided to our Committee by various federal law enforcement agencies, tells me that ya were a *very active Texan* in the campaign that just concluded last November, about nine weeks ago. Would ya agree, Mr. Madison that ya worked almost full time in the campaign to defeat our incumbent President and to deny him, I might say, his well-earned second term?"

Chuck Webster had warned his client about compound and loaded questions, so he was ready for the Senator's initial jab. "Senator, let me take the various parts of your question. First, I was not a full time, as you say, campaigner in last year's campaign. I have a job as an executive officer of an insurance company, so what I did in the....."

"Come on, now Mr. Madison. Ya gonna tell this Committee, this Congress, *under oath*, that ya weren't active in the campaign, even though ya gave over, I hear, a hundred or so speeches?"

John Madison instinctively bristled at having his words misinterpreted. In practice sessions in Tyler, the local county prosecutor that Chuck Webster had recruited to help prep his client for the hearing had done exactly the same thing – make it sound like he was lying, when he wasn't. So he was ready for the Senator.

"With all due respect, Senator Blevins, I gave forty some speeches, best I can recall. I did not work full-time, though I was active in the campaign. I was merely exercising my First Amend...."

"Fine, Mr. Madison, just fine, we're not here today to hear lectures on ancient documents. No sirree, we are here to talk about guns and hate speech...so, Mr. Madison, let's talk first about --- your guns. How many guns ya own and or possess, Mr. Madison, and I remind ya, *ya're under oath.*"

"Senator, it's hardly relevant how many guns I may or may not..."

"Suh, ya lawyer there sittin' by ya will tell ya that relevancy is *our call*, not ya all's call. Now answer my question, if ya would be so kind – and listen carefully to what I asked ya – how many guns do ya own and or possess?"

Attorney Webster leaned over to his client, cupping his hand around his ear, and gave him hurried advice. John Madison frowned slightly, started to whisper to his attorney, apparently had second thoughts, then addressed the Chairman. "Mr. Chairman, I own two handguns, and also a rifle, a shotgun and an antique long rifle, alleged to be from the Revolutionary War, that had passed down through the family to my father before he died."

"Is that *all*, Mr. Madison? Sounds like ya got yaself a veritable *arsenal* there. Ya worried about somethin? Or Someone? "

60

"Senator, in Texas, and I think in lots of areas of the country mine would not be an unusually high number of weapons for self-protection and as part of a collection." Webster flinched slightly, a movement picked up by his client, causing him to raise his guard for how the Senator would likely respond.

"*Self-protection*? Is that what ya said, Mr.Madison? *Self protection*? When was the last time you shot somebody comin' in ya house? Is that what you intend to do, Mr. Madison, shoot people that come in ya house? Ya call shootin' people just 'cause they might drop by ya house *self-protection*? Ya make me sick, Mr. Madison, sick with fear that people like ya want to hang onto ya many guns....It's the law-abidin' citizens of this country that need to be protected against ya, and all ya many hate weapons....I....I'm so....why, ya just..."

A Senate staff member hustled forward and handed a note to the Chairman, whose face had visibly reddened. He glanced at the note, banged his gavel loudly and announced, "We'll take a brief recess, I've got a call from the President that I need to return." A wire service photographer with access in the Committee room casually walked up during the recess and read the note that the Chairman had left after reading it at his seat at the committee table. It read "SENATOR – GOOD TIME TO CALL A RECESS."

ELEVEN

Washington, DC – Russell Senate Office Building

The members of the Senate Judiciary Committee were slow to re-convene, most using the recess as an opportunity to grant interviews to favored reporters, giving their spin to the high-profile Committee hearings. Returning to the Senate Caucus Room, Senator Blevins rolled his wheelchair the length of the massive oak table, and positioned himself in the center seat, the location with the Chairman's gavel, and the Chairman's power, unequalled by any other Member.

"Mister Madison, suh, are ya ready to continue ya testimony?"

John Madison was technically ready, he thought, but it was obvious from the brief brush up with Senator Blevins already this morning, that he was in for what he would call in Texas, a tussle. How could anyone, he thought, really be ready for a tussle with a varmint committed to his destruction? Nevertheless, he was committed to as much civility as he could muster. "Yes, Mr. Chairman, I'm ready to continue. Thank you so much for the timely recess."

The Chairman started to give a flippant response, then decided the better course was to move on. "I would remind the witness, suh, that the oath ya took this morning still applies to anything, that's *anything*, that ya may choose to offer to the Committee in ya further testimony today. Do ya understand that, suh?"

"Yes, sir, Mr. Chairman."

"Mr. Madison, on October 22nd ya delivered a much-reported speech to the gun lovers, uh, 'scuse me, let me rephrase that, to the Austin chapter of the National Rifle Association. Isn't that right, suh?"

"Yes, Mr. Chairman, and it was much-reported, as you said. I've seen short excerpts from that speech on several occasions broadcast by the nation's media. What the news clips don't show is what I said about..."

"Ya'all answered my question, Mr. Madison....just wanted to be sure that ya were the same person whose speech, many folks believe, may have led to the shootings, four days later, on October 26th, the President's shooting, mine and the murderous shooting of Director Larry McAlister, for whom we have named this hate weapon and hate speech elimination law to honor his memory. Now, what I want to ask next..."

"Mr. Chairman, please, you have to give me the opportunity to respond to your..."

"Mr. Madison, I don't *have* to do anything. I asked if you gave that hate weapon incitement speech and you admitted that you did. My next question, though, is about...."

John Madison was close to losing it. He had been well prepared for the likelihood of this specific attack, the accusation of his complicity in the shootings, but that didn't make it easy to take. He remembered his lawyer's advice, he took two deep breaths, and again interrupted the Chairman of the Senate's most prestigious and powerful committee. "With all due respect, and I do respect your position as Chairman of this Committee, I want to state, on the record, that I had *absolutely no prior knowledge* of the tragic shootings of October 26th, including yours, Senator, which I sincerely regret. No knowledge. None. Nothing."

"Now, suh, that was a mighty fine statement. Well-rehearsed and well stated. It suhtainly was. I expected no less. No less, indeed. I am not accusing you, suh, of any *direct involvement* with my shooting, nor the President's nor Larry McAlister's. If there were even one shred of evidence connecting you with the shootins, what's been called the Gun Conspiracy Against the Gubment, you wouldn't be settin' here, suh, ya'd already be in a federal prison, yes suh, ya would. No, Mr. Madison, what I want to know more about, and what the members of this Committee want to know more about and frankly, what Americans want to know more about, is how ya hate speech on October 22nd may have motivated the triple shooting of high government officials, just four days later. We not only want to know *what* ya knew and *when* did ya know it, we want to know *what* the shooters knew and *when* did they know it, and how much was based on *your* provocative little hate speech."

"Senator, since I have no clue who the shooters were, and apparently the FBI doesn't either at this point, how can I be expected to know how my speech affected them, or may have affected anybody else, for that matter."

"Now, Mr. Madison, that's right convenient, yes it is. Ya make ya little hate speech in Austin, poisoning the public discourse, throwin' unfounded accusations at our Commander in Chief, then when ya followers take to heart what ya said, and try to assassinate the man ya said the hateful words about, then ya just duck and hide, and say ya just can't be responsible for ya own hateful words. That won't wash, Mr. Madison, ya gonna have to face the music for what ya said in that...."

"Mr. Chairman, if I may. Please....please....Sir, you have called my words in Austin hate speech and hateful words, but anyone who has read the words, or watched the speech, realizes that I was only saying in the middle of a heated campaign that the President would likely try to take away our right to keep and bear arms if he won a second term. To use your phrase, that's political discourse. My words are by no stretch the use of hate speech. I know from the media reports that the Department of Justice is supposedly looking into whether or not I can be charged with violating the federal Hate Crimes Act, and that..."

"And, suh, that doesn't concern ya?"

"Of course, Senator, it concerns me. I'm not a lawyer, but I'm told that there was a judge a few years ago who said that a grand jury would indict a ham sandwich if the District Attorney requested it. Of course, I'm concerned, I just don't think there's any basis for such a charge."

"Very funny, Mr. Madison. Very funny, indeed. A ham sandwich, hunh? Well, we will see what we will see. I am told that there are more federal agents working on the campaign shootings than have been assigned to any other investigation since 9/11. This, suh, I can assure ya. This government will find and prosecute those who fired the actual shots, but we will also put away for a very long time the lunatics who set the stage for the assault on the government. We cannot, we will not allow the overthrow of the government by violent means, even when it's all masqueraded as protected campaign speech. Not gonna' happen, Mr. Madison, suh."

John Madison felt sick at his stomach. Virtually everything his attorney had warned him about was unfolding before him, and being broadcast to a nation demanding answers. How long had this been going on this morning, he wondered? He glanced at his watch, another thing his attorney told him *not* to do.

"Mr. Madison, suh, are we keeping ya from an important appointment? Are ya missin' a meetin' with a gun manufacturing lobbyist? Do ya need to make a call to ya gun groups?"

Feeling humiliated that the pressure and stress of the Committee hearing had made him forget even the most basic prep, like not looking at his watch, John Madison could only say, "No, Senator, you have my full attention."

"Why, I thank ya for that, I really do. Moving on Mr. Madison, the Committee staff has prepared some basic questions for ya to submit to ya little tax payer, tea party, patriot groups that ya are affiliated with down there in Texas. We'll give ya plenty of time to respond, say twelve, no...., let's say ten calendar days. But, before I pass the questionin' to the distinguished Rankin' Member, the gentleman from Minnesota, I have one other area of questionin', suh."

"Yes, Senator."

"I take it that ya are well acquainted with the Second Amendment – it's kinda like ya holy grail and ya holy Bible all rolled into one?"

"No, Senator, I wouldn't put it that way. I'd just say that the Constitution grants us as citizens of the United States the right keep and bear arms, as it says in the Second Amendment."

"Well, let's look at your precious Second Amendment, suh. Not exactly, wouldn't you agree, a model of precise, careful use of the English language. It starts out by referring to the militia. *The militia.* Quote. *A well regulated militia being necessary to the security of a free state.* Unquote. Do ya belong to a militia, Mr. Madison? Of course, ya don't. Nobody does any more, over two centuries after the words were written with a quill pen, except for some lunatics running around in the woods shooting at pumpkins and hiding ammunition in logs. There might, I say, might, have been a valid reason to own weapons of violence when the country was still gettin' rid of the Brits, but today? Give me a break. *The militia?* Because they needed an armed militia over 200 years ago doesn't mean every man, woman and child should have the right *in the 21st Century* to own instruments of mayhem and murder. Now, that just makes no sense to me, none at all. If ya want to arm the National Guard in each State, I have no problem with that, they are today's militia, I believe, but my neighbor shouldn't own an armory. Ya would agree that the many legal scholars that have been calling for a legal re-interpretation of this clumsy language have a point, wouldn't ya, suh?"

"Senator, far be it from me to criticize the founding fathers for their language. Sure, the language used might have been a little more precise, but it's clear enough. Read the balance of the Second Amendment - *'the right of the people to keep and bear arms shall not be infringed'.* The people, the citizens, of this nation, have a basic right to defend ourselves, by force of arms, if necessary. You don't have the right, Senator, to warp the clear intent of the Constitution by just saying you are re-interpreting the Bill of Rights. When they wrote those words, I'm sure they never thought that some future Congress would someday say that the black letters on parchment had *no meaning*."

Senator Blevins just sat back in his Chairman's chair and smiled. He knew that he didn't need to reply to Madison's words, as the witness had just given him tomorrow's headlines, and those words would help push the Bill towards passage. John Madison had fallen into the classic Congressional trap for witnesses, of agreeing with a statement worded against the witness's own interest. The nation's leading liberal media lost no time in headlining Madison's testimony to advance their undisguised anti-gun agenda:

New York Times

MADISON AGREES 2ND AMENDMENT IS FLAWED

Boston World

PRO-GUN LEADER TESTIFIES NO BASIS
FOR GUN RIGHTS IN 2ND AMENDMENT

CNN

CONGRESS POISED TO PASS HATE WEAPON ACT

TWELVE

Website Blog dated January 9th

Whew! I think I would rather have a really bad cold or a bout of the flu than to have to go through that again. Testifying before the Senate Judiciary Committee yesterday was like taking a beating, but without all the grins. The Hearing started on Tuesday, January 8th and I was in the hot seat most of the day. When I say the day, of course, that's not like a normal person's day. In Congress, they take lots of recesses, so they can talk to each other, and the media and who knows what else. We probably got in three hours, plus or minus, of actual testimony time.

Senator Blevins was tough on me, asking about my gun ownership and hitting me hard, as we knew he would, on my Austin speech. He really didn't want to know what I had to say (I understand that's usually the case with witnesses they call before the Judiciary Committee), he just used me, and my much interrupted testimony, to make points for his anti-free speech and anti-gun bill. To tell the truth (if you can't tell the truth to yourself, who can you tell it to?), I think he did score some points. I never should have said that the language used by the founding fathers in the Second Amendment could have been a bit clearer, that was a mistake, and the media, as we know all know, ran with it. The language is more than clear that we have the right to keep and bear arms. It's only those who want to take away that right who see vagueness in the first phrase regarding the militia in the 2nd Amendment.

My other mistake was when that Senator from Rhode Island, I've forgotten his name, asked how I could oppose a bill that allowed a specific exemption for hunters. What a joke - the so-called exemption requires an ATF employee or a government game warden to accompany every hunter. Say what? Only a government paid genius could come up with such an insult to every hunter in America. And the purpose of the hunting license exemption has to be for food purposes, only - come on. When the Senator asked me how I could oppose the exemption language, I should not have called it the most idiotic idea I'd heard in years, but it is. They're going to use this as a not very clever fig leaf to cover up what they are doing – taking away our right to defend our families against people who won't obey the law, who won't turn in their guns.

The Senators guffawed and laughed me to scorn when I said that the old bumper sticker had it right when it said: WHEN GUNS ARE OUTLAWED ONLY OUTLAWS WILL HAVE GUNS. They apparently don't believe it. Senator Blevins exploded with rage, sputtering about how no criminal would ever take a chance of a felony conviction for owning a gun. How out of touch with reality can these guys possibly get? Criminals who commit crimes are already facing felony charges if they're caught, so what's a little more prison time for owning a prohibited gun? These lawmakers ought to look in depth at what happened in Australia after they outlawed guns. The crime rate didn't decline. In some areas, criminal activity actually increased. If this bill passes, I hate to think what will happen. Most guns used by private citizens are used to protect themselves from wrongdoers who want their property or their bodies, for their own pleasure. If it becomes a felony to own a gun in America, crime rates will soar.

But, I'm preaching to my own choir, here. What we have to do, and do it very quickly, is convince enough Americans to convince enough Congress Critters to vote against this bill. Everybody in the media keeps saying that's it on a 'fast track' in the Congress for passage. They're so sure of a quick vote and passage in the House that they only intend to hold two days of public hearings, in the third week of January. Speaker Pelham has publicly told the President, in her words, that "America will be a hate weapon and hate speech free nation" well before Labor Day. At least on this bill she didn't announce to Congress that Congress would have to vote for it *first*, before they could see what's in the new law. The Lawrence McAlister Hate Speech and Hate Weapon Elimination bill is a stunning piece of clarity. We all know what it says, and we all know what it will do.

THIRTEEN

Washington, DC – Russell Senate Office Building

The Senate Committee on the Judiciary was about to conclude almost two full days of grilling John Madison. Exercising his prerogatives as Chairman, Senator Blevins concluded the questioning of witness Madison.

"Mr. Madison, suh, do these words sound familiar to ya? Ya complained yesterday that I had not used ya actual words, so let's listen to a recording of ya actual words." The Chairman nodded to his aide, who motioned to a sound engineer, who pushed the appropriate button to play an audio recording, which boomed across the marble hearing room, purposely played louder than it needed to be.

"Modern democracies like to brag, with some historic justification, that they reflect the will of their governed. The key word, of course, is historic. That's because in recent years those in power, those in control, of the levers of power of western nations have learned how to warp and maneuver the system to get around the pesky requirement that the governed should give their consent to their own governing. The trend lines don't look good for any improvement in obtaining the consent of the governed in this country. They don't care what we think, or what we want our government to do.

"It's good to be king. It's even better to be President of the United States of America. You can ignore the voters, once you have wooed them into electing you President twice, gaining their votes with the most transparent campaign promises, and then just do what you want to do. The most dangerous time, of course, for America, with any President is in his, or her, second term. With no requirement to ever face

another voter, or campaign opponent, the second term President is a potential tyrant, available for any scheme hatched by the White House staff, or outside ideological bed fellows, to radically change the Constitution of the United States, as it was written. We have to take him out!

"If this President should be elected to a second term next month, don't be surprised if he tries to re-interpret out of the Constitution the guarantee of our right to own a gun. He may even seek to alter our right to speak, or meet or worship as we see fit. That's what's on the line on November 6th. That's why we must insure that every member of our families, all of our employees, in fact every one that we know, comes out and votes to deny the President a second term, which would be a very dangerous second term for America, indeed."

"Did, the recording accurately record ya words, Mr. Madison, from ya little speech down there in Austin? Accurately recorded, suh?"

Like any person who utters words before crowds of people, or even small numbers of listeners, John Madison was stuck with his words. What could he say – no, I didn't say those words? Or, could he say if he could do it over, he wouldn't use the word tyrant or say that we should 'take him out'? Or if he had known in advance about the shootings, he wouldn't have even showed up in Austin? Camera phones had made private speeches a thing of the past. And now, Senator Blevins, freshly wounded and still healing, from his own shooting, was using John Madison's own words to advance the Senator's favorite cause – the abolition of gun ownership in America, while piggy-backing in his bill a significant restriction on the right of free speech.

"Do ya think it's *patriotic,* to use one of ya favored words, to call our elected President a *tyrant,* Mr. Madison, suh? Ya think that encourages civility and respect for our leader, suh? Ya think it's good to suggest *assassination* by sayin' *'we gotta take him out'* Suh, ya were the right-winga' who suggested *'takin' out'* the President just four days before he was shot, isn't that the case, suh?"

"Those words were spoken in another time, *before* the shootings, Senator. I meant taking him out in the election, not by shooting, of course. But I do think my words are all protected speech, under the First Amendment, discussing the Second Amendment. That's all I would say, sir."

"I didn't think ya would deny ya own words. I have no more questions of this here witness. This Committee stands adjourned until further order of the Chair."

Most impartial observers thought that Madison had held his own against rough, even rude, questioning by Committee members, some from both political parties. Public sentiment, measured by most polls, even seven weeks after the shootings, was still decidedly running in favor of the President and Congress, and their plan to abolish private gun ownership, the small problem with the Constitution notwithstanding. Attention continued to focus on the gun abolition portions of the McAlister Bill, with little public debate of the free speech issues, most likely due to public reaction to the October 26th shootings.

All members of the Committee had now asked their questions, some questions asked more artfully than others, but almost all questions calculated to make the questioning Senator look good back home to voters, to the media, to their staff members and to their significant other or spouse, or both, as the case may be. Very few questions were asked in order to actually help shape the legislation pending before the Committee. The days of the Committee on the Judiciary seeking to learn the truth from witnesses had long passed. The Republic had suffered as a result.

FOURTEEN

New York City, NY – Fox News Studios

What does a national debate on an urgent issue which has captured Americans' attention look like? Before the internet, the issues debated were framed, and presented, by the media. After the advent of the world wide web, many people, average, normal people could share their ideas with their fellow citizens, without going through the editor of the 'letters to the editor' section of their local newspaper. The internet, as many have observed, has empowered people in ways never previously thought possible. Anyone with a laptop can now launch a revolution, as they learned in Yemen, Egypt, Libya, and _____, fill in the blank, which country will be next?

This inconvenient truth has transformed national debates, in America and many western nations, on any issue that may attract the attention of bloggers and e-organizers. The blogosphere did in fact light up, and stayed lit up for a time, once gun-owning Americans realized that they stood close to losing their Second Amendment rights. Most Americans were shell shocked, so to speak, by the pre-election assassination attempt of their President, the shooting of a Senator and the killing of the federal official responsible for the regulation of firearms. The three shootings had more than a chilling effect on those normally expected to fight gun abolition, or expected to lobby against allowing the federal government sweeping powers to regulate speech. Many Americans could see beyond the current crisis, and the prevailing public mood against gun ownership, but, increasing numbers of Americans appeared to be intimidated into silence. The prevailing national culture was trending against gun ownership, aided and abetted by the daily drum

79

beat of media pressure and pronouncements from the White House and Congressional leaders.

The noted exceptions, those who were willing to openly declare their opposition to the anti-gun and speech curtailment bill, were often the subject of highly unflattering media attention. A Wisconsin television news interview typified the coverage.

"Jane, I'm here with Bill Brinkerstaff, a gun supporter from Racine, with his take on the bill being considered by Congress to make America safer." The unshaven interviewee was dressed in camouflage and was wearing a bright orange baseball cap on which was stenciled WHEN GUNS ARE OUTLAWED - I'LL BE AN OUTLAW.

"Yeah, like I said, if they take away our guns, we will take away their miserable lives."

"Who are you threatening, Mr. Brinkerstaff? Who should be afraid of you if the Congress adopts the McAlister bill into law and abolishes gun ownership by private citizens?"

"That camera's on, right? You're recording this? I'm not saying anything more. I'm not going to jail. I'll just say we're not going to give up without a fight. Got it?"

"Thank you, sir, now back to you, Jane." What the interviewer did not report was that he had interviewed eight gun rights supporters, all of whom made cogent, non-threatening arguments, before he located his target, a gun rights supporter, in camouflage, who would threaten violence, on camera. None of the eight favorable interviews were ever aired by the station.

The national media followed the same pattern, during the time the Congress was considering the gun bill. There were few favorable interviews with gun ownership advocates carried by national media. Fox News was an exception, as its President, Roger Ayres, wouldn't bow to pressure from federal agencies. Fox aired several pro-gun ownership interviews and segments covering the legal and practical arguments against passage of the McAlister bill. One such interview featured Jon Voyles, a Hollywood actor of some reknown:

"Mr. Voyles, you're widely known in Hollywood as a conservative, so, what makes your newly announced opposition to the gun ban bill news worthy?"

"Harrison, that's a real good question, yes, it certainly is. You're correct, I am a conservative, no secret there, but what I'm announcing tonight, exclusively on Fox News, is that I making a good sized financial contribution, from my own funds, to try and stop the McAlister bill.

"How much are you contributing to the pro-gun groups, if I may ask?"

"One dollar. That is, one dollar for every dollar contributed by pro Second Amendment Americans like me. A matching grant."

"Wow, Mr. Voyles, that's a serious commitment. Is there an upper limit to your generosity?"

"Let's wait and see. I'm willing to give well over a million, maybe a lot more. I truly believe that the fight over the abolition of ownership of guns by Americans is only the beginning. If we lose this fight, since the Second Amendment is so clear, the Constitution will be shredded, and it won't have any meaning in the future. This bill also goes after the freedom to speak your mind freely in this country, which Hollywood and the media seemed to have overlooked. Those speech review panels in the bill will just be used to censor Americans who want to discuss controversial subjects. Our founding fathers must be spinning in their graves. If this bill passes as its written, forget freedom of speech and worship and of the press, along with all those due process rights we have relied on for centuries. We can't lose this battle."

"But, Jon, aren't you concerned about pressure on you from the White House, and the Administration's friends in Hollywood?"

"Look, Harrison, I made my last major movie several years ago. Once it got out that I wasn't drinking their liberal kool aid, I was blacklisted, and I have been ever since. That's OK, I'd rather be right than to have to thank the Academy. We have to defeat this dangerous bill. If we don't, we'll always regret not doing everything we could to stop this assault on the Bill of Rights. Mark my words, if we don't stop this bill, the government will be deciding what we can say on shows like this, in books, in speeches and even from the pulpits of our churches. I'm very concerned, which is why I'm backing my words with my money. I invite others to join with me."

"Thanks, Jon, we'll be watching how many Americans make contributions to stop this evil bill. We've put your website link on the screen for those who want to have you match their contribution. God bless."

By the time of the vote on the McAlister bill, Americans had given over four million dollars to the Voyles fund, which he matched, dollar for dollar. Most of the funds given in opposition to the bill were used to encourage calls, letters, e-mail and other communications by voters to their State's Senators and to their District's member of the U.S. House of Representatives. Later studies confirmed that most of the funds spent, however, had little effect, as those Members of Congress who were committed in favor of the bill routinely instructed their office staff to round file written communication against the bill, to delete electronic communication and to spike telephone messages. Representative government in action.

Members who had declared their opposition to passage of the bill, and who were known from past votes on other conservative issues as Members who would keep their word, were not targeted for voter pressure, for obvious reasons. They were the safe votes in opposition, not requiring any expenditure of funds by gun rights, religious groups and other conservatives.

The undeclared Members, those who refused to pledge to vote for or against the McAlister bill, numbered approximately twelve in the Senate and forty-four in the House, give or take, depending on the day. Of the fifty-six in both Houses, some were genuinely not sure how they intended to vote. They didn't arrive in Congress because of gun rights supporters, nor were they elected with the support of opponents of gun rights. On the other hand, a few of the fifty-six uncommitted Members were known in Congress as 'perpetual undeclared Members', who had learned that holding out until right before the final vote could reap large benefits. Not only in meals at DC's finest restaurants, but also invitations to speak at expensive U.S. resorts and exotic overseas locations to various associations' annual conventions, all expenses paid. The most important rewards, however, for a last minute decision by these hold out Members were the campaign contributions bundled from the executives of companies and pressure groups, frequently totaling many tens of thousands of dollars, the 'mothers' milk of politics'. Ah, they would frequently muse, there are many advantages of taking one's time to decide important issues facing the Congress.

FIFTEEN

Phoenix, Arizona – State House

Arizona Governor Mike McManus was a hunter, a collector of antique firearms, a member of the NRA, Gun Owners of America and the Arizona state gun owners association. He was, therefore, an unlikely public official for the President to threaten, at least on gun ownership issues. Nevertheless, the President, in his telephone call to the Governor, made clear what he thought of the Governor's plan to gut the McAlister Bill, should it become law.

"Governor, we don't know each other all that well, I think we've met twice at the Governors' Conferences, but I feel like I can just be real candid with you. I can level with you, you know."

"Mr. President, in Arizona that's what we expect. Straight talk. People out here don't usually say, 'well, to be honest with you', because that's just expected. So let's talk turkey, which is something we *do* say."

"Good, Governor, here's the deal. We can't allow your State to get away with adopting your militia bill. It's not gonna' happen, not while I'm the President."

Governor McManus, as a skilled hunter, knew that sometimes the best thing to do was keep quiet, so as not to scare away the game. So, he said nothing. Seconds passed....still nothing...."

The President was the first to give in, to break the heavy silence.

"Governor. Are you still there? Phyllis, I think we've been dis-conn...."

"No, Mr. President, I'm still here, but you're right that the two of us *are* dis-connected. We'll pass whatever laws we want to in Arizona. Do you recall the immigration enforcement law fight under Governor Brewer. We don't much care out here in the desert what you all think about our State's laws back on the Potomac."

"Un-huh....Well, they told me you didn't have much respect for authority."

"Got that one right, sir. I repeat. *We don't care* what you think out in Washington about our militia bill. We are basing the bill on the most American of ideas, that every able-bodied man should be a member of our State's militia. Check your history, the Massachusetts Bay Colony required every man from 16 to 60 to be a militia member, and of course, to bear arms to defend the State. Our militia bill only applies to Arizonans from 18 to 50, and what we are...."

"Look. We *don't give a rip* about who you conscript for your militia, or don't. Governor, you are quite well aware that this is all about your planning to buy up the guns in your State from their owners, and then handing those same guns back to the *same people* you just bought them from, except you'll call them *militia armaments*. All this is to try and avoid the McAlister Bill, when it passes, from applying to Arizona. That's a bunch a horse puckey, Governor, and we're not gonna' allow it. *Are you hearing me?*"

Governor McManus started to give the President the silent treatment response again, but he couldn't restrain himself. In college he had been a wrestler, competing in national tournaments. Now he felt like his arms were being pinned behind him. It was time to make a reverse move on his opponent.

"Well, *we're gonna' pass the bill into law*, and you can *just get used* to the idea. And you might as well know, since it's been rumored in the news, that I've been in touch with a number of other Governors who are giving very serious thought to following Arizona's lead. You got ya'self a good old American *rebellion* on your hands."

"No, Governor, I'm well aware that Arizona is leading this, this....rebellion....as you call it. I would call it by another word, maybe....insurrection....maybe trea....well, let's just say we're not going to let you get away with gutting the McAlister Bill when it's a law."

"With all due respect, Mr. President, which I am quickly losing, how do you plan to stop us? Invasion? Throw us out of Union?"

"I instructed the Attorney General about an hour ago, once I confirmed that there may be other states willing to jump off the cliff along with Arizona, to prepare suit to ask the Courts to...."

"Ha! That's some threat. So if we pass a militia bill and arm our militia, you're gonna' get some liberal federal District Court Judge, probably appointed by Carter or Clinton, to tell us we can't do it? Fine...that's just fine. Do you remember Mr. President, that a Pope once famously ordered a British King to take a certain action? And the King's response was to tell the Pope to enforce his order with his non-existent armies, or something like that? Our response to the Judge will be very similar – if you want to prohibit our militia from bearing arms, which is the ultimate purpose of a militia, of course, then Mister Judge, Your Honor, sir, you just come out here to Arizona and pick up those guns yourself, one at a time. Good luck with that."

"Two problems with your little story, Governor. Unlike the Pope, I *do have* armies, and I will use them. Second problem, it won't be one singular judge picking up your guns. Now follow this, because I don't want you later on to say you didn't know what was coming....I have the Constitutional right as President to nationalize the National Guard of any State. Remember President Eisenhower and Little Rock in the 50's? He federalized the Arkansas National Guard and then sent in 1,000 Army paratroopers from the 101st Airborne Division. I can nationalize state militias. I will nationalize your state's newly created militia. All several hundred thousand of them. And, listen carefully, Governor, I will require each member of the nationalized militia to turn in their guns, to comply with McAlister, and to comply with my order, as Commander in Chief. For those who may try and be brave and dis-obey my direct order, we will arrest them, we will try them in a military court of justice, you probably know what that means, and then we will either imprison them or we may execute some."

"*What? Are you completely ins....*"

"I'm *perfectly* sane. President Lincoln strung up deserters on the White House lawn. If we have to *make an example* of a few of your Arizona rebels, in order to enforce the law, and rid this nation of hate weapons, then so be it. That would be *a small price to pay* to save the nation from continued widespread gun violence. I didn't run for a second term in order to set back for four years and watch the haters continue to spew their hate speech and fire their hate weapons. So forget your little plan to avoid complying with what will almost certainly become the law of the land. Have I made myself *sufficiently clear*, Governor McManus?"

This time the Governor's silence wasn't calculated, he was genuinely unable to speak. He wanted to throw back a clever counter-argument, but he knew he had none. He was pinned to the mat. He had just been threatened with a highly credible threat by a President who would undoubtedly do precisely what he had just told the Governor he would do, if Arizona adopted its militia law. Match over.

Arizona State House reporters that afternoon noticed the Governor huddling in his office with Arizona Legislative leaders, although the official schedule instead showed a ribbon cutting in Flagstaff. Early the next day, Governor McManus' Press Secretary issued a terse written media statement.

TO: ARIZONA MEDIA

SUBJECT: MILITIA BILL (HCR-13-927)

After discussions with the Governor, sponsors of HCR-13-927, (Establishing and Arming the State Militia), have agreed to withdraw the bill from further consideration. The Governor's Office will have no further comment on the Bill, nor on its withdrawal. Likewise, neither the House or Senate leadership, nor Bill Sponsors, will have any further comment.

90

SIXTEEN

New York City, NY – Fox News Studios

Fox News, which the White House had once suggested was not a legitimate news organization, stepped forward as the only national news service willing to air a debate in prime time on the McAlister Bill. Other broadcast and cable networks who favored passage of the bill, and who didn't attempt to hide their support for the bill, declined to give any significant air time to its opponents. Their thinking was not complex. Why stir up the right wing over imagined threats to their free speech and worship rights? Why give a platform to the Neanderthals fighting the eradication of hate weapons? The average American occasionally watching television news would have to conclude that there really wasn't much of a debate taking place on the bill, as almost everyone they saw on their home screen was in favor of its adoption into law. That may not be what they heard at work, or at the local bar or even at some churches, but it certainly appeared from news coverage of the issue that America wanted Congress to pass the bill.

Fox had promoted the prime time debate for several days, scheduling it on March 5th, knowing that the final votes in the two chambers of the U.S. Congress were likely by the end of March. The proponent of the bill in the debate was none other than South Carolina Senator Jim Blevins, the choice by the White House, as the person who would gain the most sympathy from viewers. The Senator was a little rough-spoken, at times, the White House was willing to admit, but he had been shot in October, so he conveyed a strong message before he even opened his mouth in the debate.

Senator Blevins' opponent in the debate was Representative Melinda Batchelder from Minnesota, an attractive and effective Member of Congress, who had impressed many in her quest for the Republican nomination for President. She had been supported by conservatives, but she was unable to gain traction in the early days of the selection process, withdrawing from the race, many observers believed, with dignity and style. Congresswoman Batchelder was an impressive debater, and thus the Blevins versus Batchelder Debate was an event that was expected to attract significant viewership. The Debate was hosted by Fox's talk show host Grenda Sandora.

"Welcome to the Fox News Debate on the McAlister Bill now pending in Congress, featuring Senator Blevins and Congresswoman Batchelder. The rules of the debate tonight have been agreed to by both debaters. Each will be limited to thirty seconds for a response to a question. All questions have been submitted in advance by Fox News viewers. If you are both ready, Senator Blevins and Representative Batchelder, let's commence this clash of ideas. The first question is from Iowa, a State with which you are well acquainted, Congresswoman. The viewer wants to know from the two of you simply why you favor, or oppose, the McAlister Bill. Senator? You go first."

"Well, Grenda, that's a mighty easy first question, I expected a real hardball first pitch with me comin' on to Fox, I really did. Not exactly friendly territory for a progressive Democrat, ya know. But, let me first just thank all the tens of thousands of Americans who have reached out to me expressin' their prayers and their hopes for my recovery after my shootin'. Miriam and I really do appreciate all those kind..."

"Senator, you have only thirty seconds, remember."

"Uh, yes, uh....of course, sorry. Where was I? Why am I for this bill? Simple question. Simple answer. No person in government should ever have to fear that they will be shot, maybe even killed, just because they are in public service. That's why I'm supportin' this bill."

"Congresswoman. Why do you oppose the Senator's bill?

"Let me make my answer equally simple, and easy to understand. Our Constitution grants the unequivocal right to Americans to free speech and also the right to keep and bear arms. If Senator Blevins, and his friends in the White House, want to abolish gun ownership or change the First Amendment, let them do it the legal way. They should amend the Constitution by having two thirds of Congress and then three-fourths of the states make the changes they want. It's been done before – when the nation repealed the 20th Amendment, which had prohibited alcohol consumption. But, let's not hide what they are doing by calling 're-interpretation', because it's not, it's tyranny, tyranny by the Congress and the White House, to deny us our God-given rights found in the Constitution of the United States of America."

"OK, well the next question comes to us from New..."

"Whoa, hold on a minute, Grenda, I can't let that one go without a response...

"Senator, the rules..."

"I frankly don't care about...my debate opponent here has just called me a name – a mighty serious name, and I

93

will respond, rules or not....Uh....she says that God gave her the right to own a gun? Really? Where's it say that? My pastor is in favor of my bill, and he would know if God said anything about guns, come on. Now, Grenda, I'm getting' mighty tired of hearin' about how we all gonna take away free speech and the right to worship and such. My bill won't take away anyone's right to speak, they all just can't say things that are against the law. No more of ya nasty, mean, hateful words attacking public officials, don't ya see?"

Congresswoman Batchelder quickly responded, "Senator, now you come on. The history of our nation confirms that the men who founded this nation were, for the most part, Christians who believed that God had granted them a special opportunity to create a free nation, not ruled by kings and tyrants, as they had experienced in European nations. Before the Constitution could be ratified, the Bill of Rights was written and included, and the First and Second Amendments in the Bill of Rights were the first two included for a very good reason – they didn't want this nation ending up like Europe. What you, and your friends in the White House, are doing is tyrannical, straight up, a tyrannical effort to take away our Constitutional rights, but without doing it the legal way, by repealing the amendments which you don't like. A tyrant despotically misuses his authority. Senator, you sir, are mis-using your authority, and you know it. Oh, yes, you certainly know what you are doing."

Camera three, which was focused on Senator Blevins, caught a well-known governmental leader appearing to be weighing his options. His first response to his opponent's words was to say nothing. He seemed to be gritting his teeth, then he narrowed his eyes as he stared hard at the Congresswoman. With an almost imperceptible nod of his head, it appeared to those who would later spin the debate, he seemed to make up his mind, but only after visible internal wrestling.

"Ma'am, I was raised to respect women. In ya case, though, based on ya cutting words and ya false accusations, I'm gonna have to make an exception to how I was raised. Ya no woman deserving respect, no, ma'am, ya are a highly-paid attack machine, working for the wealthy gun makers and ya supporters in the NRA and such. I am *not* goin' to allow myself to be subjected to any more of ya scurrilous attacks. Ya can just debate ya'self, cause I'm stoppin' this sham debate. I'm leavin' this here Fox News organized ambush."

With that burst of agitated words, the Senator pulled off the lapel mike clipped to this tie, spun his wheelchair backwards and out of the studio, leaving Grenda open-mouthed, along with a perplexed Congresswoman, wondering what she should say next, if anything.

The studio floor manager signaled Grenda to go to a break, which she promptly did. After two minutes of commercials, Grenda informed viewers that with the Senator's departure from the studio, the Blevins-Batchelder Debate was concluded. Most of the mainstream media who commented on the debate, and its abrupt termination, blamed Batchelder, many (not coincidentally) using the same description of her, i.e., 'a right wing pit bully'. The White House Press Secretary in his daily briefing suggested that "no self-respecting Democrat, liberal or progressive, should ever again appear on Fox News". One unnamed, undisclosed Democrat Senator who opposed Blevin's bill, leaked to a Fox correspondent who covers the Senate, that he had understood before the debate even started that Senator Blevins would look for an excuse to terminate the debate, and would leave it before it was concluded. Blevins' press spokesman called the report 'another radical right wing attempt to smear a fine public servant.'

SEVENTEEN

Dallas, Texas

Human beings generally prefer to lead a peaceful, quiet existence. Get up, go to work, come home, spend time with the spouse and the kids, go to bed. Repeat. Thus, it requires something extraordinary to make a normal human being go into the streets to protest some action or another of the government, or of some other major institution. For many Americans, the McAlister Bill was the incentive they needed to do just that. Since it became known soon after the Presidential election what the bill would do if it became law, increasingly more Americans took to the streets to protest. The demonstrations were predominate in the southern and western states, but demonstrations took place in many rural communities even in traditional blue states, such as up-state New York or in rural Maine. There were no visible protest marches in New York City or in much of California or in many of the northeast and northwest states, where anti-gun sentiment, and support for the McAlister Bill, was more sizeable.

At first, the protests took the form of organized marches and rallies, usually held on Saturdays, and including large numbers of people carrying protest signs. Most involved speeches by gun owners opposed to the pending anti-gun bill and by free speech advocates, generally conservatives and Christians and Jews, worried about the Bill's effect on religious rights. Most included chants, such as:

KEEP YOUR HANDS *OFF* MY GUNS, KEEP YOUR HANDS *OFF* MY GUNS

I SPEAK, YOU SPEAK, WE ALL SPEAK FOR *FREE SPEECH*

Some were throw-backs to the anti-Vietnam war protest of the 60s:

ALL WE ARE SAYING IS - *GIVE GUN RIGHTS A CHANCE!*

Some sang *We Shall Overcome*, with revised lyrics:

Gun rights shall overcome,
Gun rights shall overcome,
Gun rights shall overcome some day.

Freedom of speech shall overcome,
Freedom of speech shall overcome,
Freedom of speech shall overcome some day.

Media coverage of the growing protests, on a national level, continued to be sparse. As far as most Americans could tell, the only people upset about the proposed law were some local gun supporters and tea party folks who marched and rallied, but they were never told about the fact that what they saw locally was happening across the country, replicated in hundreds of protests, rallies and marches, which included hundreds of thousands, and ultimately millions, of participants. The Nation's mainstream media chose not to report what Americans were saying with their feet, their signs and their voices about the McAlister Bill's sponsors' plan to define away their rights enshrined in the Constitution.

As the vote on the bill neared, and as the debate that was being covered on a limited basis intensified, the nature of the peaceful protests began to change. Leaders and supporters of the gun rights movement increasingly began to realize that the threat to take away their firearms was more than serious, and that if they didn't stop Congress from passing the Administration's bill, they would soon be unarmed. That conclusion was rapidly reached by national, regional and local leaders involved in the effort to defeat McAlister. Rank and file members of gun rights organizations increasingly besieged the leaders of their national organizations, asking what they could do to help stop McAlister and how they could best lobby their local Members of Congress. Busloads of opponents were organized to come to the Capitol to lobby their Members. The national leaders, though, were limited in how far they could go to oppose the McAlister Bill. They could coordinate protest and lobbying efforts, which they did frequently and effectively. But, they couldn't, nor would they, call for any level of violence. Instead, they were careful that almost every member letter, news release and press conference included an obligatory warning to avoid any form of violence.

The national gun rights leaders warned their members that any act of violence would immediately be used by the backers of the anti-gun bill to persuade Congress of the need to rid the nation of what the Administration labeled in every news conference as 'hate weapons'. One national leader, Harry Flatt, warned his members, *"Even one bullet fired in anger over this evil anti-gun bill will be used against us, and used to justify taking away our firearms. Don't help the White House pass their bill by using your defensive firearm in an offensive way. We are peaceful Americans who just want to be able to obey the law and defend ourselves."*

However, in a nation with as many firearms as Americans, it was inevitable that the anti-gun debate would eventually turn violent. Bullets were fired at several federal installations, usually at night, with no recorded arrests.

When windows were blown out of federal offices, the national media was there to show the nation's viewers, and to interview distraught federal employees. Since no one was ever apprehended for the late-at-night shootings, there was no real assurance as to whether the bullets were fired in anger by out of control opponents of the McAlister Bill, or instead, by supporters of the Bill, trying to demonstrate to Members of Congress the urgent need for passage of the Bill.

One tactic used by the opponents of the Bill was borrowed from American teenagers who used what they called 'flash mob messages' to call out hundreds, even thousands, of supporters on a moment's notice, using Twitter, cell phone texts and instant messaging. With no advance warning, entire plazas or office parking lots full of opponents of the McAlister Bill were called out, when it was learned that a Congress person was expected to be at a specific location in his or her Congressional District. Nothing got their attention like thousands of their constituents showing up at their District office or outside of a Lincoln-Reagan or Jefferson-Jackson political dinner. The only media who bothered to cover these demonstrations of public opposition were local.

Since most owners of firearms, as Flatt had said, were peaceful, and since they understood that using their weapons would help them lose their weapons, there were no confirmed organized acts of gun violence. It seemed as if American gun owners were holding their breath, hoping against hope that the Bill would fail. They wrote letters and made calls to their own Members of Congress. They protested, peacefully. They contributed funds for lobbying. They prayed. But....they were scared. Scared that America would become like Australia. Scared that they would be like the Brits in the 2011 riots who could only buy baseball bats to protect their homes and families. Scared that they would soon lose the weapons that they owned to protect their families. Scared that they would be unarmed in the face of criminals who would rob, hurt, rape or kill. Scared.

Likewise, religious leaders were worried that the seemingly innocent language of the McAlister Bill punishing speech deemed to be hate speech would be used against them, restricting the contents of sermons and religious writings. Conservatives of all stripes and from organizations across the country saw the Federal Hate Speech Review Panel as a direct violation of the First Amendment and an attempt to censor their religious views, if they conflicted with prevailing government policy. Most were scared that if the McAlister Bill became law, it would be used to punish them, including imprisonment, if the courts ruled that their words were illegal, in violation of McAlister's definition of the phrase 'hate speech'. Since the Bill categorized hate speech as written or verbal speech that unfairly or illegally attacked a federal public official, or which unlawfully denigrated or negatively criticized any public official, they were scared that any critical comments about public officials could land the speaker or the preacher or the writer in prison. Scared that any sermon, speech or book dealing with gender, race or sexual orientation could have the same result. Scared that the federal government would become the federal censor. Scared.

EIGHTEEN

Omaha, Nebraska

The law of unintended consequences may have been meant for just such an occasion as this – the Omaha Gun Supporters Parade. The idea behind the newly-formed *Omaha Gun Owners Against Seizing our Guns* organization was simple. The organizers announced that the "Parade was to demonstrate to the people of Omaha, and of Nebraska, and to that Crazy as a Loon Congress, that the people of mid-America aren't about to voluntarily give up our firearms, even if the anti-gun law passes". At least that was the underlying concept. The leaders of the group, as they planned the Gun Supporters Parade, didn't think, however, to contact any national pro-gun organizations to get their input. Hindsight being what is, they should have made the call.

The Mayor of Omaha was more than happy to have his offices help the parade organizers obtain a parade permit. On first application, they had been turned down by a city hall bureaucrat who supported the McAlister Bill pending before Congress. Once the Mayor found out about the denial, though, the permit was swiftly granted. In return, the Mayor was invited to march in the front ranks of the Saturday noon event, an invitation he was pleased to accept. "Let's send a message to DC," he told anyone who would listen, including local media, "we aren't going give up our guns, no, not under any circumstances, nor any threat, nor any federal government pressure. Not in Nebraska."

In the planning for any public event, the event organizers reach a point where the early decisions made for how the event will be conducted are either affirmed, or changed at the last minute. In the very first meeting of the parade organizers one member of the group casually said, "Won't it look great when they show on TV all the thousands of Nebraskans carrying our firearms? Just seeing all those guns and all of us carrying them will make quite an impression, won't it?" Many in the group nodded their assent, and the meeting moved on to picking a date for their parade. No one at that meeting, nor at any subsequent meeting, ever thought to re-examine their initial decision to openly carry their guns in the Omaha Gun Supporters Parade.

The organizers chose Saturday, February 17th for the Parade. It was sunny and crisp, but not too cold, as tens of thousands gathered at the Heartland of America Park, as planned, to assemble for marching down Farnam Street to Central Park Plaza for speeches. Many marchers brought their children to make it a family event. All were there to demonstrate their opposition to federal gun control. The Mayor had his first inkling of personal doubt when his driver let him off at the Park. As the Mayor looked across the Park at the large crowd, he heard an organizer on a bullhorn say "Show us your guns". As the marcher/demonstrators responded, the Mayor saw the sun glinting off of what at first appeared to be hundreds, but then from thousands of rifles, shotguns and raised pistols and revolvers. The Mayor was one of the State's highest profile supporters of gun rights, but it occurred to him as he walked across the Park to greet the marchers that *maybe* this wasn't the *best* way to gain support from the general public. Seeing an individual defend themselves against a mugger or rapist, he thought as he walked, was fine for the cause, but this looked like an armed mob. This will feed into the White House's propaganda machine. Oh well, maybe, they won't be watching, he hoped.

But, of course, at the same time, he knew that wasn't at all likely. Why didn't they just march, and carry signs, not guns? This will give the nation's anti-gun President, who was from the Mayor's own political party, he was sorry to say, ammunition for several speeches in support of the McAlister Bill. Ammunition indeed.

What the Mayor did not know, nor did anyone in authority in Omaha, was that the President's Chief of Staff had quietly hired three camera crews, none known to the others, to thoroughly videotape all aspects of the Omaha Parade. The White House hoped for footage that could be used to try to persuade a majority in Congress to vote to take away individual ownership of guns. What happened during the Parade, though, turned a photo op into a full scale disaster for supporters of the Second Amendment. The much publicized events on that sunny Saturday afternoon in Omaha was later cited by a handful of previous swing vote Members in Congress as the key determinant in their final decision to vote in favor of the McAlister Bill.

Soon after noon, on schedule, the marchers began to leave the Park and started to fill Farnam Street, on their trek to Central Park Plaza, and some hoped-for 'whooping up the crowd' speeches. Within half an hour, the entire length of the east-west thoroughfare was full of people and their uplifted guns. It was quite a sight, and one that many observers thought had never been seen before, not like this. Most large numbers of people who carry weapons in public are dressed alike, in military uniforms. These gun carriers wore the full variety of what everyday people wear when they are in public, but they certainly didn't look like an army. Historically, people who showed their guns and who weren't in military uniforms, didn't usually march or pose for photographs.

The official explanation for what happened next in Omaha was first given by federal officials. The Mayor's Office refused comment and Nebraska law enforcement authorities weren't talking to the media. That's largely because neither had a clue as to who or what caused the panic in the crowd.

About the time that the large crowd of marchers was fully stretched out from Heartland Park to the Central Park Plaza, shots were fired, several shots, heard all along the seven block stretch of marchers. Analysis of audio recordings later indicated that over thirty shots, possibly more, with some overlapping shots, were fired in a 45 second period. The result, the immediate result, was pure panic. The gun owners were, for the most part, trained and quite knowledgeable about what the shots they were hearing meant, though all marchers had been told not to load or bring any ammunition. Most immediately knew that they were being fired on. They fell to the pavement, where they were able to so, or they ran as fast as possible away from the Parade route on Farnam Street. The Omaha Gun Supporters Parade was over. The fallout from the Parade wasn't.

About half of the Parade route adjoined an open area park attached to Heartland Park. Marchers along this section were able to swiftly escape the Parade route heading north across the open grassy areas. However, in a section of Farnam Street between 13th and 14th Street, buildings were located on both sides of the route, enclosing the marchers, and effectively preventing their exit. When hundreds tried to escape, but couldn't, and hundreds of others tried to fall to the ground to avoid being shot, chaos and panic ensued. In the ensuing melee, several marchers were injured, many severely. Some who fell to the pavement were trampled by others who meant to do no harm, but who feared for their lives and for those of their family members. The death toll from trampling injuries came to five, including two children. The number injured who were treated for their injuries at local hospitals exceeded one hundred and twenty, though none were treated for gunshot wounds.

In depth reports by law enforcement agencies confirmed that none of the weapons carried in the Parade appeared to have been fired, either intentionally in self-defense, nor inadvertently, as marchers fled, fell or were trampled. The reports took several months to conclude. What the mainstream media reported immediately after the Parade panic, though, was a completely different story:

New York Times

GUNNERS DEATH MARCH IN OMAHA
Five Die as Thousands Brandish Guns

NBC

OMAHA MASSACRE

CBS

SECOND AMENDMENT REBELLION

MSNBC

OMAHA INSURRECTION BACKFIRES
Polls Show 7% Increase in Support for Anti-Gun Bill

FOX

FREEDOM MARCHERS AMBUSHED

The Fox News on-air story, reported three days later, was based on the later documented fact that no marcher interviewed by either the media or law enforcement agencies could recall seeing a fellow marcher fire his or her weapon. No shell casings or other evidence that marchers fired shots from their weapons were ever located. A detective with the Omaha Police Department, not content with finding no evidence of fired weapons on the street level, decided on the Monday after the Parade, to search the rooftops of adjoining office buildings. He found what he was looking for on the gravel roof of the Woodmen of the World office building on Farnam Street at 13th Street. Incendiary devices of some sort, not unlike an M-80 firework, had been serially wired and ignited, causing distinct gunfire sounds, reverberating from the building across Farnam Street, and leading to panic and death below. The detective's findings weren't reported outside of Omaha, where they were mentioned only in passing in a later follow up story. In the interim, the national media ran with the Omaha gun story as Exhibit A for passage of the McAlister Hate Weapons Elimination Bill.

Unintended consequences for the Parade organizers.

Intended consequences for those igniting the explosives.

NINETEEN

Washington, DC – The Oval Office

'Pay no attention to the man behind the curtain.'

Public opinion polls by late February were still showing close to 40% of Americans opposed to, or with misgivings about, the McAlister Bill, even after the October 26th shootings, the Omaha deaths and subsequent non-stop media support. The percentage, by itself, was not of major concern to the President and his advisors. He was, they persuasively argued, now in his second term, he was safely re-elected, and he couldn't be removed from office In addition, his Party controlled both Houses of the U.S. Congress. There were, however, still ten to twelve votes needed in the House for passage of McAlister, mostly due to reluctant Blue Dog Democrats. Many adamantly unconvinced Americans tended to live in higher numbers in those House Members' Districts, in states like Montana, Utah and Wyoming. So it was that the President's advisors pushed for something to be done to distract the voters in those Districts, and thus provide cover for those Members of Congress whom they were pressuring to vote for the gun bill. Since major changes frequently occur while the nation's attention is distracted by a crisis, real or imagined, the President's political advisors argued there would need to be a significant diversion. America needed something else to worry about besides the McAlister Bill.

'Nothing's happening here, move on.'

The President's Chief of Staff supported his argument with the obvious - that the occupant of the most important office of the most important nation on the globe has an almost unlimited ability to shape events, certainly to direct attention to perceived events. The producers of the movie *Wag the Dog,* he said, certainly understood the principle that nothing grabs the attention of people more than war, or the threat of war. In the movie presentation, an embattled President launched a war to divert attention from his own political problems. President William J. Clinton, he argued, followed the script of the movie in his actions in launching three military campaigns in 1998 and 1999 in the midst of his Lewinsky scandal.

But, China?

The Presidential speech was aired to the nation from the Oval Office, a setting generally reserved for the most somber addresses by America's Commander in Chief.

Four...Three...Two...One...

"Good evening, my fellow Americans. I am addressing you tonight, as your President, on a matter of the utmost seriousness. No, it is not about the McAlister Hate Speech and Hate Weapons Elimination Bill, which our nation must enact into law, and which I again call on the Congress to pass, and pass soon, to protect all Americans from gun violence motivated by hate speech. Instead, I come to you tonight about China, the People's Republic of China. For years now, America has had a tenuous relationship with this four thousand year old, large and powerful far Eastern nation. We are a major, actually *the* major, customer for products produced by the billion, three hundred million people living in China. In turn, China has been the largest purchaser of U.S. government bonds and other debt

110

instruments. This relationship has been mutually advantageous for several decades.

"That began to change, however, when China, France and Russia let it be known at the G-8 conference held in Italy that they were concerned about the American dollar continuing as the world's reserve currency. A reserve currency is the currency that the world uses to value goods for international trade, such as oil, grain and other commodities. In the history of the world, there have been several reserve currencies, the most recent before the dollar being the pound sterling.

"You may be wondering, why your President, in my first major televised address to the nation in my second term, is talking with you about this issue. I am doing so simply because of the critical importance of the dollar remaining the world's reserve currency. If China, and the other nations which China has asked to join it, are successful in their efforts, the dollar will be replaced as the world's reserve currency by a basket of other currencies, including the Chinese currency, the Renminbi, also referred to as the Yuan.

"What would such a move by China mean to you, an average, hard-working American? Simply stated, it would raise the price of almost everything you buy and use. Because oil would no longer be priced in dollars, the price of oil would jump, jump dramatically. That energy cost increase would raise the price not only of transportation, but everything that is transported. As much as I regret saying it, as your newly re-elected President, I must report to you that these proposed acts by China would constitute an act of war – a war on the American dollar, a war on the American people. Hopefully, China will re-consider, which I am now calling on their government to give very serious consideration to doing. I call on the government of China to realize that peace with America is more important than its financial plans. As President I, of course, favor peace, but I must protect you as Americans, and I must protect our faltering economy. I can do no less.

"May God bless America. Good night, my fellow Americans."

Overnight polling showed three quarters of Americans were worried or very worried about a possible war with China. The airwaves were filled with coverage of the growing *"Crisis with China"*. One unnamed Pentagon source leaked that two carrier task forces were being re-positioned near Taiwan. The European Union called an emergency parliamentary meeting to discuss the growing international concern over the potential for war between the world's two strongest powers. The Secretary General of the United Nations issued a call for a meeting of the UN's Security Council on an urgent basis. The world was transfixed over the possibility of war as it stared at the increasingly hostile relationship between America and China.

What the world was not staring at, however, because it went unnoticed at the time, was a late night visit by the Assistant Secretary of State for Far Eastern Affairs who paid a visit to the Chinese Embassy in DC, three nights before the President's oval office address to the nation.

The State Department official had previously arranged the meeting with China's Ambassador to the United States, suggesting that the conference was of utmost urgency, and requesting that China's President be available by secure line for a brief conversation, following the Assistant Secretary's

112

meeting with the Chinese Ambassador. Upon entering the Ambassador's Embassy Office, the Assistant Secretary made an unusual request.

"Mr. Ambassador, I have with me a secure cell telephone. I'm going to call a number at the highest level of our government, and hand you the phone. Is that acceptable, sir?"

"Mr. Secretary, this is your meeting, you called it. That's fine. I will be speaking with....?"

"I'll let him identify himself. I apologize that this is a bit unusual, but I think you'll understand soon."

With this, the State Department official, his dialing hand trembling slightly, a fact that did not go unnoticed by the Ambassador, punched in a seven digit number, a local call, then handed the cell phone across the desk to the Chinese Ambassador to the United States.

The Ambassador took the phone, listened as it rang, then widened his eyes with obvious recognition of the person answering on the other end of the call.

"Why, yes, I do recognize your voice, Mr. Pres...I understand....yes, no names need be used. Yes. I am assured that you are ..who you are.... Yes....He's here with me....Yes, I understand that what he will tell me is what you have asked him to convey to me to then be conveyed to our government....Yes, sir...yes, I will be sure to immediately repeat his message to our honored President...No, he's in Beijing at this time, waiting for my call, as we were previously advised....Yes, thank you sir. It's been an honor to speak with...Of course, with full discretion and confidentiality, as you have requested....well, sir, good night, and let me just...".

"Oh...unh...I think he's completed the call, now. Here's...uh... your cell phone back, Mr. Secretary. Umh....he was very cordial and quite specific that you had a message to give me for my government, for our President."

"Mr. Ambassador, on a matter of this urgency I will *read* to you the message I have been asked to convey to your government, from the highest level of our government, as you have just heard confirmed. You may wish to take notes, as I will not be leaving the document with you."

"I fully understand. Please proceed."

"I quote. 'The government of China is unofficially advised, in the strictest confidence, that what will be stated by the American government in the next few days is not the official position of the American government as regards the nation of the Peoples' Republic of China. Due to domestic policy considerations of the highest order and importance, the American government finds it necessary to make statements regarding the Peoples' Republic of China which will assist the government of the United States in those domestic issues, but which will not affect the long-standing friendly relationship between our nations. Once the domestic matters are resolved, the American government will take all steps necessary to repair and restore the public perception of the long-standing American-Chinese friendship. The American government regrets that these actions must be taken, but assures the government of China that in the future it will more than compensate China for its understanding.' Unquote. That's the full statement."

"I've made careful notes, Mr. Secretary," the Ambassador responded, not mentioning what they both knew, that their words were all being carefully recorded. "Is there anything else that should be conveyed to my President."

With his duties now fulfilled, the Assistant Secretary exhaled a long sigh, then asked, "Mr. Ambassador, how long have we known each other now?"

"Leonard, I'd say over fifteen years since I was first assigned to the UN delegation. You have been a trustworthy friend to me and to my country. You've given me the unofficial official statement, now what's this really all about?"

"Junjie, because of that friendship I wish to personally apologize for this somewhat unusual approach tonight. I can only say, off the record, of course, that there are some in our nation's Capitol who are still learning how foreign relations work. As for the statement, I can only add the obvious. We're going to kick China around a little bit, not too bad, though at first it will sound like it. We need to get a bill passed that you've undoubtedly followed, and we need to change the subject while we're doing it. Then, we'll be back to normal. Everything will be the same. Hunky dory, Junjie my friend."

Unfortunately for America, though China was pre-informed, its government was not amused at being threatened with war. The results of the Administration's diversionary speech suggesting war were put in place by China within the next two months as China accelerated its plans, along with France, Russia, India and Brazil, and replaced the dollar as the world's reserve currency, with a basket of their own currencies, plus gold. The Dow fell by the largest daily drop in its history. The President suggested to House Speaker Pelham at a later White House reception that finally getting the Congress to come to a vote on the bill to eliminate hate weapons, and curtail scurrilous attacks on the Administration, was an acceptable trade-off for the change in the status of the dollar, which he said was headed for trouble in any case. The Speaker heartily concurred.

TWENTY

Website Blog Entry – March 3rd (Early AM)

Plan X was not my idea. Even today I don't know if I'm in favor of it, though I helped with input of some of the words at yesterday's supposedly secret meeting in Chicago, but I didn't come up with the idea. That may sound like John Kerry's infamous *"I voted for it, before I voted against it"* line, but it's really not. I'm belaboring the point because I fully expect to be blamed by the media for hatching *Plan X*. Since I'm writing this all down to set the record straight, someday, if anyone even cares about the facts, someday, let me just explain what actually happened. It started out as a terrific plan, we thought. How it will turn out, of course, may be another matter entirely. We'll see.

So, starting at the beginning (was it Julie Andrews who sang 'which is a very good place to start'?) Alright, I'm a little tired, OK? I'm writing this early Sunday morning after I got back to Tyler from Chicago. The first I knew anything about the meeting in Chicago was a phone call from Charlie Waggoner, one of the early tea party organizers, who heads up one of the largest tea party groups in Ohio. He swore me to secrecy (I'll get back to that later) and asked if I could attend a meeting of tea party, patriot, pro-gun and conservative leaders in Chicago on March 2nd, which was a Saturday. I checked my trusty digital calendar, saw that I was clear and then I asked Charlie the purpose of the meeting. He got very hush-hush on me at that point. Only a select few leaders are invited, he said, only the top guys in the country, he flattered me by responding. OK, but with everything we've got going right now to try and beat the McAlister Bill, I asked, should we be taking the time to fly to Chicago?

I knew Charlie, of course, from meetings and contacts during the last couple years of campaign efforts, but we weren't what I would call tight. Nice guy. Smart. Good tactician. But, that's about all I knew. It just seemed to me that I needed to spend time trying to line up, or shore up, as the case may be, our Texas Congressional guys and gals, and not be flying up to the Windy City, in late winter, of all times, with a forecast of a snowstorm. Burr.

Sensing that I had the time available, but that I wouldn't commit to the meeting without more information, Charlie gave me the 'double dog/hope to die secrecy oath' and then he told me the true purpose of the March 2nd meeting. Was I a bit surprised? You could say that. Up to that point we were still repairing the damage from my testimony before the Blevins Committee. Essentially, we were fighting a defensive action, trying to convince the swing votes in the Congress that we could retire them in the next election if they passed the bill and took away our guns and free speech. The problem with that approach, obviously, was that if they passed the bill, we might, and probably would, defeat a few members of Congress next time, but we would still have an enforceable federal law on the books making it a felony to criticize a public official or own a firearm. And, oh yeah, giving my neighbor a cash incentive to turn me in if I didn't turn over my guns. Repealing an adopted law, once it's the law of the land, even if you win control of a house in the Congress is just about impossible. So, we needed a plan *if* McAlister should pass and become law. The hook that Charlie used to get me to Chicago was that he wanted us to discuss and agree to a significant plan to be pursued in the event that McAlister was adopted by the legislative branch, signed by the executive branch and confirmed by the judicial branch. A terrible trifecta, so to speak.

Why did they pick Chicago? Simple. Hundreds of flights into O'Hare and Midway every day. Middle of the country for some to just drive in. No one in the media would be watching, in a City that large, on the weekend, for a handful of political leaders. We had reason to be concerned because our mugs had been plastered on TV and in newspapers, even *Time* magazine (remember the cover headline - *Enemies of the State?*). Our meeting of the major leaders in our movement had to be confidential. What's the best place to not be seen? In a big crowd. Charlie had arranged for a small conference room – which was carefully checked for bugs – the electronic kind – at the Hilton Chicago Hotel, which used to be called the Conrad Hilton Hotel, on the lake shore in Chicago. Big old enormous hotel, with lots of elevators, people milling through its large lobbies, you get the idea. Those of us who were invited were told to make our own Friday night sleeping arrangements, scattered in other hotels, again, for security purposes. Once I knew what we were going to do at the meeting, I was fully on board with all of the security concerns, as the last thing we wanted was a leak.

The other leaders at the meeting will probably write their own memoirs someday about what happened in Chicago. Here is what I remember happening. We started early on March 2nd, which was a blustery, snowy day, no surprise. Charlie Waggoner summed up where we were on efforts to beat the pending Bill. Everybody agreed that the vote would be very close, but we also all concluded that if the vote were the following week, the Bill would probably pass. This was very smart group of political leaders, even though most of us just a few years before had no, or very little, political background. I mention this because we didn't waste any time asking 'how did we get to this sorry situation' or 'what's happening to our freedoms in this country' or anything like that. We all knew how it had happened and we all were very well aware that the nation was very close to becoming an America that none of us would recognize, certainly not 'the land of the free'. But, we *did* think we were the 'home of the brave.'

Here's what I do recall Charlie saying, as best I can recall his actual words, the words that led to *Plan X*, and everything that followed after that. I've put his words in quotes, since this is what I recall him saying:

"Unless something major should happen, by the end of March, maybe sooner, Congress will pass the anti-free speech and anti-gun ownership felony bill. The President will, of course, sign it. The feds will begin to fully enforce it should the Supreme Court decide and rule that McAlister is Constitutional. The current bill, unless it's amended, will give Americans only about six months to turn in our guns or be charged with felonies, with mandatory ten year sentences. So, by the first of October, give or take a few days, keeping a gun, and not turning it in, will result in federal prison. Under McAlister the feds can go after any outspoken conservative, or preacher, whom they don't like, as soon as the Bill is signed. I doubt if Rush will stay on the air. Talk radio and cable news will be toast.

"If we lose our cherished First and Second Amendment rights so easily, just by the passage of a simple bill, we'll all know that the Constitution is essentially worthless, irrelevant and disposable. If all it takes to remove a right provided in the U.S. Constitution is simple majorities in both Houses and at least five Supreme Court Justices agreeing, then our Constitution will have been effectively set aside.

"Here then, is our Plan. If the McAlister Bill should become the law of the land, the various like-minded organizations of the country and others that will join us, will use what's left of the Constitution to save the rest of it. What does that mean? We'll jointly propose that a Constitutional Convention be convened, under Article V of the United States Constitution. Under this brief provision, there are two ways to call a Constitutional Convention. The first is for Congress, by a two thirds vote of both Houses, to do so. We all know that will never happen, as Congress itself is the problem. The second way to convene a Constitutional Convention is for two thirds of the legislatures of the fifty states, that is, a minimum of thirty four states, to pass resolutions calling for a Constitutional Convention, which the Congress then 'shall call'. It has no choice.

"Since the founding of the United States there have been occasional efforts made to try and get enough states to petition for a Constitutional Convention, but there were never enough that did so. The Liberty Amendment, which would abolish the 16th Amendment's power to tax income, among other restrictions on the federal government, has been passed by nine states, the most recent being Indiana in 1982, but not by enough states. Thus, some might say that a Constitutional Convention could never happen. We beg to differ. There are enough Americans who are concerned about our loss of freedoms, not just our right to own weapons, but also our unsustainable national debt and runaway spending, all adopted by our out of control Congress at the urging of the White House, that we may now have sufficient *people power* to make this happen. We could encamp in the State Houses of this nation, night and day, as did the unions in Wisconsin in 2011, until the legislatures of thirty four states, and hopefully more, adopt resolutions calling for a

Constitutional Convention of these United States of America. If a passed and confirmed McAlister Act shreds the First and Second Amendments, then our last hope of saving what remains in the Constitution may well be a Constitutional Convention.

Charlie continued in his pitch for *Plan X*, "What amendments will the Constitutional Convention adopt, to send to the states for adoption? That, will of course, be up to those who are sent to the Convention. We would encourage our folks in the states to be selected as Delegates. We would that propose that Delegates to the Convention consider, and hopefully adopt Amendments to the Constitution that would put term limits on Members of Congress and would provide that every law passed by Congress must apply equally to all Americans, with no exceptions for Members of Congress, or for judges or any other federal employee. We would expect to see a balanced budget amendment that would prohibit the federal government from spending more money than it takes in. No federal government debt, unless approved by 34 states, and only if in a national emergency, like war."

After Charlie gave us his plan there was a very spirited discussion....okay....a real donnybrook of an argument for over three hours. Some of those present fully agreed with the plan, as Charlie spelled it out. Some wanted to make sure that other amendments would be considered by a Constitutional Convention, like abolishing the IRS in favor of a flat tax, or requiring that only a declaration of war could send Americans into war. Several argued for returning to a gold backed currency and abolishing the Federal Reserve.

Some of us, about half of those present, as I recall, were a bit more reluctant. We argued that a Constitutional Convention could become a Pandora's Box, some said a can of worms, pick your metaphor, at which anything could be adopted, even booting the entire Constitution. The proponents of *Plan X* responded that the way the country's going now there won't be anything left in the venerable old document, anyway. I said that I hoped that the House wouldn't have the votes to pass McAlister and if it did that I prayed the Justices on the nation's highest court would strike it down.

Charlie's response was that I was engaging in wishful thinking and that we'd better be ready with an alternate plan if I was wrong and we lost our free speech and gun bearing rights. I don't know yet if I favor a Constitutional Convention. I can understand the arguments both for and against. But, I do agree that we need a plan if McAlister is imposed on the nation and parts of our Constitution are blotted out, gone.

In any case, these notes reflect what I can remember took place on a snowy weekend in Chicago in early March. Seemed like a harmless meeting. Really.

TWENTY-ONE

Website Blog Entry – March 3rd (early afternoon)

The prior blog was written early this morning, after I got back from Chicago, and before a short sleep before Church. As it turned out, while we were at worship services I had some frantic calls, left on my voicemail at home, most from Charlie Waggoner. The first message, which must have been recorded as we were pulling out of the drive, reported the very bad news that Alex McDaniel had crashed his plane late last night, a Cessna, leaving Chicago. Alex, one of the leaders who met at the Hilton, was a major tea party organizer, a real prince of a guy, from Iowa. We had spent all day Saturday, and late into the night (with pizza brought in) debating the wisdom of a Constitutional Convention should McAlister become law. Then we hashed out how we were going to circulate the details of *Plan X*, on a confidential basis, to key conservative leaders across the country. We knew we couldn't keep it secret very long, but we wanted to get the word out to the nation's major tea party, patriot, pro-gun, Christian, conservative Jewish and even some Republican committees before the Administration learned about it and tried to stop others from joining up. The idea was great, but who could have known that Alex McDaniel would crash his Cessna leaving Chicago?

The second call from Charlie, about an hour later (that must have been about when my wife was elbowing me to stay awake during the Pastor's sermon), informed my VM that the airport authorities had recovered Alex's briefcase last night, which we knew contained his notes from the meeting at the Hilton, and had then immediately turned them over to the NTSB, a federal agency. Alex was the unofficial secretary of the meeting, and he had taken several pages of notes, which we assumed were in his briefcase. We each had a copy of the final version of *Plan X,* which we had carefully copied in the guest office center at the Hotel, as we were leaving. There were no other copies. Charlie's voice mail said that he was really worried that Alex's notes would be used to try and prove that were attempting to overthrow the government, or something stupid like that. That seems far-fetched to me, but we <u>were</u> kind of strong in what we discussed, but all within the law. At least, I think so.

The third call, which came in as we were at lunch after church at the Black Eyed Pea, was not a call you would ever want to receive. I wrote it down exactly as it was recorded:

Mr....John Madison....this is Special Agent Charles Bock....of the FBI in the Dallas regional office. I need to speak with you, sir, as soon as you can return this call....It's an urgent matter, I'm informed by our offices in DC. Please return this call....promptly. (He left his number, twice).

It didn't take a genius to figure out why the FBI wanted to talk to me on an urgent matter. Of, course, it might have something to do with the testimony from last month, or it could be...ooops. I'm writing this in my den. I'm writing fast. I'm looking at two black Suburbans, government vehicles of choice, which have just pulled up to our curb. My Sunday afternoon surprise? How many suits did they send? Four? No, my goodness...three in each vehicle. Two talking into their sleeves. Not a good sign. Another checking, no, he's unsnapping, his shoulder holster. A worse sign. I do wish, though, that they would have just waited until I called back, and not sent their squadron of agents to my house to arrest me, in front of my family, on a Sunday afternoon. I'll get one call to my lawyer -- I hope Chuck's at home -- more later, assuming there is a later.

TWENTY-TWO

Journal Entry – March 10th

While I've been here in jail, I've been thinking a lot about MLK. Martin Luther King, Jr. used his time while in jail in 1963 in the midst of the civil rights struggle, to write what became known as the *Letter from Birmingham City Jail.* He wrote that "one has a moral responsibility to disobey unjust laws". I certainly agree with Rev. King. As a created human being I have the moral right to defend myself, and my family members, from another human being who may want to harm us or take our lives. It's immoral to prevent me from defending myself and my family. I have the God-given right to speak my mind on who should be the leaders of my nation's government.

I'm writing this as a journal entry, instead of a campaign website blog, since I don't have access to a computer. I recognize that these words may never be read. Security in this Houston, Texas Federal Detention Center is quite tight. King faced a similar problem, of course. He smuggled his letter out of the Alabama jail in a toothpaste tube.

The news they allow us to see here indicates that the House will vote on the McAlister Bill soon. I'm only allowed one call a day, which I normally use to talk to my beloved Debbie. So, I've not been in a position since I got here to be involved in any way in either the debate on the gun bill, or working with my buddies to try and influence Members of Congress to oppose the McAlister Bill. Not that they missed me all that much. I'm the one that Senator Blevins tricked into saying that the Second Amendment was vague. Genius, right?

Most of my hours since I've been here have been spent working with Chuck, my erstwhile legal beagle. My arrest made some splash in the local media in Texas, though the President's pals in the national media squelched any national coverage. I'll have to say that was a shock, after the coverage given to my testimony before the Senate Judiciary Committee, but I understand how things work in the liberal mainstream media. An occasional news magazine or newspaper article, though, quotes me, I'm told, which must irritate the White House. One article accurately reported that my dad named me John in honor of John Adams, one of his heroes. He thought that Adams and James Madison were key to the formation of the nation that we became, so he wanted me to have both names. The media can get it right, sometimes.

My first question to Chuck was how quick he could get me out on bail. How hard could that be? Well, as it turned out, it was very hard. In fact, impossible. Normally a lawyer can file a writ of habeas corpus and spring his client from the slammer, or at least force the authorities to file charges. By the time any one reads this, it should become known that Chuck's writ of habeas corpus was denied. Habeas corpus essentially means 'bring forth the body' or 'you may have the body'. The purpose is to make the authorities bring forth a prisoner to the court and justify their detention.

The Administration, though, had its Department of Justice file a pleading opposing our writ of habeas corpus. On what basis? Article I, Section 9 of the U.S. Constitution allows the government to suspend the right to a writ of habeas corpus "in cases of rebellion...when the public safety may require it." The Administration, without revealing the actual details of our Chicago deliberations, warned the Court that national security issues were involved, and notified the Court that my right to a writ of habeas corpus was suspended, because I was part of a "rebellion". They said the "public safety" required that I lose my right to file a writ. We're told that the only person more shocked than Chuck and myself was the federal district court judge, who told one of Chuck's lawyer friends that he had never seen anything like it. He had his staff research whether it had happened before. They learned that it hadn't happened since Abraham Lincoln suspended the right to habeas corpus writs for Confederate soldiers. No question that the South in the 1860's rebelled, but our efforts to use the Constitution to change how things work in DC could hardly be called a rebellion.

Great. Now I'm in "rebellion" against the United States. Give me a break. Chuck says that the conservative commentators and bloggers are calling me a "political prisoner". I can't read the blogs, incidentally, because we don't have access to the internet in the slammer, which I can understand. These guys, with all their free time, would figure out how to hack every bank or government office in the country. "Political prisoner"? That has an ominous ring to it. I guess that's what I am. I haven't done anything to break any laws, at least any that I know of. I know, I know, I hear it all the time here from almost every inmate in here that he's an innocent man. But, I think I really am innocent. They won't tell us what laws I am accused of breaking, and since my habeas corpus petition rights have been suspended, Chuck says they can just keep holding me here on unspecified charges. We both think that will eventually change and they'll file charges, but they're holding up, we believe, until after the McAlister Bill passes, or gets defeated, as the case may be. They don't want to stir things up any more than necessary, until the vote is taken. Likewise, I didn't want to go completely ballistic public-comment wise, as much as I can from the slammer, until after the vote on the Bill. That would be a complication that the opponents of the bill don't need, to be saddled with official charges of "rebellion", or whatever they decide on, filed against one of the leaders against the Bill.

Bottom line, right now it looks like I'm not getting out of federal prison until I'm tried by a jury of my peers, hopefully, and found innocent. When will that be? Unknown, according to Chuck. Obviously, they need to keep me bottled up here until the Congress votes the McAlister Bill up or down. If it passes, I'll be tried and the Department of Justice will throw the veritable kitchen sink at me. If the Bill fails, it could be a long time before my case comes to a public trial, for obvious reasons. They wouldn't want to try a leader of a cause that had just won, if the Bill is defeated. A defeat of the McAlister Bill would make it harder to get a jury to convict me.

My primary heart ache in jail has not been myself (I somewhat knew what I was getting into, sort of), but instead, my ongoing disagreements with our son, John Madison II, a/k/a Jack. Jack, our oldest child, is married and has fathered our two grandchildren. He is the pastor of a fast growing church in the Dallas area, and is starting a new television ministry. Jack is a great kid (though at his age now the word kid might not apply). We have a good relationship, and have had since he was birthed, but that doesn't mean he agrees with his dad on what I have been doing for the last few years. His view is that as Christians we are to 'render unto Caesar'. I agree with that, but only as I think Jesus used it, in regard to paying taxes.

My opposition to the President in the recent Presidential campaign, which admittedly was fairly high profile, led to several somewhat intense arguments with Jack. He just feels that we should live under whatever government we get, and not ever oppose Caesar. In one of our debates, I reminded him of Dietrich Bonhoeffer, the German theologian who was executed for his involvement in an attempt to assassinate Hitler. He admitted that Bonhoeffer was a good example of a principled Christian who acted out of a desire to save the lives of Jews who were being slaughtered in concentration camps, but he argued I was no Bonhoeffer. OK, agreed, but I am worried about how this Administration is treating Israel, pushing it to give up its land. If we curse Israel, we will be cursed, I argued to Jack, citing one of the verses I've actually memorized. Genesis 12:3, I reminded my son, which promises blessings to those who bless Israel and curses to those who curse Israel. He said America would never abandon Israel, but I replied that may not be the case under this Administration. But, simply stated, Jack's not in very much agreement with me on very much that I've been doing.

Debbie and I love Jack, and his terrific wife, Allison, who doesn't say much on the subject, but who seems to agree with her husband. We pray that they will eventually understand why his dad took on the President. In the meantime, we'll just agree to disagree, and try to do it agreeably, as they say. But, it still hurts every time Jack asks me if I really know what I'm doing. Our other child, Katie, is working overseas and not too much affected by her dad's problems. We only briefly discuss the issue in our weekly Skype calls. But, she says she prays a lot for us, which is good to hear.

Well, that's enough candid blathering for now. Sorry I ran on, but what else are you going to do with your time in the joint?

TWENTY-THREE

Dallas, Texas

Pastor Jack Madison was having a good day. He'd met with his men's discipleship group for breakfast at La Donni's, his favorite morning restaurant, he'd finished his sermon notes for Sunday and had just started reading a contract from a local television station to carry his church's services on air. Then his day changed, abruptly. His long-time assistant had just buzzed him to tell him that there were two unsmiling, dark-suited federal agents in her office demanding that they see him. The agents had arrived at his church, without an appointment. Great, he thought, I' m not dressed in business attire today, just jeans and a polo shirt, since it's Friday. How was he going to be perceived by his unannounced visitors? He was taller than his dad, due to his mom being nearly as tall as her husband. He had a full head of dark hair and his wife, Allison, regularly told him knew she thought he was quite handsome. But, his looks he quickly concluded, would have nothing to do with why he was being visited by federal agents. He had a distinctly bad feeling about what was about to occur.

After perfunctorily apologizing for coming to his church office without an appointment, the older of the two agents said, "Pastor Madison, we've dropped by to advise you, as a representative of the family, that the government plans to indict your father for several federal crimes, not the least of which is expected to be a charge of conspiracy to overthrow the government".

Jack was not pleased at having federal agents descend on his office, unannounced, nor with their attitude and general demeanor. His earlier thoughts were confirmed, as he sensed that this meeting would not yield positive results. Thus it was that Jack flippantly responded, "Well, any candidate who runs for office is trying to overthrow the government".

"*Really*, Pastor Madison?" Jack noticed that they were definitely not amused. "Your father wasn't a candidate for office. If he had been a candidate, maybe some of his incendiary words, though not his seditious plans, might have been protected speech. No, Pastor Madison, your father is expected to be charged with these several federal crimes because he went over the line. He clearly violated the federal hate crimes law. He'll be charged with even more serious crimes than hate crimes. He's an enemy of the state."

Jack was raised to be polite, but he was at the outside limit of his ability to restrain himself. He wanted to reach across the desk and smack these guys silly, but he knew that striking a federal agent would earn him an adjoining cell next to his dad. Instead, all he could think to say was, "May I ask why you are here? And why are you telling me these things? I'm not my dad's lawyer. Call Chuck Webster in Tyler. I don't control what my dad says or does. Talk to him."

"Pastor Madison, you make a valid point, you are not legally representing your father. But, as his son, you have contact and you communicate with your father, as we, of course, know from monitoring all of your father's communications with anyone outside the federal facility."

"You read everything he writes? Everything, even to my mom?"

"Of course, Pastor. Your father is expected to be charged soon as an enemy of the state. Under the Patriot Act we can do what we need to do to protect America."

"Look guys. I'm a busy pastor of a fair-sized church. You've got lots of federal criminals out there to catch, I'm sure, so can we either wind this up, or can we get to the point?"

"No reason to be testy, Pastor Madison. The *point* that you want us to get to is simply this. Three things. Number one. Encourage your father to back off his trouble making. Knock it off.

"Number two. Advise John Madison to stop writing letters and articles that are being used to stir up the gunners across the country. Stop writing.

"And number three. Suggest to him that if he ever wants to live someplace but a prison cell, he should consider a plea bargain once he's charged. Agree with the Department of Justice that he's violated the law, take his lumps, and maybe, with some good behavior, he'll get to spend some time, on the outside, with your children, Josh, Sarah and Thomas, that is while they're still children."

The agent's last comment, specifically naming Jack's three minor children, was too much for Jack. "We're *done*, gentlemen. You found your own way in, you can find your own way out."

The agents were trained to carefully watch and evaluate the reaction of interviewees that they were attempting to intimidate. After they were abruptly evicted from the Pastor's office, they both agreed that it had been a fruitful visit. Pastor John "Jack" Madison II had been intimidated. He would talk to his father and convey everything he had heard. However, the older agent, upon reflection, said as they were driving from the church parking lot, "I agree that he was intimidated, he'll pass it all on to his dad. But.... I saw in his eyes something that concerned me. He's no wimp, no roll over. The powers that be had better never push this young man *too far*....or....they may wish they *hadn't*."

TWENTY-FOUR

Houston Federal Detention Center

Jack Madison enjoyed visiting with his Dad even though the visit was at a federal prison. What he was not looking forward to was telling him what the FBI agents had revealed to him in their recent unpleasant visit to his church office. He knew he had to share what they had said, but he dreaded being the bearer of serious news, that agents of their nation's government had confirmed to Jack that his father would be charged with several federal crimes, not the least of which was conspiracy to overthrow the government. How many sons, he wondered, as he checked through security at the Houston federal detention facility, have ever had to tell their father he was going to be formally accused of serious federal crimes. Not many, he thought, as he realized he needed to pray before he entered the prisoner/visitor contact area of the prison. He had been so wrought up over what he would say, that he had forgotten to turn the matter over in prayer. I'm a pastor. I should know how to approach tough jobs like this, he thought. So, he prayed and then went in to deliver the news.

Jack's dad was upbeat, as was his normal approach, happy to see a visitor and to be with his son. "Jack, my son, great to see you....though, to be frank, you look like you ran over a cat, or a good-sized dog, on the way here. Why the sad face?"

"Oh, sorry, dad. I should be the one trying to cheer you up, not the other way around. No. I didn't hit any animals, but I kinda feel like I've been run over a bit."

"Oh? Is Allison OK? The kids' fine? Everything all right at the church?"

"Well, that covers what it's important, and they're all just great. No major issues. Thomas got into a playground fight with some abrasions, but mostly hurt feelings. No big deal. No, I may not be as smiley as usual because I had an unannounced visit by two federal agents late last week."

"Really? Seriously? Why did they visit you? What did they want?"

Jack then explained all that had taken place, emphasizing the statements made by the agents threatening John Madison with upcoming serious federal charges, along with their three warnings to lay low, keep his mouth shut and their final suggestion that he plea bargain, once he was charged.

"Well....hum....now I see why you looked glum coming here today. I guess none of this surprises me. Chuck's been saying for some time that they would get around to charging me....and that it wouldn't be friendly or fair. They've definitely targeted me to try and send a message to others who are like-minded. What I *do* object to, however, is using you to try and get to me. That's reprehensible. They have something to say to me....they know where I am. They shouldn't try and pressure me through my family."

"I don't mind that, dad, but what concerns me is the suggestion that if you don't plead guilty and accept a plea bargain sentence, that you may be in prison for many, many years. That's not a happy thought. As you know, I'm still worried about your case, and how you got yourself into this position...."

"No, it's not a happy thought, that's for sure. But, I'm had many days to think and pray about this, Jack. I've come closer to the Lord in all of this than I ever was before. Yes, I've had my rare moments in the past of having to realize that I couldn't pull something off and I needed divine help. But those were few and far between. In order to get out of this mess, I know it will have to be an act of God, not of John Madison, not as a result of my schemes and plans. I can't smart my way out of this, He'll have to do it, if it gets done. And, frankly, I've decided that if He doesn't do it, get me out of here sooner rather than later, I'm okay with that. Obviously, I think I can be used better on the outside. But....if His plan is for me to minister to the guys in here, or wherever I end up, I think I can live with that....I hope I can....that is."

"My suggestion, Dad is that you pray, then talk to Chuck about what they said. Ask him for his insight. These can be very serious criminal charges. One of the lawyers in my church told me that if the feds want to convict somebody they almost always are able to do so. On the other hand, does the visit by the agents show that they think they have a weak case, so they're trying to get a plea-bargained conviction on the cheap, so to speak. That was my thought anyway. But, try not and lose sleep over it....as you say, if He wants you out of here, no power on earth can keep you behind these bars. Look at what He did with Paul and Silas, Busted them right out the front gate."

"You're exactly right, Jack. I won't lose much sleep. I actually sleep better in here than I used to, when I tossed and turned over office issues, missed sales quotas, and all that. There's a certain peace about this place, strange as that sounds."

Jack was struck with how much his dad had grown spiritually in his few months of confinement. He had worked with prisoners in the past, but he couldn't recall any who had experienced such a level of trust as what he was witnessing in his father. Jack knew that before John Madison became a federal prisoner he regularly, and many times irregularly, read his Bible. But his dad shared with him that after he changed his address to a federal facility, given his increased free time, he had become an avid student of scripture. He candidly told his son that he was now spending long hours of reading, study, cross-referencing and prayer, all of which had led to his deeper understanding of the Word.

One area of scripture that had captured John Madison's attention was prophecy. He had always been interested in prophecy, but once imprisoned, he decided to extensively look into what the Bible said would happen in the end times, in the last days. One area of last days revelation that had he had focused on was the role of America in prophecy. Knowing that his son Jack would be visiting him soon, and knowing that Jack was not in total agreement with him on the political issues that landed him in the pen, he had prepared several questions for discussion on a different, non-political topic. He hoped that by talking about a spiritual subject, they could avoid clashing over the political reasons he was not a free man.

"OK, Jack, we've talked that visit by the feds to death. I appreciate your taking the heat for me, we'll just have to see what happens, and what He wants to do. It was no surprise to Him. So, I'd like to change the subject to a more pleasant topic. I've been studying prophecy, as I told you on your last visit. I've prepared a list of questions for my seminary graduate son. I want to see if all those bucks we spent on books and classes had a good result....But, seriously I have some questions....let me just start with the biggy....the primo question. Why isn't America in prophecy?"

"What?"

"I mean....well....given that we are obviously at the beginning of the end times....and "

"Dad, stop....I don't disagree. But, what leads you to you say that now? When I wanted to talk about prophecy as a teenager, you never seemed very interested in the subject."

"Well, Jack, I wasn't. I didn't know much about it and it just never grabbed me like other parts of scripture. But here in prison, I've had a lot of time to read and think. Every time I'd read about Jesus talking to the fig tree, I'd stop and try and figure out what He was telling us. Jesus said to watch for the re-budding of the fig tree, as the beginning of the last days. Israel has used the fig tree as its symbol for centuries. Israel, contrary to all odds, is actually back in the land, just as Jesus said it would be."

"True. He did say to watch for the re-budding of the fig tree. Israel was dead, dead, dead....that is, until 1948. Anyone who has any doubts about the accuracy of the Bible has a big obstacle to overcome when it comes to Israel. No nation in the history of the world has ever gone out of existence for 2,000 years and then come back into the same land, populated by the descendants of the same people who lived there two millennia before. It even has the same name. Never happened before."

"And, since Jesus said, several times, that Israel would be re-born in the land, and Israel has, in fact, been re-born in the land, an indisputable fact, how can anyone not say that God has revealed Himself in our times? Today?"

Jack was a graduate of a Bible-believing, conservative seminary and had been a pastor for twelve years in Dallas. He replied to his Dad's softball question, "No question about it. Israel is Exhibit A for Biblical prophetic fulfillment in our time. He said Israel would come back in the land and they did, against all odds, and contrary to the world's plans. You know, the test for whether a prophecy was from God was whether or not it was 100% accurate. If a prophet was only partially accurate, he was stoned."

"That was certainly a dis-incentive for making up stuff. But, Jack, let's come back to the first question I have written on my 'Stump the Pastor' list....why isn't America in prophecy? All those hundreds of verses telling us about the last days, the end times, the day of the Lord, but none about the most important country on the globe? I don't get it. What did they teach you in seminary about that?"

"Pops, you bring up a really challenging issue because Jesus also told us that the generation that sees the re-budding of the fig tree won't *all* pass away until the end times prophecies He gave us are fulfilled. Your generation, the generation that was alive in 1948 when Israel was re-born, is clearly the generation Jesus was referring to.'

"OK, Jack, I'm tracking with you, here. I think. Since my generation saw Israel return, and Israel has survived over sixty years, we won't all be gone before these other end times prophecies are fulfilled? Am I getting that right?"

"Yup. That is exactly what the Lord said....so....back to your question. Given that we are living in those last days, why doesn't scripture talk about the world's most powerful nation around today?"

"That, my son, may be the key. In my research, I came across an article by Dr. Lester Sumrall who said that he thought that meant that America would cease to exist before the end of the last days. He said....let me find my notes here....'Simply put, the United States will no longer be a world power in the end times. It will not be a significant enough nation to play a major role in the events of those days – that is the obvious answer.'"

"Pleasant thought. Any other cheery results of your research?

"Maybe not so cheery, but Dr. Tim LaHaye, you know him, he wrote that Left Behind series, asked, 'Why would the God of prophecy not refer to the supreme superpower nation in the end times in preparation for the one-world government of the Antichrist?' Good question, hunh?"

"Well, generically, America is included in the end times verses that refer to all of the nations of the world, of course, but that doesn't answer your question."

"Nope, it sure doesn't. I finally decided to start digging deeper, which leads me to my next several questions on my 'Stump the Pastor' list.

"Fine, go on, Pops, but I'm not doing too hot so far."

"OK, here's what I've come up with, I'm giving you a copy to take it along, and when you have a chance, take a look at it, in light of what you know about prophecy. Then, next time you visit, we can talk about it. This research took my mind off the debate over the McAlister Bill. By the next time I see you we should know whether or not the Bill has passed. Agreed?"

"Deal. What'd you find?"

"Take a look at these 223 verses in prophecy I've listed, written by five Prophets, both Old and New Testament, all of which describe a rich, powerful and influential end times nation. The name the Prophets used for that nation is both the Daughter of Babylon and Babylon the Great. That last one is in the Book of Revelation. Look at the verses, I've detailed them on this list I'm giving you, and tell me who you think they are referring to, America, or to somebody else?"

"This next month is a killer on our church calendar, but, Pops, you taught me to always set aside some time with just me and the Lord. I'll use some of that time to study the verses."

"I'll pray for wisdom for you. See you in a month. Give my usual hugs and kisses to Allison and the kids."

"Will do. Love ya, dad."

The list that John Madison gave his son included the following prophetic verses detailing the future of the Daughter of Babylon/Babylon the Great.

Psalm 137:8
Isaiah 13; 21:1-10; 47 and 48
Jeremiah 50 and 51
Zechariah 2:7
Revelation 17 and 18

II.

Congress
Votes on the
Lawrence McAlister
Hate Speech
and
Hate Weapons
Elimination Bill

TWENTY-FIVE

Washington, DC – U.S. House of Representatives

Under the arcane rules of the United States House of Representatives, the Speaker has sole discretion on many matters before the House, including when the Members may engage in a floor debate over pending legislation, and how many minutes they each may speak. The Speaker alone decides.

Having been a Member of the House for almost two decades, the Speaker was well aware that she could help frame how the nation views bills being considered by her chamber of the Congress. She did it by scheduling long floor debates, in good viewing times, for legislation she favored. She diminished Americans' exposure to the details of legislation she didn't favor. Generally, legislation that she didn't favor would never come to a floor debate because the bill would never make it through the House Committee to which she had assigned it. She would suggest to the Chairman of the Committee to which the unfavored bill was assigned that the Chairman either never set a hearing to consider the bill, or alternatively, vote down any bill that was not favored by House Leadership. Either way, the Speaker ruled. It was good to be Queen.

With the McAlister Bill, though, the Speaker was faced with a slightly different situation. She did not want to increase public visibility and perception of the Bill for quite obvious reasons. Those Americans who favored passage of the bill were already in support and didn't need to be persuaded by a lengthy prime time floor debate. On the other hand, those who were opposed to the Bill didn't need to be stirred up any more, as they would then increase pressure on her Members. The vote was going to be razor thin, either way, she knew from early head counts, so she concluded that scheduling a high visibility, lengthy formal floor debate would not serve her purposes. In addition, though she was firmly committed to the Bill's passage, she knew enough American history, from having once been a high school history teacher, to convince her that the opponents had by far the best argument against passage of a Bill seeking to re-interpret the first two key provisions in the Bill of Rights. So why, she thought, give them a forum? Let them go on Fox News. This is my House, and you don't use my House for your hate speech, she concluded as she signed the floor debate notification. The Speaker, who was tall and thin, was widely-known for her extravagant wardrobe, her acerbic tongue and her general dullness when it came to nuanced policy issues.

When the Speaker posted the notification of the floor debate there was a hue and cry from the Members of the minority the likes of which and not been seen or heard since the 1960's, when Vietnam and civil rights issues reigned. The Speaker had scheduled the floor debate on the McAlister Hate Speech and Hate Weapons Elimination Bill for 8 AM on Monday, March 18th, allowing only three Members to speak from each side, and for only three minutes each. In her notification the Speaker cryptically said, *"This Bill has been thoroughly debated in the media. It's time to vote."* Republicans and Tea Party Members were outraged.

The Minority Leader in a hastily called news conference summarized their anger, "Nine minutes? Nine minutes? That's all the time we get, total? To debate a bill that purports to take away our Constitutional rights to speak as we see fit and to keep and bear arms? This is utter nonsense. It's the tyranny of the majority in its worst possible form. Thomas Jefferson said it best when he said, 'When people fear their government there is tyranny. When the government fears the people, there is liberty.' We know under the House Rules the Speaker can get away with this high-handed act of oppression against free speech, but she should know that in doing so she is feeding a growing awakening sleeping giant, the American people, and they will not let her get away with it. No, sir, not by a long shot. This government had better start fearing the people, just as Jefferson said."

MSNBC's most liberal talking head in his commentary that evening accused the Minority Leader of threatening the Speaker with violence. "When the Republican leader said 'not by a long shot', is that actually code, for calling for gun violence? If it is, we just can't have that in this country any more. Then, when he said the government should fear the people, is that a call for armed insurrection? These are scary comments, sure enough."

Most House Members travel to their home Districts over the weekend, returning to DC late Monday or early Tuesday. By scheduling the brief debate for 8 AM on a Monday morning, the Speaker purposely forced the Members to return on Sunday, which did not set well with most, even many in her own Democrat caucus. Her point was to schedule the debate early enough so that potential viewers in the nation's eastern time zone would be getting ready for work and sending kids off to school. In the other times zones, millions would sleep through this momentous House expression of free speech. Perfect timing. That is, if one didn't want a lot of attention.

At 8:10 AM the Speaker gaveled the House to order and recognized the first Member to speak on the bill. "The Chair recognizes the distinguished gentleman from California for three minutes, speaking in favor of 113-S.-1."

"Madam Speaker, thank you for allowing me to address the reasons for passage of this most important bill. All Members here this morning recognize that we are in this Chamber in historic times, as we will soon have the opportunity, to actually make, that is, to help in making history. History will record that as we adopt this....." The Member from California consumed his full three minutes describing the historicity of the debate over the gun bill, but without advancing any legal, political or policy arguments for its adoption.

"Thank you. The Chair now recognizes for three minutes only, I would remind you, and time will be strictly enforced...Uh...I recognize...who is it?...yes ...The gentleman from Ohio, in opposition to the Hate Speech and Weapons Elimination Bill...uh...113-S.-1."

The Congressman from Ohio was briefly tempted to point out how the Speaker's introductions of himself and the Congressman from California varied so greatly, but he knew it would just consume part of his time, and fair-minded viewers would have caught it in any case.

"Madam Speaker, I rise today to oppose the McAlister Bill. Not because I favor gun violence or hate speech, but because I favor the rule of law. Let me be crystal clear in my brief time. If this Congress, the White House or the American people, for that matter, want to amend our Constitution to repeal our right to own firearms, or to curtail free speech, then they know how to do that. This bill is a reprehensible attempt to do an end run around our sacred founding document, by a mere simple majority vote of Congress. In their wisdom, our Founding Fathers knew that a day could come in this nation, as has been the case throughout history, in which the passion of the moment would be used to strip citizens of their rights. When times are scary, when the blood runs hot, when the mob demands that action be taken, they knew that it would be in those times when our freedoms would most be at risk. The writers of the Constitution knew this and required super majorities of the Congress and of the states in order to dissolve a fundamental right. They allowed it to be done, but they made it almost impossible to do in order to prevent government by mob action.

"Let us not set this most dangerous of precedents. Today, the right that may be lost is the right to express your opinion openly and the right to own firearms. Gun ownership is now not popular with the governing authorities, nor with the media, and likewise not so popular with some Americans, the truth be told. The authors of this Bill have tied together changing the First Amendment right of free speech with the more popular ban on gun ownership. What rights will we take away tomorrow, next year, the year after that? Which due process rights in our Constitution do we lose by simply voting them away, as we threaten to do with the McAlister Bill? Can we so easily 'reinterpret', and then lose, those rights that were won for us by the many who gave their lives, their fortunes and their sacred honor? May God forbid that it would ever be. Let us kill this dangerous precedent before it is born, before it becomes the roadmap for the loss of all of our rights as Americans. Those rights are all now hanging by a thread. Your vote, your single vote, could literally decide the fate of this Bill. Your single vote could decide the very future of our rights as Americans. Cast it wisely, my dear colleagues, cast it *very* wisely. A final point....Don't let the threat of a possible war with China divert our attention from preserving our rights as a free people. Thank you, Madam Speaker, I yield back the balance of my time."

"The gentleman from Ohio's time has expired. The Chair recognizes the distinguished gentle lady from New York."

"Thank you, Madam Speaker. I'll use the time that you have so graciously given to me to talk about hate.

"Hate...is...what...brings...us...together...today. What is hate? Hate is what makes us pick up a firearm and take another person's life. Hate makes us think we should be allowed to live, while others die. What makes a person hate? We may not know all of the reasons why people hate enough to kill another human being, but we do know that guns kill people. So to stop the hate killings in America I am a proud co-sponsor of the Lawrence McAlister Hate Speech and Hate Weapons Elimination Bill.

"Our colleagues who oppose this noble bill are skilled at raising legal objections about amending the Constitution. But, if you are like me, you know in your heart that we have to ban guns in America, except of course the guns we have entrusted to our military, who may well be needing them if the current crisis with China worsens. Legal technicalities shouldn't stand in the way of protecting us from gun violence. The gentleman from Ohio suggests that we have to wait, for who knows how many years, for the various states to consider a formal amendment to the Constitution. That could take possibly several years before thirty four states have the chance to consider and vote for an amendment banning hate weapons, and shutting down all of this rampant hate speech that we hear on cable TV and on the radio. We can't wait that long. How many hundreds or thousands of our neighbors, our friends, our public officials, even our family members will die, from gun violence, instigated by hate speech, while we wait on those legal technicalities?

"No, Madam Speaker, waiting is not the answer. We must prohibit the private ownership of guns now, because if we don't take this unique opportunity, we may never again be in a position to take away the firearms that are too frequently used to kill others. At a time when the world is worried about a possible war with China, we need to get this matter resolved now. No more delay. Madam Speaker, you should order a vote sooner rather than later. Stop the hate – stop the killing – vote yes on the Lawrence McAlister Hate Speech and Hate Weapons Elimination Bill. I yield back the balance of my time."

Tensions on the House floor were at a breaking point. If the final vote was a foregone conclusion, the Members would have been considerably less tense, knowing the outcome. But, both sides had head counts, as recently as that morning, showing a dead heat. One Member's vote, therefore, took on critical importance. The Members of the Minority knew that the Speaker was abusing her authority, but they also knew that when they were in the Majority they had been accused of similar actions. One thing that the Members would agree upon if polled at this early morning session was that no one would change their vote based on a total of eighteen minutes of floor debate, which was just as the Speaker intended.

The Speaker then recognized the second opponent to the McAlister Bill, Representative Adam Nation, a leader in the Tea Party Caucus of the U.S. Congress. Congressman Nation had seated himself close to the podium so that he could quickly begin his remarks once he was recognized by the Speaker, who clearly did not like this new Member of what she thought of as *her* House.

"Madam Speaker. Members of the House. My fellow Americans. There are two surprising aspects of this floor debate being held on this early morning. First, that this OBGYN from the Midwest is speaking in this Chamber today. Except for the American people rising up and electing me, and many other Tea Party supporters, I would still be treating hot flashes in Michigan. The second surprise to me as a new Member of this body is that I even have to defend a right as foundational and fundamental as the right to free speech and the right to defend oneself from a weapon-bearing assailant, that is, with more than one's bare hands. What could possibly be more important to one's life than the right to stay alive, to defend oneself, with a firearm, if necessary, and when assaulted by a criminal using a firearm? Name any right more important than the right to stay alive.

"Madam Speaker, my second argument is also a fundamental truth about governing. An elemental truth of governing a free people is that when a nation is divided, when as many people favor a change in the law as are opposed to changing the law, nothing should be done, until or unless there is a consensus of the governed. We should have learned from the healthcare debacle that forcing through massive changes in the laws of a nation, when about half of all Americans are opposed to the change, only invites trouble, and an increasing suspicion and disdain for their government by the governed.

"Lastly, Madam Speaker, I hesitate to raise this argument, because it will undoubtedly be misinterpreted. But, the truth is that this country was founded by men with muskets, to whom we owe our freedom. If this free nation passes this anti-gun legislation, we should not be at all surprised if men with today's form of muskets try to regain their freedom. I'm not threatening anyone. I have no inside information as to any armed resistance that may occur. But we've all heard rumors that if this Congress passes this law and takes away our right to be armed, and to speak our mind freely, there are strong rumors that there will be persons who will not abide such a decision, who will not turn in their firearms and who may even use those firearms. How would they use them? I don't know, but I am strongly suggesting to this body of legislators that before it crosses the line of public opposition to banning guns, that it first look to see what's on the other side of that line. Be warned, my colleagues, you are warned. I yield back the balance of my time."

As the Tea Party Caucus leader concluded his remarks, the Speaker's facial expression could only be described as hateful.

Spluttering, she said, "I have never....in all my years in this....I can't recall ever hearing a Member threaten violence against our government, before. Never. I just can't believe....Why, I should ask the House Ethics Committee to investigate the gentlemen's threatening remarks....I....The Justice Department should....Sir, you should be very...."

"Madam Speaker, I didn't threaten anybody, let alone our government..."

"Yes, you did, you very clearly said that...."

"If the Speaker would let me finish, I only suggested what everybody has already heard, and probably already discussed, and that is, that if this bill becomes the law of the land, that the new law will *not* be universally obeyed, and it may lead to violence. That's not a threat. That's reality, Madam Speaker, and we had better be aware of reality before we..."

The reality was that Speaker now had what she needed.

"The gentlemen will desist. Your time is expired. I am exercising my prerogative to terminate debate in this House when it appears that decorum has been disturbed, under Rule XVII. There is no right of a Member to engage in seditious comments in this House. There will be no more floor debate. The last two Members who were scheduled to speak can submit their remarks for the Record. We will vote tomorrow, Tuesday, March 19th at 5 PM. This House is adjourned." With that the Speaker slammed down her Speaker's Gavel, and walked off the Speaker's platform.

"Madam Speaker, I challenge the...you can't..."

"I appeal the Chair's ruling and ask for a division."

The motions were to no avail, as the Speaker had adjourned the House. No further business could be transacted. The floor debate on the Lawrence McAlister Hate Speech and Hate Weapons Elimination Bill was over. What remained was the vote.

TWENTY-SIX

Dallas, Texas

Pastor Jack Madison had a free evening, due to a cancelled counseling session, which allowed him to look more extensively into the 223 prophetic verses that his Dad had asked him to study during his last visit. After a very long night of study, prayer and research, he wished he hadn't done so. He didn't sleep well in the remaining hours of the night.

The next morning he decided to expand his study of the prophecies by asking his senior accountability group to also look into the verses. The six men in the group were all involved in leadership in Jack's church in the Park Cities suburb of Dallas. Four had seminary training. All were students of the Bible. None were prepared for what their Pastor was about to ask them to do.

"Men, I didn't sleep well last night...."

"Unconfessed sins, Pastor?", asked Scott Banks, the comic member of the group.

Always ready for a laugh, Pastor Jack joined in the general mirth, "No, Scott, but if I think of some to confess, you'll be the second one I call, after the Lord, of course....OK, seriously though, my sleep deprivation was caused by a late night Bible study. My dad, you've met him and you all know why he's in prison, gave me several prophecy verses to study. I finally had a free evening and I did so, though I frankly wished I hadn't."

"Why's that, Pastor?"

"You'll soon see. Here's a list for each of you of 223 verses. All of them are about a single end times nation. Very powerful, called the hammer of the whole earth. Extremely rich, living in luxury. Influential, referred to as the great voice. The nations of the world stream there to meet. Has a large Jewish population. A supporter of Israel. There are over thirty clues to what the Bible calls the mystery of the identity of this end times nation."

"Very interesting, Pastor. Sounds like you may have solved the mystery already?"

"It might sound that way, but I haven't come to any final conclusions. Yet, that is. I want you each to take the list, look up and read the verses, do whatever research you have time to do, then let's discuss it next week. I'm very interested in hearing what you come up with. This subject is obviously important, otherwise God wouldn't have devoted so many verses to it, and they may answer the question that many American Christians have asked."

"What question is that, Pastor?"

"Is America in the Bible? If it is, what happens to it in the last days?"

Thus the members of Jack's most trusted church leaders were given what would prove to be a very challenging assignment. None would ever forget how they started down this path pursuing the contemporary application of prophecy.

TWENTY-SEVEN

Washington, DC – Chambers of U.S. House of Representatives

While the nation worried about a possible war with China, Speaker Pelham, not coincidentally, scheduled the final vote on the McAlister Bill. The pending vote drew several tens of thousands of protestors and supporters to Capitol Hill. The signs being carried on the plaza in front of the U.S. Capitol were many, varied and, in some cases, hateful and vitriolic, and those were the signs in *support* of the gun bill. Not to be outdone, opponents of the McAlister bill showed their entrenched positions against the bill, with signs such as:

ONLY WHEN YOU PEEL AWAY
MY COLD, DEAD FINGERS

AN ARMED MAN IS A CITIZEN
AN UNARMED MAN IS A SUBJECT

DEFEAT GUN ABOLITION
DEFEAT SPEECH CENSORSHIP

GOD, GUNS AND GUTS MADE AMERICA GREAT!

KEEP YOUR LAWS OFF MY GUN!
KEEP YOUR LAWS OFF MY SPEECH!

ONLY CROOKED POLITICIANS FEAR ARMED CITIZENS

THE ORIGINAL HOMELAND SECURITY
THE RIGHT TO KEEP AND BEAR ARMS

Gun bill supporters' signs generally ignored the philosophical issues involved in the gun debate and, instead, reviled the opponents of the gun bill:

DON'T LET THE PEOPLE HATERS & GUN LOVERS WIN

SAY NO TO SLOPEHEADS

BAN GUNS AND HATE SPEECH NOW

ENOUGH IS ENOUGH – PASS THE BILL – STOP THE KILLERS

NO OLD DOCUMENT
CAN GRANT THE RIGHT TO KILL OR HATE

GOD MUST HATE GUN OWNERS

"The House will be in order."

"The House will be in order!"

"The House *will* be in order!! All Members please take their seats. All Members *please* be seated, so that we can begin the vote tally. This is a *truly* momentous vote for our nation, so I would like to start..."

The only persons who were actually listening to Speaker Pelham try to call the House to order, were not those excitedly milling in the chamber, but were instead those watching her on the big three, C-Span, MSCNB, CNN or Fox, all of which were covering live the historic vote on the McAlister Bill. The House session had originally been noticed for 1 PM, but it was abruptly moved to 5 PM, when the Speaker realized that she might be as many as three votes shy of the votes necessary to pass the hard-fought, and heatedly debated, bill.

160

The Members of the House, particularly the undecided, had been lobbied, and lobbied hard, but of course, that's the price they paid in personal stress to be in public service, as they could be expected to argue in their own defense. Some might respond that the money, perks, staff, vehicles, fame and health and retirement benefits provided to Congressmen and Congresswomen more than justified the pressure and stress associated with having tens of thousands of people tell you what to do, and how to vote.

Voting was why the Members assembled together tonight on Capitol Hill, in the historic shadow of the Members who had come before them, who also cast votes through which America was changed. With some votes the nation changed for the better, with other votes, the results were not so good. The true believers on both sides of the speech and gun issues who were assembled in the Chamber knew that it was their votes that would ensure either that America would be free of guns, or alternatively, that America would lose rights guaranteed by its Constitution. They knew those rights could vanish with a simple bill, should it become a law, and be upheld by the U.S. Supreme Court. Such were the stakes facing the Members, as the Senate had yesterday voted in favor of 113-S.-1 in sufficient numbers, and the President had let it be known that he had several honorary pass-out signature pens lined up on his desk, prepared for signing the McAlister Hate Speech and Hate Weapons Elimination Act. What was needed was 218 Americans, Members of the U.S. House of Representatives, willing and able to vote yes on the pending bill to change Americans' rights to speak freely and to keep and bear arms. An historic vote indeed.

Speaker Pelham earlier in the afternoon informed her House majority leadership team that she intended to use the "Hastert Hat Trick", if necessary, to get the votes needed to pass the McAlister Bill. She was referring to controversial legislative actions taken by Speaker Dennis Hastert in 2003 to pass the Bush Medicare Prescription Drug Act. On the first vote in the House in June, 2003 the bill failed by 218 to 214. After some arm-twisting, three Republicans changed their vote, passing the bill by 216-215. After several months of debate and eventual passage by the Senate, a revised version of the bill came back to the House for consideration. Voting on the bill started at 3 AM on November 22nd, but the initial vote tally showed the bill losing by 219-215.

Contrary to the traditional House voting limit of fifteen minutes, the vote was held open for several hours while Speaker Hastert and Majority Leader Delay sought two more affirmative votes. During the vote delay one Congressman alleged that he was offered campaign funding for his son, who wanted to run to replace the Congressman in the next election. At 5:50 AM the Speaker found two more votes and the bill passed. Democrats called foul, but the precedent had been established, allowing the Speaker of the US House to hold open a vote on pending legislation, as long as necessary, and to do whatever was necessary, to get the votes necessary, to pass the bill and thus make a new law. Now, if the vote promised to be close, the Chair could instruct the House Clerk to suspend the clock countdown at one minute yet to go, to ensure that the Speaker had sufficient votes to either pass or defeat a bill, as the case may be.

Within a half hour, the Speaker had gaveled the Members into their seats and into enough order and

162

decorum for the Clerk to read the title and synopsis of the bill upon which the Members would soon vote.

"The question is upon the passage of 113-S.-1, A Bill for an Act to Eliminate Hate Speech and Hate Weapons, be it enacted by the Congress of the.... "

"Thank you Madam Clerk, the Bill is upon the table, the Committee of the Whole having considered and acted upon all amendments submitted by Members, the question is on consideration of the Bill. All those in favor, say aye, all opposed say Nay. In the opinion of the Chair, the ayes have it, and the bill..."

"Madam Speaker," the Minority Leader made the obligatory motion for a recorded vote by individual Members, "I move for a recorded vote."

"The Gentleman's motion is granted. The Clerk will open the voting system for voting by Members."

The time was 6:05 PM. As Members began to vote, they didn't do so in a vacuum. Not only were the eyes and ears of the world focused on their vote through electronic media, the multiple thousands of Bill protestors and supporters outside the U.S. Capitol insured that the Members of the House heard their respective messages.

The House of Representatives vote tally device posted votes as they were entered by Members, each using the encoded card given to them upon being sworn in as Members. Television screens carried the ongoing totals, as votes were added. Those who were strongly in favor and those who were adamantly opposed to the Bill cast their votes quickly, each side showing their voting numbers strength, as an early indicator.

163

With just five minutes to go on the countdown, almost all Members had voted, showing a count of 205 in favor and 207 opposed, leaving 23 not yet voting. At one minute and fifteen seconds yet to go, the count had risen to 212 in favor and 215 opposed, with 8 not yet voting. At almost one minute, 3 of the 8 had voted, but all had voted no, bringing the tally to 212 in favor and 218 opposed, a margin of 6 against, but with only 5 not yet voting. Alarm bells sounded behind the Speaker's Rostrum, as the Speaker alerted the Clerk to stop the countdown, until further order by the Chair. The backers of the McAlister Bill had a problem, a big problem. They didn't yet have the votes needed for passage.

The task was easy enough to understand – the Speaker needed all five Members not yet voting to vote yes, and one Member of the 218 voting no would have to switch their vote, a maneuver that was allowed under the House Rules as long as voting had not yet been closed by the Chair. The Speaker was not about to close the voting until she had 218 votes cast in favor of the Bill. How to accomplish that task was now her immediate task.

The five Members who had not yet voted were invited to leave the floor of the House and meet with the Speaker, "Congressman Scott, the Speaker would like to see you in her Chamber Office, if you have the time." The Members not yet voting had the time.

The five Members of the House who had not yet cast their votes were assembled in the Speaker's private office just off the House floor. Congressman Scott later told his colleagues that it was almost like school children being chastised in the Principal's Office for their behavior on the school grounds.

The Speaker even used language to that effect. "Alright, now children, what have I possibly done to you to lead you to disappoint me so greatly? This Bill is the most important since healthcare reform, and here we are, with your Speaker six votes shy, and you are five of those six votes. What am I to do? Could I conceivably be more embarrassed than to have five Members from my own Party who won't vote for this bill?"

Speaker Pelham had developed through the years a reputation for personalizing every vote, whenever and however possible. She had been told that former Speaker Sam Rayburn had used the technique to great effect in his 17 successful years leading the House in the 40's and 50's. Since amending the Bill was out of the question procedurally at this point in time, the only thing the Speaker could offer to pick up votes now was in the 'sausage making category'. Otto von Bismarck, Chancellor of German, had once famously said that if one ever wanted to respect the law or eat sausage again, one shouldn't watch either one being made. It was sausage making time for the Speaker.

"I don't have all night, so let's just do this. Write down what it will take on the back of your Member business card, drop it on the desk, and I'll call you back in individually. But, don't get greedy and don't be stupid, there is actually a limit on my powers, there's even a limit on the President's ability to get what you want. He's on standby at the other end of Pennsylvania Avenue, so we're prepared to deal. But, before you leave, I still need a switcher, so also put on your card the most likely Member to switch, and I'll call them in. Now get out of here, you guys have caused enough trouble tonight."

Between the Speaker, and her ability to substantially advance a Member's career and standing in the House, and the President, and his almost unlimited ability to bring federal benefits, grants, contracts, campaign contributions and Presidential visits to a favored Member of Congress, the five visitors to the Speaker's Office eventually saw the light, and voted yes on the McAlister Bill. U.S. Senator Everett Dirksen, former majority leader of the Senate, had frequently observed that "when they feel the heat, they see the light". His commentary on lining up votes was from a by-gone era, one in which political pressure to conform was more prevalent, times in which monetary and power enticements were the norm. The vote on the screens was now 218 opposed and 217 in favor. The Speaker needed one no vote to switch to yes. Now, finally, she knew she would win.

The Speaker's words to her caucus leadership team and the bill's floor leaders were certainly succinct, "This is the word. Circulate it. The first one to switch, the first one to change from no to yes, *the very first one*, gets a choice: a.) their spouse or significant other gets appointed to the Board of Directors of America's third largest multi-national corporation, guaranteed 400 K per year for four years, plus perks, or b.) appointment by the President to the empty Ambassadorship to Italy, upon resignation from the House, all done within sixty days, with a guarantee of confirmation by the Senate. After the Court of St. James, our Ambassador to Great Britain, Rome is the best Embassy post in the world. After that, whoever switches, I don't care. They get nothing special. Let's get this done."

Within minutes, three things had changed in America:

a.) A Congressman from New Jersey switched his no vote to yes, immediately after which the Speaker declared the vote closed at 6:18 AM, with 218 in favor and 217 opposed;

b.) America's Congress had adopted a new law allowing the federal government to decide what constituted free speech, prohibiting private ownership of firearms and making it a felony to own a firearm, in spite of the Constitutional Amendments granting speech and gun ownership rights; and

c.) The President signed and faxed to the Speaker's office the necessary appointment documents naming a new Ambassador to Rome, a man whose sole prior experience in foreign affairs, and particularly international relations with the nation of Italy, was as a frequent diner at Newark's several Italian restaurants.

TWENTY-EIGHT

Dallas, Texas

The longevity of an American protestant pastor can frequently be stunted, cut short by internal issues. It doesn't have to be that way, as many evangelical churches with long-serving pastors can attest. Pastor Jack Madison had originally started at his Dallas church as a youth pastor, but when the senior pastor retired, he was the natural choice for the job. Since becoming senior pastor Jack Madison had developed a close relationship with his members and they with him. He was trusted, respected and considered to be a reliable expositor of God's Word. Thus it was that Jack Madison strived to insure that the messages he delivered to his congregation were as consistent with scripture as humanly possible. The last thing he would knowingly do would be to misinterpret scripture. He knew that he would someday answer for each word, so he anguished at great length as he studied what the Bible said about the last days.

The seven members of the weekly senior accountability group had convened in the Pastor's office, right on schedule at 6:30 AM, with hot coffee and Krispy Kremes in bountiful supply. What was also in plentiful supply were opinions on the prophecy verses they had all been studying during the prior week. After prayer, the Pastor kicked off their discussion.

"Men, you can't say I didn't warn you, now can you?"

Jim, consistent with his known proclivity for prodding the Pastor, though in good humor, responded, "Pastor, if I had known what you were getting us into, I would have missed the meeting last week. Thanks a bunch."

"I know, I know. I had the same reaction, as I told you last week. I couldn't sleep most of the night trying to figure out what other country those mystery identity clues could apply to, except for the U.S."

"Pastor, when I was a young Christian in Idaho we studied prophecy and our teacher told us that those verses applied to the Catholic Church. That seemed at the time to make sense....but as I re-read them, as a group of verses, that doesn't really work. Most of the verses refer to a nation, and the cities, plural, in the nation, with ports and an army, all clues that can't apply to a church."

"You're right, Jim, that for a long time, since the mid 1800's, most Christians were taught that the Babylon the Great verses in Revelation 17 and 18 applied to the church in Rome. What I discovered in my research was that a pastor named Alexander Hislop in 1852 published a book called *The Two Babylons*. What he argued in his first page or two was that the prophecies about Babylon the Great applied to the Catholic Church, based on just one of the several identity clues."

"Which one was it? I didn't see any of the clues that applied to a church, frankly."

"Well, he took the reference to seven hills in Revelation 17:9 and ran with it. Rome has seven hills and the Catholic Church is based in Rome, so he made a leap of logic, though not based on anything but location, and he argued that because of that one clue, Babylon the Great had to be the Catholic Church."

"That's faulty scriptural analysis, isn't it Pastor? How did he explain all the other clues that obviously don't apply to a church?"

"He didn't. He ignored them. The balance of his book was just an attack on the beliefs and practices of the church in Rome. The principle of scriptural analysis that he violated is that no scripture is of *private* interpretation. All scripture is God breathed, and it all hangs together. When you try to base an argument on just one or two verses, and ignore other verses on the same issue, you get in trouble and do violence to the Word. Not a good idea."

"Pastor, admitted that the identity clues don't work for a denomination or a church, but why don't they apply to ancient Babylon? The name of Babylon and the two names given in these verses are very similar."

"Great question. That's an issue that occupied my study and research for several hours. There are several reasons they don't apply to ancient Babylon. First, of course, is that the Daughter is not the same as the Mother, obviously. If the Lord had meant these verses to apply to ancient Babylon, all He had to do was refer to Babylon, and leave off the Daughter of Babylon reference. Secondly, ancient Babylon has been gone since 331 BC when Babylon fell to Alexander the Great. Why then did the Lord give us the several end times prophecies in Revelation 17 and 18, a book that was written three centuries *after* Babylon became a pile of rubble? Why did He give us prophecy at about the time of Christ that Babylon the Great will someday fall, if it had already fallen three hundred years before?"

Scott added his take on the issue, "Well, that makes sense to me. The verses that grabbed me were the references to cities, plural. Babylon was one city. Plus, there were references in the verses you gave us to being on many waters. Revelation 18 refers to the ocean offshore from Babylon the Great. Ancient Babylon was not on the sea, or even near the sea, nor on many waters, just at the junction of two rivers."

"True, but be aware that the Revelation 18 verses refer to the fall of a city, singular, when it refers to the merchants of the earth weeping and wailing once Babylon the Great, the source of the business is gone."

"Is that a contradiction?"

"No, I think it clearly refers to a huge trading city that is destroyed, along with the other cities the verses refer to in Babylon the Great. They don't contradict each other. If Babylon the Great is America, New York City, the center of world commerce, is an obvious candidate for the city pictured in Revelation 18 that the merchants of the world weep over when it falls."

"Alright, Pastor, this is the first time you've indicated in our two meetings that you think these prophecies may refer to the good ol' U S of A. Do they? In your opinion? That's kind of heavy, you know, with what the verses say will eventually happen to this prophetically described nation."

"Over the next few weeks I want us to concentrate on these prophecies, what our research shows us and what we conclude, after a lot of study and prayer. I'm not ready yet to come to a final conclusion, frankly, because I'm not finished with my research, and I know you're not. What I suggest we do is to divide this up into bite sized pieces and look at different parts of the mystery. God didn't give us a mystery without the ability to figure it out."

"Didn't he say that He always tells his prophets before He acts, or something like that?"

"Correct. Amos wrote in 3:7 that "Surely the Sovereign Lord does nothing without revealing his plan to his servants the prophets."

"Well, then, let's study these end times verses and see to which nation they could apply. I suggest we start by looking at what's happening and has been happening in the streets and public buildings. You know, all the civil disobedience in Madison, Wisconsin, the large Tea Party rallies and the hundreds of demonstrations across the country by the Occupy crowds. Let's go through the 223 verses and see if there's anything in them that looks like civil disobedience in the Daughter of Babylon/Babylon the Great. Check it out, and we'll talk about it next week."

174

TWENTY-NINE

Washington, DC – White House Rose Garden

Within twenty four hours of the First Lady's GW Hospital bedside announcement, in late October, that the President would prioritize the abolition of guns upon his re-election, virtually every box of ammunition in America not yet sold after the earlier shootings, was then sold. The same phenomena had occurred during his first campaign four years earlier, so no one was greatly surprised, and just as then, no media outlet felt it worthy of reporting. Americans buying guns and ammo? Ho hum, so what? Later, within forty-eight hours of the introduction in Congress by Senator Blevins of the McAlister Bill, virtually every firearm not yet sold by retailers, was then sold. Again, no mainstream media attention.

One late show comedian did mention that there were no guns currently available for purchase from retailers, comparing the lack of supply to the rumor a few years ago that toilet paper was no longer going to be available, thus clearing store shelves nationwide. The comedian, not known for his propensity to favor conservatives, said that guns and toilet paper served pretty much the same purpose, so it was ok with him. His audience dutifully laughed, but supporters of the Constitution were not amused. The highly paid comedian may have made light of firearms, and their owners, for his late night audiences, but he was highly unlikely to reveal that he was routinely driven to and from his studio by a driver and an aide, who were both armed in order to protect their celebrity boss.

Within twenty-four hours of the March 19th narrow, one-vote margin adoption by the U.S. House of

Representatives of the McAlister Bill, the President had signed the Bill, making it into law. The widely covered signature event took place in the White House Rose Garden, the weather cooperating, so that several hundred gun ban and Administration supporters could be crowded into the event. After the President handed signature pens to Senator Blevins, who was no longer in his wheelchair, and Speaker Pelham, the next pen was handed by the President to Patrick Humless, the Director of the Bradford Center to Prohibit Gun Violence through Abolition of Guns. Humless frequently described the Bradford Center as the nation's largest grassroots anti-gun organization. His role in assisting the President in lining up critical votes for the McAlister Bill was acknowledged by the President, but with more than a ceremonial pen.

"Pat, we couldn't have done it without you and your Center. We needed votes. You and your people worked tirelessly to get us the votes, and America will be forever grateful. I'm a big believer in rewarding those who deserve rewards. So, besides my signing today the McAlister Bill into the McAlister Act, which makes it quite an historic day indeed, I am also announcing that I am today nominating Patrick Humless as the next Director of the Bureau of Alcohol, Tobacco, Firearms and Explosives, the ATF. Patrick will fill the position made vacant by the senseless murder of Director Lawrence McAlister, the same day that I was shot, along with Senator Blevins, of course.

"In making this announcement today of my nomination of Pat Humless as the next Director the ATF, I want to state clearly what I expect him to do as Director. I'm stating it, here, on the record, and for all Americans to understand, and understand it without any question or doubt. Director Humless *will enforce* the hate weapon elimination aspects of the McAlister Act. Not just on passing occasion, and not just when gun owners feel like complying with the law. No, Director Humless and his ATF agents, and other federal law enforcement agencies as needed, *will* find and destroy *every* illegal hate weapon in this nation.

"It's now illegal, a felony, for a private citizen to own and or possess a firearm in this nation, except under very limited circumstances that we all know about, similar to the exceptions in other countries. I won't allow America to become a nation of law breakers. This new law that I have just signed as President requires that every American turn in their firearms, and that they do so within the time limit set in the McAlister Act, that is, within 180 days. After the 180 redemption period, I have instructed Pat to instruct his ATF agents and employees that they are to vigorously follow up on *every tip* the Bureau receives that an American has violated the law by refusing to comply with the law and failing to turn in their firearms. Our government employees will enter any home, business, farm, church, synagogue or other building where we have reason to believe there is being retained an illegal firearm. We will not abide any violations of the law that I signed today as your President.

"Monetary rewards will be promptly paid to Americans who turn in law breakers, once the hidden firearms are located. I have also instructed my Attorney General to prioritize the bringing of felony charges, by the various District Attorneys across the nation, against any American who does not comply with the law, and who is found to still have a firearm in their ownership and or possession after the 180 day redemption period. The Speaker and the Senate Majority Leader have assured me that the funds to be paid to

Americans for their firearms will be appropriated next week. These funds will be made available to pay Americans for their firearms because our Constitution, requires that property owners be paid just compensation for their property when seized by the government. We honor our Constitution and its requirements, when those requirements, of course, conform with the vital needs of our current culture. We will shortly detail our Administration's efforts to enforce the hate speech aspects of the McAlister Act. Ridding our nation of hate speech goes hand in hand with abolishing hate weapons.

"Finally, let me just say that as your President I am pleased that the American economy will get yet another jump start when these gun funds begin circulating and Americans all across the country use these dollars to buy goods and services for their families. It's a win-win, as I see it. No more hate weapons, no more gun violence and an improved economy. Thank you for coming today to the White House on this very historic day in my Presidency. Patrick, any brief comments on your new job?"

Humless, an enormous smile across his face, stepped forward to the Presidential podium, the world's most watched. Humless was stocky, with greying curly hair and was liked by his gun abolition supporters for his ribald sense of humor. This was his day. "Mr. President, you not only do me great honor with this nomination, you also are acknowledging and honoring the tens of thousands of supporters of gun control across the country."

The President's Chief of Staff, standing a few feet from the podium, inwardly groaned. Humless, he thought, was not off to a very good start. He had been well briefed before today's announcement to avoid the use of the phrase, 'gun control'. After the McAlister Bill was introduced, most areas of the country were flooded with bumper stickers opposed to the Bill, which said:

THE AMERICAN REVOLUTION WOULD HAVE
NEVER HAPPENED WITH GUN CONTROL

GUN CONTROL IS USING BOTH HANDS

GUN CONTROL IS HITTING YOUR
TARGET REPEATEDLY

Yet, here was the President's nominee for the job of taking away Americas' firearms talking about *gun control*, a phrase the President was careful never to use publicly. Humless bubbled on effusively for a time about how his nomination meant so much to so many (particularly, he was thinking as he spoke, to enhance his ability to sell books after he left office, detailing how he had disarmed an armed nation). Then he came to remarks that had been carefully scripted by the White House.

"Our President has given me specific instructions to fully and timely implement the McAlister Act, passed yesterday by Congress, and signed into law here today here at the White House. Let's be very, very clear on this subject. I didn't spend the last seven years of my life fighting to rid America of hate weapons, weapons of violence, to now fail to finish the job. So, my suggestion to any gun owner who is *even considering* not turning in your gun, is, *think again.* This nation has spoken through its elected representatives. It has spoken through our President, who has been elected by the people twice now, and who has just signed the law. This nation will witness *the ATF enforce the law.* Turn in your guns in *the next 180 days* at the designated redemption centers or get ready to spend *over 3,650 days* incarcerated in a federal facility. It's your choice.

"Thank you again, Mr. President for your confidence in me and in the Bureau to get the job done. *We will get the job done.*"

Many of the gun owners watching the news event from the White House felt like they were now living in a different country, certainly not the land of their youth. The days ahead would only confirm their worst fears.

THIRTY

Dallas, Texas

Pastor Jack Madison had a rough few days between the weekly meetings of his senior accountability group. He preached two funerals, one for a close friend who unexpectedly died at work, performed a wedding, attended a regional pastors conference, counseled with three couples in his church with family issues and prepared his Sunday sermon. He realized late Tuesday night that he had not yet examined the assigned verses for prophecies of civil disobedience. He also knew that with his schedule he couldn't hit the books for an extended late nighter, and still function on Wednesday. He did a quick overview, found an obvious verse that seemed to apply, said his prayers and collapsed into bed, hoping the guys would understand the next morning.

After explaining his difficult week since they last met, Jack asked their forgiveness, which was quickly granted.

"In the very few minutes that I did have, men, I found a verse that seemed pretty obvious to me. It's in Jeremiah, in 51....look at verse 38....'Her people all roar like young lions, they growl like lion cubs'. America has had a reputation as rebels since its founding. Still does today. This verse says that the people of the Daughter of Babylon will all roar like lion cubs. That sounds like widespread dissension."

"Pastor Jack, I came across the same verse, and I agree with what you're saying, but if you'll look at the next verse, verse 39, that makes an even stronger case."

"What does it say, Max."

"Jeremiah in 51:39 describes the people of the Daughter of Babylon as being 'aroused'. That's the NIV translation. The King James describes the people as being in 'heat'. Sounds like a nation that's in turmoil, at least."

"What else did anyone see?"

"Well, Pastor, moving down a little further in chapter 51 of Jeremiah, we come to verse 49, 'One rumor comes this year, another the next, rumors of violence in the land and of ruler against ruler'. The phrase violence in the land is kind of dramatic. As bad as things have been in the streets, this seems to indicate that it will get worse, if America is the Daughter of Babylon. More, that is, increasing levels of violence."

"Yeah, and look at the last phrase of that verse, 'ruler against ruler'. Think about that for a minute. This can't just be rumors of politicians arguing with other politicians. That always happens. This implies violence between rulers, *within* the nation described as the Daughter of Babylon. That would be like one State's governor fighting another, or like a mayor using his police department against a national guard of his own State. It would be like a mini-civil war inside the end times nation. We haven't seen anything like that....yet."

"But, Jim, look at the verse. It describes rumors of these things happening. What does that mean? Do they actually happen, or do people just pass on rumors that they happened?"

"I don't know. This is all we're given on this subject. What we can validly assume is that the people, all of them, in this rich, powerful, influential end times nation, will roar, as in widespread societal discontent. And the land will be filled with rumors of violence, which apparently won't come as a surprise, so there must be violence in the land, as well as officials fighting each other, or at least widespread rumors that they are. That sounds to me a lot like what we've been experiencing across the country. We've seen tens of thousands of people in the streets, all over the country, in about every State. If we are in fact the Daughter of Babylon, it sounds like what we will witness more of that in the future."

"You guys are a bundle of joy. Can I just say I hope that these verses apply to ancient Babylon, and not to us, today? But, we covered that last week. The verses just don't work for what is now just a pile of rubble in Iraq. But, they clearly do apply to an end times nation. These prophecy verses, after all, are set in the end times."

"I'm with you, brother. Every time I read how these five Prophets described the Daughter of Babylon and Babylon the Great, I get chills, or goose bumps, or however you would describe a serious case of the heeby-jeebies. John, Jeremiah, Isaiah, Zechariah and the writer of Psalms were all in agreement about this end times nation. Scary."

"I think we agree that internal dissent and violence is one of the several clues that the Bible gives us for the mystery identity of the rich, powerful and influential nation that's described by the Prophets in these verses. We've seen some of that in the US, particularly lately, and are quite likely to see more. Let's keep studying and keep our antenna up for anything else that looks like fulfillment of prophecy in our times.

"Because of the upcoming holidays, we won't meet for a while. I'll send out an e-mail. But, I can tell you what our assignment is in the prophecy verses for when we do meet next. Let's all make a list of today's nations that the verses might apply to. Particularly look at these four clues: 'the hammer of the whole earth'....'the great voice'....'significant Jewish population'....'center of world commerce'. Let's all list any other country in the world that these prophecies could apply to, that is, besides America....OK?....Let's pray, guys. 'Lord, give us wisdom as we study the prophecy that you have given to us. Keep us from error. Direct us to the research you would have us study. Keep our hearts and minds on You in these upcoming holiday weeks. In Jesus' name, amen.' See you all in January."

THIRTY-ONE

Richmond, Virginia

Coincident with the White House plans to formally sign the McAlister Bill into law, the nation's gun rights leaders convened at the same time a few miles south of the Rose Garden in the Capitol city of the historic Commonwealth of Virginia. They did not meet to plan, nor to strategize. Those days were over. Gun abolition would become the law today with the President's signature. The gun rights leaders met to be told, on a strictly confidential basis, about a movement that had only recently developed in several parts of the nation. Prior to today they had each heard various rumors, and received numerous calls, about the secret effort. Today, they would learn the facts. Each would leave the meeting in Richmond convinced that there might still be hope for their nation.

Harry Flatt was the head of one of the nation's largest gun rights organizations. He had been fighting efforts to deny Americans to defend themselves with firearms for almost thirty years. He commenced the meeting by explaining why repeal of the McAlister Law was not feasible. "I'm getting 10-12 calls and three times that many e-mail a day asking us to crank up an effort to *repeal* the McAlister Bill, uh....sorry, it's now called the McAlister Law....now that the President is signing it into law, as we speak. The same calls were raised to repeal the healthcare reform law. I've gone over the reason why we can't get it repealed so many times that I've practically memorized it. There's really no hope of repealing it. Once both the Senate and the House pass a bill, even if by one vote, the adopted bill goes to the President, and he can sign it or veto it. Then it's the law of the land. To repeal it requires *both* the Senate and the House to repeal the law and the President to sign the bill repealing it. So, if either House or the White House is opposed to repealing the new law, then it remains as a law. That's it. Unless the Senate *and* the House *and* the White House are *all* controlled by guns rights supporters, McAlister will remain as the law of the land. It's that simple."

A gun rights leader from Nevada asked, "Harry, I know what you're saying is correct, but it's still a bummer that one vote in the U.S. House took away our Second Amendment gun rights. Worse yet, a 5-4 vote in the Supreme Court could affirm that it was okay to get away with it, if the Court votes like the media are saying. That's just not right. I know the majority rules, but what about the rights in the Constitution that were supposed to only be changed by super-majorities?"

"You're preachin' to the choir. We all agree, but what to do next is the real problem. That's one reason I asked you all to come here to meet, away from DC, in the Commonwealth of Virginia. It's appropriate that we meet here, because on Virginia's State Seal is the statement *Sic Semper Tyrannis*, which means Thus Always to Tyrants." Little did Harry Flatt know how his uttering this simple State motto would haunt him in the days ahead.

Flatt, who had been experiencing serious cardiac problems coincident with the filing and passage of the McAlister Act, explained the purpose of their meeting, "I've invited to our meeting today two men who will remain unidentified. They're waiting for us in the room next to us. When we go in, you'll see that they are faced away from where we will be sitting. We won't see their faces, though we will hear their actual voices."

"Harry, why all the mysticism? We can keep a secret."

"That's not the issue. They would only come to speak to this group of gun rights leaders, whom they trust, or they wouldn't have even contacted us, under the two conditions that they not be identified and that no one see their faces, for the same reason. You'll understand when you hear what they have to tell us. For some of you, I suspect you won't be terribly surprised. Let's go hear what they have to say."

True to Harry's description, two men were seated at the far end of an adjoining narrow room, facing away from the chairs positioned so those in the chairs couldn't see the two men's faces. Once the group was seated, Flatt led off, "Gentlemen, these are two gun rights leaders who have organized, very quietly, and without any disclosure, a new movement. You may never hear anything in the future publicly about them or their plans. Alternatively, depending on what happens in the months and years ahead, you may hear about very little else except what this group may be doing. As you see, there's a small sign behind the man on the left that says Rifle, and on the right saying Pistol. They have no connection with either type of weapon, we just put the names there so you could direct your questions later to the man you are addressing. Rifle, do you want to start?"

"OK, sure. For background, without any details, I've been in the Second Amendment protection group in our area since I was a teenager. In our part of the country, we've been saying for several years that they would eventually get our firearms, take them away from us, just like in those other countries. We just didn't know when or how. Now we know. When that idiot Senator from South Carolina introduced his gun abolition bill we immediately kick-started plans that we had been discussing and that we had partially implemented over the prior years. I'll let Pistol tell you what we've done."

"Thanks, Rifle. I'm also a veteran of fighting to uphold the right to keep and bear arms. Our organization has no name, nor will we ever name it. We are a resistance movement, in the classic, historical model of citizens organized to oppose tyrants in their own government. We are in every State. We don't hold meetings, except the top guys, and then not often. We don't maintain membership lists. We don't seek publicity. What we do, though, is real easy to understand. We have stored away enough firearms and ammo to take this country back, if it comes to it. American gun rights supporters all over the nation have buried 55 gallon drums, full of firearms and ammo. Buried them in places that they would never be found, under almost any conceivable circumstance. Only the individual resistance members who buried drums know where they're located. There's no master list. No way anyone can rat out somebody else under the pressure of torture or whatever. Questions"

"Yeah, this question is to Pistol. What are you gonna' do with all that firepower?"

Pistol took his time responding, "Well, sir, good question, but the true answer is maybe we will never use the weapons."

"Hunh? I'm afraid I don't understand that. Why sock away guns and ammo and never use them."

"I didn't say we would never use them, I said *maybe* we would never use them. If the American people wake up and change the government, either through elections, or a Constitutional Convention, there will be no need to ever bring these weapons up out of the ground. On the other hand, if the asylum inmates that are running the government now continue destroying our rights, shredding

188

the Constitution and turning the nation into a tyrannical despotism, then we may be the nation's *only hope* to take them out of office, and save the country. The guys who banded together and took out the Brits, would expect no less from us. It was ol' Tommy Jefferson who said that the tree of liberty occasionally needs to be watered with the blood of patriots."

The meeting continued for another thirty minutes with most questions centered on the details of what they had just heard. The gun rights leaders present felt encouraged that there might be a future for a nation they saw hurtling towards disaster. But, at the same time most were concerned that they now knew enough about the resistance organization to ensnare them in any federal government investigation that might someday occur. One leader present didn't stay present very long, as he appeared to be angry, and left the meeting soon after hearing what had been said. Another leader stayed after the meeting and quietly offered a large personal financial contribution to the movement. Over the next few days, in private discussions between those who attended the Richmond meeting, the consensus was that the resistance effort would never be heard of publicly and that it would not be required to unearth its considerable firepower. Time, of course, would tell if their conclusion would prove to be correct.

It didn't require much time, though, for the Department of Justice to pursue Harry Flatt. Shortly after details of the Richmond meeting were reported to agency superiors by an undercover federal agent who attended the Richmond meeting, Flatt was incarcerated and ultimately charged with threatening the life of a federal official, the President of the United States. The indictment claimed that

Flatt in a secret meeting held in Richmond, Virginia encouraged violence by a group of anti-government leaders. Flatt was charged with incitement of violence against the President for using the same words, *Sic Semper Tyrannis*, uttered by John Wilkes Booth as he jumped to the stage of Ford Theater, after he shot President Abraham Lincoln. Flatt's arrest and the charges against him were widely reported in the mainstream media. Flatt's attorney released a statement to the media that Flatt was not guilty and expected to be exonerated if the case went to a jury; that Flatt had not known about Booth's use of the Virginia motto in connection with his assassination of President Lincoln; and, in any case, his words were not aimed at, nor meant to encourage violence against, the nation's chief executive. In prison, after several hours of questioning about his personal knowledge of the resistance movement, Flatt collapsed and was taken to a DC government hospital for treatment for what was diagnosed as a heart attack. Other gun rights leaders who attended the Richmond meeting whose names were known to the undercover agent were either arrested and held without bail or subpoenaed to testify before a federal grand jury to be convened in the District of Columbia. The federal government took a dim view of reports that Americans might have made preparations to someday overthrow it.

THIRTY-TWO

ATF Redemption Centers

The next day after the appointment of ATF Director Humless, who would serve in an acting capacity until the Senate confirmed him, the ATF issued a list of 'ATF Hate Weapon Redemption Centers'. It had been previously determined by bureaucrats at the ATF that establishing a sufficient number of new locations for turning in guns would not be cost effective. Therefore, the ATF list included virtually every existing federal facility in the nation, in order to obtain the widest compliance with the new law. On the list were all post offices, military bases and installations, federal courthouses, FBI offices, Social Security centers, EEOC offices, Department of Agriculture facilities and other offices operated by the federal government. Left off of the list were any offices related to Medicare, as it was felt that the turning in of guns at such facilities could be seen as inconsistent with their medical purposes.

ATF planners devised a system for collection of guns that they hoped would avoid the highly likely possibility of some federal employees at the Redemption Centers pilfering guns as they were redeemed by their owners. Each gun was tagged with a digital read bar code specific only to that gun, with a copy of the same bar code imprinted on a receipt given to the owner and also on the federal check reimbursing the owner for the owner's redeemed weapon. Guns were deposited in a triple locked metal box for later disposal. As the checks were cashed or deposited, they made their way back to the issuing agency, the ATF, who would then check the bar code numbers with guns that were redeemed. Any discrepancy at a redemption center would soon show up and alert ATF headquarters in DC that it had a problem at that

Redemption Center. The system was supposed to be fool-proof, but like many fool-proof systems it didn't turn out exactly as planned. Many guns turned in by their owners seemed to just disappear before they could be smelted down, with police departments in many cases turning up the missing guns in the hands of criminals who admitted they had purchased them from federal employees.

After Australia banned most private gun ownership following the 'Port Arthur Massacre', many thousands of guns were turned in to their government, by Aussies, who were then paid from the levy imposed on Australian Medicare. By all reports, compliance was steady and effective during the time period allowed to turn in weapons. On the other hand, no one could know how American gun owners would respond to the new law. ATF records eventually would show that compliance looked like a ski slope upward shaped curve with increasing numbers each week. In the first two months of the six month period redemption was modestly low in numbers. It apparently took owners some time to decide to comply with the new law. There was a drum beat for redemption which increased in intensity from the mainstream media and from all government agencies, steadily increasing the number of firearms turned in by their owners. Public service messages conveyed by the Administration to American gun owners varied, but they had three common themes – safety, patriotism and fear of prison:

TURN IN YOUR GUN - IT'S THE LAW!

TODAY'S PATRIOTS OBEY THE LAW

SAVE A LIFE – TURN IN A GUN

IS IT WORTH TEN YEARS IN PRISON?

JOHN WAYNE WOULD HAVE REDEEMED HIS GUNS

MAKE AMERICA GUN VIOLENCE FREE!

Television spots claiming that John Wayne would have redeemed his guns were pulled when his heirs filed suit, claiming that the Duke "would have gone down shooting before he would have turned in his guns". The other public service announcements appeared to have an increasing effect, though, as more guns were turned in each week than the preceding week. The ATF was faced with a difficult accounting problem, of course, because no one knew, with any reasonable specificity, how many firearms were owned by Americans, or by persons illegally in America. Estimates had always varied widely, and there was literally no way of determining the actual count, as gun registration had never become the national law that some had tried to impose. Because of this fact, widely known to be true, many gun owners thought they would be safe in holding on to their firearms. After all, many thought, 'who knows if I own a gun?' It was this 'nobody will know' reluctance that led Senator Blevins to include Section 4.4 in his bill, to reward tipsters turning in non-compliant gun owners, with large monetary payments.

With two months to go in the Redemption Period, ATF officials were concerned. Over one hundred million guns had been redeemed, as far as they could calculate, but they estimated that left almost the same number still not turned in. So the agency began to air public service announcements in all areas of the country, promoting compliance by stepping up the 'fear factor'. A typical thirty second spot asked how sure gun owners were that they wouldn't be turned in, by friends, by neighbors, by shooting buddies, by their own family?

SCRIPT FOR TV AD - GUN REDEMPTION

Setting - Jail Cell - Low Lighting - Inmate Speaks - Cellmate in background of shot - heavy beard - cellmate frowns through most of shot - wicked grin at end as he puts his hand on shoulder of speaking cellmate. Both in orange jail attire.

"I know, I know. I didn't think I would get caught. I thought that I was the only one who knew that I owned guns. I only had two guns. But, I forgot that I went shooting at the range a few times. I didn't remember that I had shown my newest gun to my brother-in-law, my former brother-in-law. Yes, I had talked about guns and ammo with some work buddies. So, who turned me in? Who knows? The tipster stays anonymous, but he gets the big bucks. I've got a lot of time to think about it now. Ten years….You'd better think about it while you still have time. Turn in your guns, for cash money, before September 13th. Don't end up like me, 'cause you will get caught....Count on it, ol' buddy."

The purchase of the television ads was a saturation buy in all mass markets. Within forty-eight hours of its airing, more Americans had turned in more guns than in the prior two months, combined. Many Redemption Center officials reported that most turn-ins were either directly by wives, or by husbands who appeared to have been hauled into the centers by their wives, not wanting to lose their spouses to prison. Petitions for dissolution of marriage shot up following the ads, as spouses couldn't agree on redemption versus possible jail time.

THIRTY-THREE

Washington, DC – Department of Justice

Throughout the history of the world, government leaders have chosen to imprison persons who opposed their rule. That bears repeating. Throughout the history of the world, government leaders have chosen to imprison persons who opposed their rule.

John Madison was one of those persons.

Early in his incarceration, the official word issued by John Madison's captors was that Madison was an enemy of the State, a danger to national security and he had possible 'ties with terrorists'. Very few people come to the aid of a person accused of such serious crimes. Over time, however, as John Madison was not officially charged with committing any federal crime, many began to change their mind, and instead saw him as a political prisoner. A political prisoner is generally regarded as someone who is in prison because they have opposed or criticized the government of their own country, and not because they have committed a crime, as such. No one was more surprised than John Madison when Amnesty Universal labeled him as "America's best-known political prisoner, who should be released forthwith." Madison didn't know much about this foreign human rights group calling for his release, but he had heard of it and vaguely thought of it as a liberal group. Now, however, he was appreciative of any help he could get.

The White House, apparently stung by criticism from abroad, issued a media release denouncing Amnesty Universal for "interfering with American domestic criminal cases". John Madison was once again in the headlines.

New York Times

ATTORNEY GENERAL DENIES
MADISON IS POLITICAL PRISONER
White House Suggests Madison is
Linked to Right Wing Extremists

CBS

AMNESTY UNIVERSAL
INTERFERES IN AMERICA

MSCNB

 JOHN MADISON - TIES TO AL QUEDA?

FOX

AMERICA'S #1 POLITICAL PRISONER

Friends of John Madison in Tyler contacted other friends around the nation and formed a FREE JOHN MADISON Committee. Though the mainstream media largely ignored the Committee's efforts to draw public attention to John Madison's extended incarceration, by e-mail and social networking millions of Americans were reminded that John Madison was still in federal prison, and was still not charged with any crimes. As more people learned that Madison's writ for habeas corpus had been denied, the drumbeat increased to either charge Madison and try him, or alternatively, to release him. Even totalitarian governments are sensitive to criticism, especially from abroad.

The heat from Amnesty Universal, and increasing pressure at home, led the Attorney General of the United States to convene a strategy meeting in his office at the Department of Justice on Pennsylvania Avenue in DC, seven blocks from the White House. To say that the AG was not in a good mood would be a clear under-statement. He had not been an early proponent of arresting and imprisoning Madison, but had taken his orders to do so from the White House, which was quite insistent on the issue. As an attorney, the AG knew that he was on shaky legal ground, but his loyalty to his old friend, the President, forced him to do what he would not have otherwise even considered. The AG had given serious thought to resigning and going to work for a DC law firm, with a large income. Of all of the President's friends, cronies and buddies serving in his Administration, the AG was the least enamored with what he saw his old friend doing. He was caught between a rock and....and he didn't like it, not a bit.

"Let's get on it, folks. Madison has been in prison too long without charges. Our end run on avoiding habeus corpus worked, but it made us look bad with people who were paying attention. We're starting to look like Guantanamo, but here onshore. I don't like it. Amnesty Universal has butted in, as you know. The President's getting heat from some of his European diplomatic buddies. The White House even had a call from the New York Times yesterday. They're considering doing a story on why we are holding a prisoner without charges. When the President gets heat, we get heat, so I'm looking here for some creative ideas. Come on, people. What do we charge this troublemaker with? Something that passes the snicker test."

The Deputy AG tasked with supervising the prosecution of Madison briefly reviewed the contents of John Madison's October 22nd speech in Austin, four days before the shootings. After he did so, he looked up at his boss, the AG, who was holding his head in his right hand.

The exasperated AG said, "Yeah, that's what I recalled. Some nasty words, but how can they *possibly* be crimes ?"

"Mr. Attorney General, I've been working on it. We have five possible options....treason, misprision of treason, rebellion/insurrection, seditious conspiracy and advocating the overthrow of the government."

The AG's mood was not improving, "Forget treason, that arises from war and giving aid and comfort to the nation's enemies. Likewise, forget misprision of treason, which means having knowledge of treason, but not turning someone in. Stop wasting our time. What about rebellion and insurrection?"

"That's all in one statute, sir, 18 USC Sec. 2383. It makes it a crime to incite, set of foot, whatever that means, assist or engage in any rebellion or insurrection against the government or its laws. Keep this in mind, because...."

"Come on. That clearly doesn't pass the snicker test. We'd be laughed out of court. What rebellion? What insurrection? This statute might work for an armed insurrection, but not to a speech by a political figure."

"OK, it was a little weak, so let's look at seditious conspiracy, section 2384. Maybe we can show that Madison conspired with one other person, that would be easy to prove, to overthrow, put down or destroy by force the US government, or levy war, or *oppose by force the authority of the United States*. He definitely opposed the authority of the United States. Judge McDermott could be counted on to deny a motion to dismiss a charge like that."

The AG looked like he might have a stroke, "Stop. Stop. You're killing me here. You left out the phrase *by force.*

Of course he opposed the government, that's what any political candidate or speaker does. But he didn't use force, at least that we know about. Even if McDermott lets the charge stand, so what? Don't forget, people, we will be facing a jury, someday, and a jury won't convict if *force* is a required element to convict. What's the fifth choice, again?"

"Mister Attorney General, our last choice is really our only choice....I think. Section 2385 of the criminal code prohibits advocating the overthrow of the government. The statute prohibits knowingly or willfully advocating, abetting, advising or teaching the duty, necessity, desirability or propriety of overthrowing or destroying the government of the United States. Yes, it does include the phrase 'by force or violence', but it adds 'or by the assassination of any officer' of the government. It also includes organizing or helping to organize any group of persons to overthrow the government. It provides for a twenty year sentence. I think we can make this one work. He did say to 'take out' the President."

"I'm listening. How do we charge Madison, or anybody for that matter, with advocating the overthrow of the government, if they don't use force and violence?"

"Admittedly, we have to be creative, but that's what I understood was the purpose of this meeting. The indictment would simply say that Madison obviously advocated the overthrow of the government in his speech at Austin. He said 'we have to take him out'. Also, we can say that he essentially advocated the assassination of federal officers by telling the nation that they would lose their right to own firearms if they voted for the President and he won. The people who owned guns, and who might lose them, he was implying, should do something about it. Which they *did*, lest we forget, four days later. He established an atmosphere of

199

violence by raising voters' fears against their elected officials. He aided and abetted the shooters on October 26th by his violence-laden speech. His speech was delivered well before McAlister was even thought of, so we can't charge him with violating McAlister, though that would be sweet if we could. What do you think?"

All eyes in the AG's Conference Room were on the AG. It was obvious he was thinking. On the one hand, if he charged Madison with conspiracy to overthrow the government, the White House would be happy, and would get off his back. On the other hand, if he released Madison, his friend at the end of Pennsylvania Avenue would be upset with him, as it would look like the Administration had no reason to hold Madison all those months. It reminded the AG of the old joke that his next attorney would only have one arm, because he was tired of attorneys always saying 'on the one hand, but then again, on the other hand'.

"Alright, people, here's what we're going to do. Draw up the indictment for advocating the overthrow of the government, but juice it up a little, plus let's add a count of conspiracy to overthrow. Do a third count for conspiracy to violate the federal hate crimes act, that statute can apply to almost anything. I'll run it past O'Dayson at the White House, unofficially, of course. If it gets approved, we'll release it Saturday night, on the media graveyard shift. We'll push it hard in Europe through our buds in the media there. That should shut up Amnesty and the diplomatic set. Tell our District Attorney out in Oregon that due to his extremely busy schedule he won't be able to try the case for several months, maybe next year. If this case goes south, I'd rather have it go south later, rather than sooner. This case is not going to win any of us any prizes for high standards of justice, you know what I mean? We're dismissed. God bless America, because we sure didn't bless it today."

THIRTY-FOUR

Letter from Jail/Journal Entry of August 27th

Jack, my much loved son, visited me again today. It was a sweet and sour experience. It was great to see him. I'm thankful he wanted to take the time to visit his dad in jail. Our time of fellowship, and prayer, was really memorable. Jack is a strong believer, and a forceful and effective pastor. I'm proud of him.

As for the non-sweet part of the visit, we clashed, again, on my opposition to the President, and my tactics in opposing our nation's Chief Executive. Jack still doesn't think that I should have gotten myself arrested for what I have done to fight to keep our Constitutional rights. I've brought up Dietrich Bonhoeffer before in my discussions/arguments with Jack. Bonhoeffer was executed by the government he opposed. Not that I'm planning on a similar end game, just that he was a principled man who was willing to do what was right to help others, in his case, to fight for saving the lives of Jewish residents of his nation. I'm fighting to try and save the rights of Americans to defend ourselves.

Jack, of course, supports our right to own firearms. He's owned a gun since he was sixteen, and we would hunt and go to the shooting range together. He told me today that he will turn in his firearm before the end of the Redemption Period. I didn't expect him to violate the law and hold on to his gun, but I thought he should make some form of protest in connection with doing so. He doesn't agree. As a pastor, it's his position that he should preach the gospel and not be involved in what he calls 'current events'. He's not persuaded when I bring up either Bonhoeffer, who was a pastor, or Martin Luther King, Jr., who likewise was a man of the cloth.

I guess I can't expect my son to be like his dad in all respects, especially when it comes to civil disobedience. But, that doesn't mean that it doesn't hurt when he gets that look on his face. You know, the look that kind of says, 'I respect you as my dad, but you're hurting our family by your actions'. Debbie has talked with him, and spent time with Allison, and expressed nothing but her support for me and what I'm trying to accomplish. So, Jack can't have any reason to think that we're not together on this. I truly don't know what I'd do if Debbie was side-wise with me. She's paying a huge price for me being in prison, naturally, but she seems to be handling it well. We have a good extended family, neighborhood and church support team. One of our small group guys hired her at his company, which supplements our daily financial needs while I'm a guest of the government. My room and board here are covered, no need to worry. The government provides me 'three hots and a cot", as they say here.

I've shared with Debbie and Jack how I've been used here. Because it's widely known that I'm in the can because of my gun rights activities, I'm a little bit of a hero with many of my fellow inmates. Probably because of that I've not experienced what I understand a lot of new inmates go through, with various forms of harassment, sexual and otherwise. They kind of give me a wide berth and a certain level of visible respect. I've had some good spiritual discussions with some guys, who have some true needs.

Our biggest argument today was when Jack asked me what I thought about the new ATF television ad, created and aired to try and scare gun owners into turning in their guns. Maybe I'm a little sensitive because the ad was staged in a jail cell. Seriously though, I told Jack that I thought it was not the role of the government in a free country to tell its citizens, using their money, that if they don't do what the government tells them to do, they can spend several years in forced confinement. What kind of a country does that?

Jack's response was that the internal revenue code works like that, and everybody accepts it. I sort of lost it at that point, and went off on IRS abuses, that led to a tiff over the Federal Reserve, and downhill from there.

So, what should a parent do when agreement with an adult child is just not happening? I changed the subject. I brought up my potential future trial. We were both happy to talk about something else, I think. I know I was, because it makes my stomach hurt to fight with my son. I don't mind at all fighting with abusive Senators or probing District Attorneys, but I don't handle fighting with Jack very well. Or Debbie, for that matter, but as I said, that's not generally been a problem, thankfully.

As I said, I brought up my possible criminal charges and trial.

Jack asked me if I thought there was any chance that any charges against me would be just dismissed, thrown out? I explained that the Attorney General had been appointed by this President, that he worked for this President and that he would do what this President asked him to do. Jack then asked if the Judge might grant some kind of a dismissal pleading. I explained that my attorney told me yesterday that my case was being venued out of Texas next week to Oregon, and that I would be transferred soon thereafter to the Pacific coast, to the federal prison at Sheridan, Oregon.

Jack immediately realized that the change of location was motivated by at least two goals, to harass me by separating me from my family and support network by several hundreds of miles and also to pick up a federal judge and jury who would not be friendly, shall we say, to a Texas gun rights leader. My attorney's conclusions, exactly. Maybe Jack should have been an attorney. I told him that his hunch was correct, as I learned right before he arrived today that my new federal judge in Oregon will be Hiram 'Hanging Judge' McDermott, a Carter appointee, who has a record of imprisoning for maximum terms persons convicted in his court of gun law violations. One blog I read said that the Judge had told an attorney in a private conversation that the payer name on his twice a month check was 'U.S. Government', and he never forgot who his employer was. So, we are not counting on any favors from my new Judge, let alone a dismissal of any sort. Debbie is looking into moving to Oregon, if she can find a decent job. It won't be easy on her, which, of course, makes it tough for me, which is the government's purpose, pretty clearly.

Well, dear journal/readers of my jailhouse letters, how am I doing, you may ask? Besides that, Mrs. Lincoln, how did you enjoy the play? Sorry, jailhouse humor, I guess. I'm human, so it's not easy. But, I know Who has control of all this, so I'm OK. Pretty much, that is. Can't mislead your own journal, right?

As Jack was here today, seeing his youthfulness and energy, I couldn't help but recall when I was that young, a long time before my eye-opening education in how things really work in government and politics. As a young

204

businessman and new father, I didn't have a lot of time to pay attention to current affairs, what has happening in DC, or Austin or even at City Hall in Tyler. Like most people, I sort of just took it for granted that people in public office were all doing a good job, for the most part. I paid my taxes, voted and hoped for the best.

Then, my life changed. Somebody invited me, as a new insurance company employee to Rotary. The first time I attended, I met two guys who both became important in my life. One guy I met was named Ralph Snyder. Ralph took me to a meeting that led me down my political activism path that I'll cover later in this journal in greater depth, but I'll need some time to get all that collected in my memory and written down, maybe next week. I've got nothing but time here.

The other guy I met at Rotary on my first visit, Fred Rose, is a Tyler businessman, a house contractor, as I recall. He invited me to a luncheon Bible Study. As an American and a Texan, I always pretty much thought of myself as a Christian. If anyone had asked me, I would have said, 'sure, I'm a Christian, I'm not a Buddhist'. Well, at the Bible Study, which was attended by about thirty some guys, some of whom I knew, somebody did ask me. But not the way I expected. Fred Rose asked me "when did I come to know the Lord?" I put his question in quotes here because that's how he asked me. I, of course, had no answer. I kind of spluttered out something like, "well, I've always been a Christian", which didn't answer his question. A slightly raised eyebrow, and then a quick smile told me that I might hear some more about this from Fred.

Sure enough, he stopped by the insurance company the afternoon of the next day and asked if I had any time to talk. Turned out I did. I expected 15-20 minutes, max. We were still talking when Sally asked if I needed anything else before she left work for the day. I couldn't believe it was quitting time. Fred told me about his messed up, booze-heavy, womanizing life that had nearly destroyed his family. He told me that a carpenter had saved him. Well, I knew he was a contractor, so I asked him if one of his workers had helped him out with some good advice. He smiled.

No, he said, this carpenter is Jewish, and he died a couple thousand years ago. I'm a little dense sometimes, so I asked how that could be and he told me that the carpenter was Jesus of Nazareth. Honestly, my first reaction when he said that was to glance at my phone to see if maybe Sally might buzz me and I could terminate this meeting. But, I'm really glad now I didn't try such a stunt. Fred shared with me the gospel. That Jesus was crucified and resurrected and through Him I can have a new, abundant life. I'd heard some of that kind of talk before – I'm a Texan, remember, but it hadn't really sunk in. My parents weren't particularly religious. The only time I went to a church when I was kid was when a neighbor or friend invited to something special.

But, this time I guess I was just ready. Once I understood what Christ had done for me, and what He expected from me, that's all it took. I still don't know how I'd been so blissfully ignorant all those years, but I was. So Fred led me in a prayer. I prayed. I repented of my (many) sins. Then I told Jesus that I believed in Him as my savior and Lord, and I asked Him to come into my life, to take over the throne of my life. No fireworks, just a totally changed life. Jesus didn't waste any time shaping me up. I don't know who all may read this someday, so I'll leave out all the lurid, racy stuff that I gave up, but I know, and my best friends

206

know, how thoroughly, and rapidly, He changed my lifestyle. Whew!

I told Debbie, naturally, that night what I had done. She looked at me like, "yeah, sure you did", but she said nothing, except "that's nice, John". But, within about a month or so, she had seen enough of her new husband ('where is my old husband and what have you done with him?') to want to know more about what happened to me. I count it a real blessing that I could share my new Best Friend with my wife at the kitchen table, and she came to know Him, also.

OK, dear journal/readers of my jailhouse letters, how did I get on this memory lane? Oh, yeah. Jack was here today. He has such potential. He loves the Lord. He's a great preacher, at least a lot of people in Dallas must think so. He draws from all over the Park Cities area. Great family man. I just wish he would agree with his ol' dad on the issues that are dividing our country. You know, the issues that landed me in prison. Oh, yeah, well, maybe <u>that</u> has something to do with why Jack isn't in agreement with me. But, there's always hope. More later on Ralph Snyder and what he did to me, make that <u>for</u> me.

THIRTY-FIVE

Des Moines, Iowa

Gary Miller had sold guns at gun shows throughout the Midwest for so many years he couldn't recall how many it had been. Through the years his inventory had grown, along with his knowledge and expertise in firearms. He wasn't always the largest exhibitor at the gun shows where he sold guns, but he was generally the vendor who attracted the highest foot traffic, due to the high quality of what he had to sell. He refused to sell junk, off brands or low-end weapons. As a result, he prospered in his business.

Gary Miller saw the first televised reports of the October 26th shootings of three federal officials, including the President, and the death of the head of the ATF, in his family room at his home in Missouri. He turned to his wife and said, "Well, honey, I'd better start looking for another line of work. Maybe, we'll sell candy and nuts at flea markets. Or, maybe, plastic potted plants." Gary Miller instinctively knew that though his business was revered by gun owners, it was also reviled by the anti-gun lobby. All it would take, he had frequently mentioned to his regular customers, would be something major like Port Arthur in the US, and we'll be out of business. But, when Columbine didn't do it, nor did Virginia Tech, nor Fort Hood, he concluded that maybe America was different from Australia. Just possibly a shell-shocked population reeling from a horrible mass shooting would resist the temptation to punish all of its gun owners for what was caused by one or two crazed gunmen.

When he saw the video of the October 26th shootings, though, his gut told his brain that it was all over. Then his brain started analyzing how many firearms that he had in inventory that he would need to sell before guns were banned. He made the decision to stay in the gun show business, that is, as long as he was allowed to legally do so. Just as he had suspected, the movement to ban individually owned firearms in America continued to grow, fed by nightly media reports of the latest local gun incidents, even if the shooting would not normally have been covered outside of the immediate media area. Nut jobs and deranged criminals seeking attention soon learned that they could make the national news as long as they shot somebody with a gun, a/k/a, a hate weapon. They could shoot the clerk at the 7-11 in Racine and then call their relatives in Tampa to catch them on NBC that night.

Gary Miller normally vended firearms, accompanied by his wife, three weekends a month, which gave him one weekend a month off the road. The routine was to arrive in the city of the gun show on Thursday, check in at a mid-priced motel, go to the gun show site and set up his tables, lights and empty cases. He would normally sell Friday afternoon and evening, then all day Saturday and Sunday afternoons. One of the aspects of working the gun show circuit that Gary liked was getting to know the other gun vendors through the years, many of whom had become his best friends. One of those good friends was Charlie Wheeler. He had only known Charlie for a couple of years, but during that time they had shared many meals, drinks and stories together. Gary looked on Charlie as the kind of guy who just seemed to get along well with everybody on the gun show circuit, making the rounds of the vendors, asking about their families and being a friend whenever anybody had a need. What Gary Miller didn't know was that though his good friend Charlie Wheeler was a firearms vendor on weekends, he was also an ATF Agent during the week.

Gary finally figured out Charlie's real occupation one night in Des Moines as they unwound after the day's gun show at the Liars Club Bar on Court Avenue. Later, he told his wife how ironic it was that he first spotted Charlie as a liar at such an aptly named bar. Gary and Charlie were seated in a booth, along with two other vendors from the Des Moines Gun Show, across from a large screen TV. Gary hushed his drinking buddies when he looked up and saw John Madison on the screen in a re-broadcast of his earlier testimony before the Senate Judiciary Committee. "Shuu...look, its Senator Blowhard Blevins reading to John Madison his speech, the one that got him arrested. I love that guy. He's Mister Guts. Listen up."

Once the Liars Club Bar waitress obligingly turned up the volume, they could hear Senator Blevins reading to John Madison a portion of Madison's speech in Austin before the shootings, *"It's good to be king. It's even better to be President of the United States of America. You can ignore the voters, once you have wooed them into electing you twice, gaining their votes with the most transparent campaign promises, and then just do what you want to do. The most dangerous time, of course, for America, with any President is in his, or her, second term. With no requirement to ever face another voter, or campaign opponent, the second term President is a potential tyrant, available for any scheme hatched by the White House staff, or outside ideological bed fellows, to radically change the Constitution of the United States, as it was written."*

Gary Miller whopped it up, *"Yeah, yeah, yeah!...You tell 'em Madison....Nobody ever talks that way anymore....everybody's so afraid that Big Brother will hear them, track them down and put 'em in jail."* His drinking buddy fellow vendors also shouted their agreement to John Madison's words, including Charlie Wheeler. They turned back to the TV, *"If this President should be elected to a second term next month, don't be surprised if he tries to re-interpret out of the Constitution the guarantee of our right to own a gun. He may even seek to alter our right to speak, or meet or worship as we see fit. That's what's on the line on November 6th. That's why we must insure that every member of our families, all of our employees, in fact every one that we know, comes out and votes to deny the President a second term, which would be a very dangerous second term for America, indeed. We have to take him out."*

As Senator Blevins asked John Madison if those were his words spoken in Austin just four days before the October 26th shootings, Gary Miller just happened to glance at a mirror on the bar wall that revealed Charlie Wheeler's facial expression, which he would not normally have seen, since Wheeler's face was turned away from their booth. At first, Gary thought maybe he hadn't seen Charlie's angry, almost dismissive snear accurately, but Gary Miller trusted his own instincts, and he considered himself to be a good judge of character. Funny how such a simple, fleeting look can put a person on alert, if they're paying attention, and Gary was paying attention. What was there about John Madison's verbal attack on the President that so obviously irritated his good friend Charlie? His next reaction was to ask Charlie what he thought of Madison's attack speech, but since he thought he knew the answer to that question, he thought his question would alert Charlie that Gary suspected him. Instead, Gary leaned back a little in the booth, slowed down on his beer consumption and waited to see if the alcohol, what he liked to call 'truth serum', would cause Charlie to slip. Quite a few Buds and a couple hours later, Charlie slipped.

The four vendors had been doing what they did a lot of lately, bashing the President and beating up on the Congress. The vendor sitting next to Charlie Wheeler was lashing Senator Blevins, wondering how he could be a gun-hating liberal, and still represent a fine State like South Carolina. Throughout the evening Charlie had, of course, agreed with everything anyone said that was critical in any way of the promoters of banning gun ownership. Continuing to be agreeable, Charlie jumped in, "No question 'bout it. Blevins is a bumbling bumpster, full of hot air and grits, but not a true Southerner. My daddy and mommy were true southerners, when they were alive, and they would have *never* voted for that bag of excrement."

Had Gary not been alerted by what he saw earlier, and had he kept up with his buds' Bud consumption, Charlie's comment would have gone over his head. But as soon as he heard Charlie's words, generously fueled by 'truth serum', he knew he had something to go on, some way to find out who Charlie Wheeler really was, and why Charlie had been so friendly to all the gun vendors, overly so, since he meet him two years ago or so. Gary Miller recalled that Charlie Wheeler had mentioned to him just last week in Oklahoma City that his parents were still living, and living in Sun City, Arizona. Couldn't both be true, either alive or dead, not both.

Gary decided it was worth a few bucks to find out the truth. What he found out was that Charlie told the truth about his deceased southern parents, they had lived in South Carolina, but they obviously didn't live in Sun City. Such a small, almost insignificant lie, but it clanged the alarm bell leading to what other lies Wheeler had told. The investigative agency that Gary hired confirmed in their search that Charles T. Wheeler was employed by the ATF as a special agent, usually working at the agency from Tuesday to Thursday. They gave Gary pictures taken at the Denver airport of Wheeler as he was dropped off at the terminal by an ATF government vehicle. They also provided photographs of Wheeler entering Denver's ATF offices, his ID badge clipped to his suit coat pocket and plainly visible. Caught.

But, knowing the true identity of an undercover agent, Gary thought, and doing something about it were two distinctly different things. He talked to his wife, his best advisor, who suggested that he seek counsel with the handful of vendors that he had known and trusted for several years, which is exactly what Gary Miller did, in his customized show van, after the Saturday night show closed.

"Charlie Wheeler's a *what*? An ATF agent? You must be kidding...Why, heck, he even arranged to let me borrow a car when I had that wreck. You remember. Plus, he sent me a bottle of Chivas for Christmas last year...nobody's ever done that before."

"No way Charlie's undercover for the ATF. I don't buy it, Gary, no....not for one minute. He's a gun guy through and through. You're smoking' somethin', Gary."

All doubts were laid to rest, though, when Gary shared with his trusted fellow vendors his agency's report, and especially the photographs, confirming Wheeler's real role in life – infiltrating Midwest gun shows as a pretend gun vendor.

"OK, I get it now....he always did kind of seem like a suck up....too much of a good thing, you know. But....I'll have to admit it, he did fool me. The question is....actually....the two questions are....Number one, why is he undercover at gun shows? What's he trying to do? And, second, what, if anything, do we do about it?"

Gary Miller had thought about both questions ever since he learned the truth, and he had some ideas, which he shared with his fellow vendors, "Look, we're not talking here only about one guy...one guy who betrayed our trust....as a snitch for an agency that we hold in minimum high regard, to put it nicely. We're talking about the whole United States Federal Government. He can pick up a phone, and call in all the firepower he needs. Our issue is *not* with Charlie Wheeler, God bless his little pea pickin' heart. The question is, what do the feds think we are doing, or are about to do, that would violate the law, and allow Charlie the snitch to bring in the feds, in full force, to hurt us, to hurt us bad?"

"Gary, it doesn't take a rocket scientist nor a brain surgeon to figure that out. He was planted with us long before the McAlister Act was ever thought of, for an obvious purpose – to catch any of us if we were to violate any firearms laws."

"True that. But, that being the case, since none of us has been thrown in the slammer since 'Good Time Charlie' joined us, that should tell us we have run good, clean gun vending businesses."

"Yeah, well, duh....we knew that. None of us is dumb enough to violate the firearms laws, and Good Ol' Charlie didn't take too long to figure that out. So, once he did, why has he stuck around? Why not look somewhere else, at somebody else?

Gary thought he knew the answer to this question which he had himself been pondering ever since he knew who Wheeler really was. He said, "It's simple. Once the October 26th shootings happened, Wheeler's assignment changed from general surveillance for possible firearms violations to a bigger assignment. He's here to try and make the case for the federal prosecution of any gun vendor who he can prove refuses to sell out or redeem our gun inventories by the deadline. He knows our mentality, we sell guns because, for most of us, it's been our lives. It's what we do, it's who we are. He knows that the chance that we will go from owning scores, or even hundreds, of guns, down to owning zero, nada, no guns at all, are not all that high."

"Gary, I think you're right on. We've talked a lot about the anti-gun, anti-freedom bill, but I don't recall any of us ever saying anything about hiding our guns after the deadline, or not selling or redeeming all of our inventory. Am I wrong? Have we ever discussed anything like that?"

Gary Miller took his time to reply, thinking about several months of conversations, "Guys, I think we *have* had conversations like that. I'm pretty sure I blasted my mouth, more than once, saying that I wouldn't comply with the new law if it passed. I still don't know, to be frank about it, what I'm going to do, as we get closer to the deadline to turn in our guns. Part of me says 'to heck with them', this is still a free country, or at least it was, and the Supreme Court can be counted on to rule that this loony law is contrary to the Second Amendment of the Constitution."

"Don't forget that one of the Supreme Court justices who voted right on the gun cases is gone. He has been replaced by that liberal woman who hates gun owners."

"But aren't they supposed to follow....what's it called? Legal precedent? If they do, then we'll be OK, and they'll toss out the law that this goofy Congress passed."

Gary tried to clarify what he was saying, "Here's the deal. I've donated, as I suspect you guys did, to the groups that fought to defeat the Bill. My Congressman and both US Senators voted no. I'm holding on to some inventory, hidden away, of course. If the Supreme Court throws out the law, which should be a really quick ruling according to that Italian judge on Fox News, then I'm back in business."

"But what if the Supreme Court upholds the new law? What'll you do? You'd be a felon the day the Court rules."

"Actually," Gary replied, "my lawyer told me I'll be a felon the day the law's turn-in deadline is past, next month, not when the Court rules. But, if the Court upholds the law, all hope would be lost. At that point, should that sad day happen, I would either toss my stashed guns in a deep lake or take a chance and hold on to them."

"But, if you hold on to them, and get caught, you're toast. You'd be a big target. They'd love to stick you in the can. You'd be a high profile prisoner. I can see the headline, *Gun Dealer Violates Gun Law, Sent to Prison for Ten Years.*"

"Isn't that why our ol' buddy Charlie is still here, still sniffing around to see what he can learn, and what he can pin on us? We all know that the feds for years have wanted to pass a law to close the so-called 'gun show loophole'. They want to put us out of business – plain and simple. Cars kill over forty thousand Americans every year and nobody's trying to close the 'car show loophole'. The feds would love to indict a bunch of gun show dealers, they hate our guts. We sell a legal product, or at least they're legal today. After McAlister – not so legal."

"But, I still say that this law won't stand. They're trying to terminate a right stated in the U.S. Constitution with just a simple bill passed by Congress. The whole idea of the Supreme Court is to strike down bad laws, like McAlister. I think they'll do their job."

"Don't let me rain on your parade....but....they said the same thing about the McCain-Finegold campaign financing law in 2002. All the smart folks said don't worry about it, it's a bad law, the Supreme Court will take care of the problem and shoot it down. The NRA, and others, filed suit to try to get the Court to overturn the law because it directly violated the First Amendment right of free speech. The law restricts when and how you can criticize a candidate for office, for cryin' out loud. The only problem was, the Supreme Court *upheld* the law that everybody said was unconstitutional. So much for the smart folks."

"So, it was easy to define away our First Amendment rights, by a 5-4 vote of the Supreme Court. I'm just saying don't get your hopes up for the Court's protection of Second Amendment rights. We're never more than five votes away from judicially approved and authorized executive branch tyranny in this country." Thus, in spite of their fears, Gary Miller and his fellow gun show vendors very hesitantly placed their confidence in their nation's highest Court to uphold the Constitutional right to legally own and possess firearms, and thereby uphold their legal right to sell firearms. They joined many Americans who expected their nation's highest Court to strike down the McAlister Act.

THIRTY-SIX

Concord, Massachusetts – Old North Bridge

The ATF claimed that its advertisements were so successful that 94% of the estimated number of guns in America had been turned in at Redemption Centers by the deadline of September 13th. Of course, like many statistics, this one could not possibly be proven to be accurate, and was by many estimates excessively high. But it sounded good, and the estimated percentage of compliance became commonly acknowledged by the mainstream media as proof of success of the new law. The seemingly impressive statistic was cited by the President when he and Director Humless officially commemorated the concluding day of the Redemption Period. They did so with a joint news conference at the historic re-built Old North Bridge, spanning the Concord River, in Concord, Massachusetts, the site of the first battle of the Revolutionary War. The President and Director Humless gave their remarks in front of the Daniel Chester French sculpture of the Minuteman.

"Director Humless, I have asked you to join me here today at this historic location, to honor you for your agency's hard work over these last six months to make America free from gun violence. I couldn't think of a more appropriate spot to formally end the era of gun violence than to commemorate its end where it began. It was here that guns were used for what we now know was the historic purpose of freeing our people from their domination by the British Empire. That Empire oppressed people on many continents.

"There are some who have objected to the McAlister Hate Speech and Hate Weapons Elimination Act based on what I think are misguided Constitutional law arguments. I know a little bit about Constitutional Law, having taught the subject. I want to assure the American public that if I thought the McAlister Bill was unconstitutional, I would not have signed it into law. The fact that it appears to conflict with some persons' interpretation of the Second Amendment doesn't mean that it actually does. We used to have slavery and people argued that it was Constitutional. The U.S. Supreme Court, as we all know, will hear arguments next week, in an emergency hearing, in a case challenging the constitutionality of the McAlister Act. I am sure that our nation's highest Court will carefully consider the arguments both for and against the new law. I am just as confident that the Supreme Court will render a Constitutionally correct decision, and hand it down expeditiously. My own view, of course, is that old words from two centuries ago must be carefully weighed in light of today's public demand to rid our nation of gun violence, which has been caused in large part by hateful speech, which we have also outlawed in the history-making McAlister Act.

"So, my fellow Americans, we are gathered here today at Old North Bridge at Concord. What started here with guns, can now end here, as we honor the successful conclusion of the Redemption Period under the Lawrence McAlister Hate Speech and Hate Weapons Elimination Act. From this day forward, any American caught owning or possessing a firearm, with very limited exceptions, will be charged with a felony, will be convicted and will serve the maximum statutory time at a federal prison. The same penalty will apply to any person who violates the law prohibiting hate speech. There have been rumors that I will allow an amnesty period for those who did not comply with the 180 day Redemption Period. I want to clear that up. That is false. I will not excuse those who, after today's midnight deadline, violate the McAlister Act. That will not happen, got it? So, for those still hesitating, you've only got until twelve midnight tonight, as I did extend the regular office closing hours for today at the Redemption Centers. Thanks, again, Director Humless. Any plans ahead for you or your agency?"

ATF Director Humless, visibly preening himself as nicely as any peacock, assumed the podium. This was the day he had sought for years as America's leading anti-gun lobbyist. His time had come to take credit, and also to send a message. "Mr. President, together with you, your staff and all the fine officials in your Administration, the ATF has managed to handle the redemption of millions of what some call firearms, but I call hate weapons, as does the McAlister Act. The final accounting isn't done, naturally, but when it is, America should be overjoyed with the results. Our nation will be safer, and America will be gun violence free, which has been my dream for the last several years at the Bradford Center Against Gun Violence by Gun Abolition.

"Phase two now begins. Our agency has been authorized by Congress, and under your instructions, Mr. President, we almost finishing hiring over fifty-four thousand new ATF agents, which greatly helps the employment situation in this country, of course. That's approximately one new ATF agent for every 5,000 Americans. This fact should make most Americans feel very secure, knowing that our agents will be out there deployed in the various states. They will be hunting down....maybe a better word would be locating....sorry....the few remaining gun owners, those whose continued ownership of hate weapons threatens all of us. This will fulfill the hopes and dreams of many former Presidents, particularly Presidents Carter, Clinton and Obama."

Two men were watching with great interest the televised coverage of the President's news conference at Old North Bridge. The first was the President's Chief of Staff, watching the news conference from his West Wing corner office, who groaned, again. Can this guy ever get his 'government speak' correct, he wondered? Humless may have been effective in the 'gun round up' for 'meltin and smeltin', as the President's top aide liked to describe the disposal process. But, he briefly pondered, is Humless up to the task of phase two. Enforcement? Getting a large number of scared gun owners to turn in their guns for money was one thing, but actually going after the hold outs, the tea party folks, the patriots, the militia groups, the angry hunters, the others they might not even know were out there, he knew that was another issue entirely. The easy part, the *I'll give you money, you give me your gun, and, oh yeah, you don't go to prison'* part, that was finally over. Now, it was time for enforcement of the criminal provisions of the new law, which promised to be a bit more difficult.

The other man greatly interested in the Old North Bridge Presidential media event was watching from his home in Billings, Montana. As he watched the President of his country discuss the anti-gun law at the site of the first shots fired in the American Revolution, in front of the Minuteman statue, he made a life-changing decision. His President, he concluded, was desecrating what the founding fathers did at Concord, as they fired the shots heard around the world. How dare he celebrate his anti-gun victory on this holy site? He then decided, though reluctantly, and after much prayer, that he would honor what they did, and he would do it in a way that the world would understand that freedom and freedom's friends were not yet dead and gone in America. It was time to assemble the posse. They had work to do.

222

THIRTY-SEVEN

Washington, DC – Supreme Court of the United States

The Honorable Chief Justice and the Associate Justices of the Supreme Court of the United States. Oyez! Oyez! Oyez! All persons having business before the Honorable Supreme Court of the United States are admonished to draw near and give their attention, for the Court is now sitting. God save the United States and this Honorable Court!

The Marshal of the United States Supreme Court thus called to order the nation's highest tribunal. His words came from an earlier time, when Americans still called on God to save their nation, and when the nation allowed His name to be used in a public setting. Constructed in 1935, the Supreme Court building displays several carvings or castings that depict the role of Moses and the Ten Commandments in the western world's jurisprudence. On the Eastern exterior pediment Moses is predominately carved in the middle of several figures, holding two stone tablets. In the Supreme Court Chambers Moses holds a stone tablet bearing Hebrew letters. Doors to the Supreme Court Chamber show two tablets with Roman numerals I-V on one and VI-X on the other. Ironically, the Court that presides from this building has more recently ruled that allowing the depiction of the Ten Commandments in a public building, such as a local court house, violates the Constitution of the United States.

After the Clerk called the Docket of the Court for the first day of the new term in October, the Chief Justice called the first case, which was on the Docket as an emergency petition for a writ from the Court.

223

"This matter comes before the Court on an expedited, I might say, highly expedited basis, with five Justices agreeing to take it up as an emergency. It's been since Bush vs. Gore that we acted so expeditiously. In light of the pending enforcement of the McAlister Act there may be some justification for the way we are addressing this case, this issue, but I would not want to establish such a fast track consideration for every suit challenging the Constitutionality of an act of the Congress. Having said that, Mr. Attorney General, it's your law to defend. Defend it."

"Thank you, Mr. Chief Justice. Associate Justices of this honorable Court. The people of the United States of America urge the Court to affirm the Constitutionality of the McAlister Hate Speech and Hate Weapons Elimination Act. The various free speech advocates, so called, and the gun owner and manufacturer groups that have challenged the new law don't dispute that the Congress can *adopt* such a law, that's what Congresses do, they adopt laws. Frankly, some better drafted than others.

"No, instead, the Appellants have only one argument. They urge the Court to strike down the McAlister Act because, they argue, it violates the First and Second Amendments of the Constitution of the United States. Their argument is that the American people *can't* rid themselves of the rampant hate speech and the millions of hate weapons that kill tens of thousands of us every year. And why not? Because of the handful of words used in these two vague, poorly-drafted, last-minute Amendments. They argue...."

Justice Scanlon had been visibly holding himself back to give the Attorney General his customary few opening words before the Justices jumped in with their probing questions. He could restrain himself no more.

"Mr. Attorney General, with all due respect, this Court settled the issue of gun rights in 2008 in DC v. Heller. We held that the Second Amendment protects an individual's right to possess a firearm for self-defense. So, how can you seriously argue that we...."

"Justice Scanlon, also with all due respect, that was five years ago. The nation has changed. Americans have evolved in their thinking about...."

"Are you saying that the Constitution, without going through the amendment process, can be changed, I think was your word, just because today's public opinion polls may show some transitory shifting opinion, which might shift back just as quickly tomorrow or next year? Is that this government's view of settled law?"

"No, Justice Scanlon, this government's view of the law is that when Congress enacts a new law the judiciary gives to that new law its highest level of deference, and will only interfere in those limited instances where the new law clearly violates an express provision of the Constitution."

"Whoa, Mr. Attorney General, you don't see a conflict between 'the right of the people to keep and bear arms shall not be infringed' and the McAlister law that imprisons those who seek to keep and bear arms? That's not a clear violation of an *express provision*? And hate speech *review panels*? What are *those*?"

"Justice Scanlon, the government is only arguing that under the principle of granting the highest deference to Acts of Congress, that this Court has almost always followed, that you should uphold the McAlister Act. Any other holding...."

Justice Alinon, who had also been itching to engage in the legal sparring, jumped in, "Mr. Attorney General, you have fully ignored Justice Scanlon's reminder to you that this Court has already ruled in Heller that the Second Amendment protects individual ownership of firearms. Two years later in McDonald v. Chicago, we held that the Second Amendment applies to the states through the Fourteenth Amendment. So, sir, what possibly makes you think that the government has any chance of this same Court upholding the McAlister Act. It's unconstitutional on its face. In addition to which, the government can't review speech to decide if it's hate speech or not. The Act is an egregious example of over-reaching by the Congress, apparently goaded on by the Administration for which you work."

The Attorney General refused to lose his temper. Court observers later agreed that the AG was uncharacteristically calm as he sparred with the Court's most vocal and persuasive conservative members. He soon revealed the basis for his confident manner.

"Justice Scanlon, not to pick a nit, necessarily, but you just said this Court is, to use your phrase, 'the same Court' as the Court that decided Heller and McDonald. It's not. The five Justices who decided those two cases are now four Justices. I know you don't like to discuss Court politics in oral arg...."

"*Nor will we now, sir.*" The Chief Justice, exercising his prerogatives, cut off the discussion. "We are here today to argue the law, not who has what votes. *Is that clear*, Mr. Attorney General. May we proceed now to discuss the law?"

"My apologies, Mr. Chief Justice, I'll move on. The Appellants in their briefs urge the Court to strike down

McAlister under the principle of stare decisis, that is, that the matter has been decided and must be ruled upon in the same way, barring certain circumstances. I think that is what both Justices Scanlon and Alinon are asserting, that under Heller and McDonald, the matter has been decided, and the Court has to follow the precedent of those two cases."

"Precisely, Mr. Attorney General, precisely," Justice Scanlon re-engaged, "and why isn't that the principle we must follow in deciding this case? Stare decisis demands that we follow our precedent and strike down the McAlister Act, just as we struck down the DC and Chicago gun ordinances. No difference. All three violate the Second Amendment right to keep and bear arms. The Act is so obviously violative of the First Amendment that a first year law student could write an opinion striking it down."

"Justice Scanlon, in every oral argument the core issue eventually emerges, as it now has. The principle of stare decisis, I say with the highest level of respect for this tribunal, has been abandoned by this Court, and no longer has the meaning and importance that it once enjoyed. When this Court...."

"What? Would you mind repeating yourself, sir? I must have not have heard you correctly. We....this Court....we have abandoned stare decisis?"

"Justice Alinon, this Court in 1986 in Bowers v. Hardwick upheld the sodomy laws of 25 states in America." Knowing where this argument was going, Justice Scanlon was seen holding his head briefly in his hands, before leaning fully back in his leather high-back chair. His facial expression was not one of joy. "Yet, just 17 years later, in

2003, this Court, *the same institution* that decided Hardwick, ruled in Lawrence v. Texas that all sodomy laws were *unconstitutional*. The Court, in an opinion by Justice Kennedy, even said about following precedent in the Lawrence case that 'Stare decisis is not an inexorable command'. Honorable Justices, when the nation changes, the laws must change and our *understanding* of what the Constitution says must also change. The Constitution must change, even if it's not actually formally amended through the cumbersome process of Congress and the states adopting the Amendment by super-majorities. The nation shouldn't have to put up with laws allowing prejudice against certain Americans, any more than it should put up with laws, or Amendments, that allow Americans to attack each other with hate speech and to slaughter each other with hate weapons."

Justice Scanlon remained silent for the balance of the oral argument. In 2003, he led the minority of the Court in the Lawrence case in the hotly-fought split decision, even accurately predicting in open comments from the bench that the Lawrence case would open the floodgates to gay marriage, which before Lawrence was rarely even discussed. His mind briefly returned to his dissenting opinion in Lawrence where he criticized the majority for using stare decisis as the primary justification for not overturning Roe v. Wade, which would have ended abortion on demand, but abandoning stare decisis in Lawrence, when it suited the majority's desire to advance what he called the "homosexual agenda".

Justice Scanlon recalled how Justice Kennedy tried to justify overruling precedent in Hardwick, writing that the nation, since Hardwick, had experienced an "emerging awareness". He knew that this was a slippery slope indeed, as the Court could abandon virtually any precedent under such an open-ended standard. Kennedy's citation of the European Court of Human Rights' view on the gay rights issue was the last straw for Scanlon, and had also been roundly criticized by many, as Kennedy based the Court's majority opinion on other nations' case law. Kennedy had even criticized a former Chief Justice of the Court for stating, accurately, that historically homosexual behavior had not been legally or socially acceptable. Justice Scanlon had observed in his hotly-worded dissenting opinion that this Court has not only re-written existing law, it also re-writes history to suit the majority's purposes.

Justice Scanlon knew he could not now argue that the Court had to follow precedent, because the Court in Lawrence had demonstrated that it had to do no such thing. The Attorney General was correct that Justice Kennedy wrote in Lawrence that stare decisis was "not an inexorable command". Well then, he pondered, what is it? We follow precedent when we feel like it, but we abandon precedent when it fits our "emerging awareness" of whatever cultural agenda is regarded to be acceptable for the day? Are we really now a *"rights de jour"* nation? We only have the rights that are felt by five Justices to be acceptable for that day only? If so, any Constitutional right would just be five votes away from drastic modification, or even extinction. Just five votes. Goodbye, Rule of Law, he thought, sadly.

The attorneys for the Appellants made their arguments, under withering questioning by the more liberal members of the Court. Veteran Court observers wrote in their articles and blogs that night that the government was expected to win the case, conjecturing that the Court would, in a 5-4 split uphold the McAlister Act. Newly seated Justice Newton, was known to be opposed to private ownership of firearms. It had been conjectured that she had written a strategy memo for the President before she ascended to the high Court, advising him on the text of the McAlister Bill to be considered by Congress. Nevertheless, she refused to recuse herself from the Court's consideration of the Constitutionality of the new law. Justice Newton appeared to confirm those views in her single question to the gun owners' lead Counsel.

"Tell me Counsel, one reason, just one, I'm only looking for *one reason*, to justify the Court striking down an Act of Congress that has the potential of saving tens of thousands of precious lives and of stopping all the hate speech that spawns violence. Just one little reason, please, Counsel?"

The other indicator as to how the vote to be taken the next day in the Court's stately Conference Room would turn out, was a rare statement by Justice Thomson at the conclusion of oral argument. "Mr. Attorney General, we all know, I think, how this case will come down. What none of us knows, *yet*, is the impact of this decision, *not only* on our First and Second Amendment rights, but on all *those other* Constitutional rights that we *used* to think we had as Americans. I shudder to think what is happening to my country."

On Friday afternoon, the Supreme Court posted an official notice in the McAlister Law Constitutional challenge case. The quasi-opinion was a model of brevity:

FOR PUBLICATION

BY THE SUPREME COURT
OF THE UNITED STATES

THIS COURT, having fully examined the briefs submitted by Counsel, the oral argument offered in open Court and having thoroughly reviewed the legal issues involved, concludes that there is no valid legal justification to extend the consideration of this case further. A lengthier opinion will be released as expeditiously as possible, authored by Justice Newton, writing for the majority. To assuage public concern in the interim, and so as not to further impede the enforcement of a law validly adopted by the Congress of these United States, this Court orders that this appeal is resolved in favor of the Appellee U.S. Government, and that, accordingly, the Lawrence McAlister Hate Speech and Hate Weapons Elimination Act is affirmed, as in compliance with the Constitution of the United States, and all of the Amendments thereto. So ordered. Copy to all Counsel.

The McAlister Act was now confirmed as the law of the land.

III.

The ATF Enforces the
Lawrence McAlister
Hate Speech
and Hate Weapons
Elimination Act

THIRTY-EIGHT

Elmhurst, IL, Philadelphia, PA & Des Moines, Iowa

The Attorney General was ready. Once the call came from the Department of Justice staffer who had been stationed at the Supreme Court, tipping the AG to the Court's expected Order upholding McAlister, the Department of Justice sprang into action. The government had learned decades before that the best way to insure taxpayer compliance with the April 15 tax return filing deadline was to file federal tax evasion charges against a few hapless miscreant taxpayers, and do it just days before the deadline. Wide media attention to the filing of the criminal charges guaranteed that tax return filing rates jumped.

Likewise, the Administration had laid careful plans for charging several gun owners, in major media markets, who hadn't yet complied with McAlister, now that the redemption deadline had expired. They knew that the mere act of showing how serious the government was, by the arrest and indictment of several gun owners, would bring in many thousands more guns, particularly now that the law had been affirmed on appeal by the Supreme Court. It was time for the 'perp walk', the televised and photographed hauling of criminal defendants, 'perpetrators' in police language, in handcuffs, into official-looking grey limestone buildings. Nothing, the AG knew, promotes compliance with the law like a good 'perp walk' viewed by Americans on their nightly televised newscasts.

Perp Walk I

Charles Robinson was a law abiding resident of Elmhurst, Illinois, a suburb of Chicago. He owned a small travel agency, which because of the growing use by travelers of the internet, was not doing all that well. On weekends, during hunting season, Charles Robinson liked to drive up to northwestern Illinois, to the Apple River Canyon area and to Castle Rock to hunt northern bobwhite, which most people just called quail. His dad had taught Charles Robinson how to hunt, and he had passed on that training to his son, Charles, Jr., now in his mid-twenties. They enjoyed the time they could spend together hunting. When Charles Robinson first read the text of the McAlister Bill in the Chicago Tribune, he was surprised that firearms might be outlawed in America. But, as he read further, he saw that the Bill had an exemption in Section 5.1 for firearms to be used for hunting.

At first, Charles Robinson concluded that he would just apply for the exemption for his firearms used for hunting, and that would be that. But, the more he read, he realized that he might not be granted an exemption hunting license because he usually didn't hunt for purposes of acquiring food, and he wasn't going to lie about it on his application. Then, he read that he could only use his firearms for hunting under the license if he was directly supervised by an ATF agent or by an agent from the Illinois Department of Natural Resources. What kind of hunting would that be? Baby-sat by a 'gubmint' employee, he thought, using his favorite expression for the government.

Charles Robinson talked to his son about what they should do. They neither one wanted to give up their primary recreation, so they decided to apply for the exemption, eat some of what they caught and see how long the government really wanted to accompany hunters out into the field. They agreed that the gubmint boys would soon tire of traipsing through the woods with hunters, and just let them go hunt. The problem developed when they tried to apply for an exemption hunting license.

Charles Robinson called his son, as it was nearing hunting season. They picked out a date a few days away on the calendar, so they could line up either an ATF agent or an Illinois game warden to accompany them hunting, under what they assumed would be a quickly issued hunting exemption license. As silly as they thought the whole process was, they were law abiding citizens, so they decided to comply with the McAlister Act, as best they understood it.

The cordial young lady at the ATF Field District office asked the Robinsons to fill out a six page ATF form. The form included several questions about the applicant, and also required details of the firearms that would be used by the applicant, under ATF supervision. The applicant had to supply the manufacturer of the firearm; the date manufactured; any known serial numbers; the price paid; from whom the firearm was purchased; the current location of the firearm; location at said address; nature of storage facility; locked or not locked; accessibility to others; any other known prior owners; address; telephone numbers; future intentions of the applicant regarding the sale of the firearm; and the intentions of the applicant regarding redemption of the firearm to the ATF under the McAlister Act. Charles Robinson read over the form, then he re-read it. None of this was mentioned in the McAlister Act, so why was the government asking so many questions, he wondered, his anger beginning to rise up within him. He asked his son, who was with him in case he needed to sign anything, to read over the form. They both agreed that it was more than intrusive, but what could they do? They loved to hunt, and this form was their ticket to hunting. Or at least, that's what they thought.

After nearly an hour, which included calls out to gather requested information, the Robinsons had completed their respective forms. They asked the young lady to speak to an agent so they could confirm a time to go hunting. She asked them to have a seat while she buzzed an agent to come out and talk to them. Forty minutes later, ATF agent Falendar found the time to meet with the agency's latest applicants for exemption hunting licenses.

"Name's Falendar. Agent here in Chicago Field District office. What can I do for you? Busy days here, what with the new law, and all."

"Thanks, Agent Falendar for talking with us. Real simple. We filled out your forms, though I think the ATF asked us for a lot of unneeded information on our firearms. We want to schedule a time, sometime in the next two or three weekends to go hunting....with an ATF agent....like it says in the McAlister Act."

Agent Falendar didn't exactly laugh, it was more like a short nasal snort. "Nuhuh....Do what? To schedule....go hunting?.....Umh, let me 'splain how this all works. Cause....you both seem like good law abidin' folks. We got here in the Field District Office a limited number of agents. We've all got important things that have to be done, a lot more now with McAlister, what with trackin' down law breakers. We got zero....that's zero....time to tramp around with hunters, holding their hands so they can own guns, and not turn them in like everybody else. So, sirs, what we've been told to do by our HQ in DC is we take your names and put you on a waitin' list. We will call you when an agent has a free Saturday and wants to spend it with hunters, instead of with his family. Not saying, you understand, that it won't never happen, just that it may be a while before it does happen. Any questions?"

"Yes, Agent Falendar, how long it will be before we can hunt – that is, with an ATF agent?"

"Like I said, you seem like nice folks. I'd give it a couple, maybe three years, something like that....maybe not that soon. That's not for publication, you understand. I'm just levelin' with you here, OK?"

"Wow....Really?....Well, thanks for being honest....I guess....So should we just contact the Illinois Department of Natural Resources down in Springfield?"

"You can do whatever you want....but, you'll just be wastin' your time. They'll give you the same response. Their guys are real busy, too, just like we are."

Charles Robinson, Jr. didn't have his father's ability to stay calm when he was tempted to be angry. His father through the years had tried to teach his son how to control himself when he wanted to lash out. He saw out of the corner of his eye that his dad, though normally calm and collected, was not calm, nor was he collected. His face reddened. He clinched his fingers around the ATF forms which they had labored to complete. His son, sensing that his dad was about to do or say something he would later regret, reached over and grabbed his arm, saying "Dad, it's ok, if they don't want us to hunt anymore, we'll turn in our guns and take up something else, like bowling, or fishing, or....".

"Chuck....we....are....not....giving....up....our...hunting ....NOT....Gonna....Happen.... I don't give a rip about this crazy new law. They can't stop us from what God has given us to enjoy. Agent Fal....whatever your name is..."

"Now, Dad, we can..."

Charles Robinson, Sr. was not about to hushed.

"As I was about to say....Mister Agent. You can take this hunting exemption form....and....file it....where....the sun....or the moon....will never shine! Got it? If my son and I want to hunt, we'll hunt. Get used to it."

Robinson crumpled the pages of the ATF forms and tossed them at Agent Falendar, hitting him on the forehead. The Robinsons stalked out. Agent Falendar made careful notes of the encounter. The notes became the basis for a rush report to ATF Counsel, who then converted the details into a formal charge by the Department of Justice. The Agent swore in an affidavit that he had been assaulted by disgruntled license applicant Charles Robinson, Sr.

The Robinsons, father and son, were arrested by the FBI three weeks later. They were perp walked, handcuffed and heads down, into the Everett McKinley Dirksen Federal Court House in Chicago, with full media coverage. When they were arrested, the warrant allowed FBI agents to search their homes, where they discovered and seized several firearms, mostly hunting rifles and shotguns, owned and possessed by the Robinsons in what was charged was a direct violation of the McAlister Act. They had no hunting exemption licenses. The Robinsons were charged with illegal possession of hate weapons in violation of the recently passed law, as well as assault on a federal official.

Perp Walk II

Not many years ago, if one wanted to share one's written thoughts with the world, letters to the editor were the major venue. Most editors limited how many letters they would publish from a single writer, which crimped the style of those who had a lot to say. Things have changed. Bloggers today, particularly skilled bloggers who have something to say, can attract more readers than newspaper columnists, and frequently do. James Elizas Brown was the pen name of one of those bloggers who attracted a following of readers, primarily because his readers loved to read his rips on the liberal left and his frequent attacks on firearm opponents. The writer who adopted and used Brown's pen name was in his real life Peter Samuel, a captain in a metropolitan fire department in Pennsylvania. Depending on the day and the heat generated by a scorching hot blog, Brown may have readers numbering in the hundreds of thousands.

One of Brown's/Samuel's columns printed early during the debate on the McAlister Bill started out with these memorable words:

WHO DO THESE PINKO/NAZIS THINK THEY ARE?

I know that Communism is, well, supposedly, dead. Tell that to the Chinese who are still in jail for their beliefs, or because of their religion. Tell that to the Cubans. But, whether you call it Communism, or Socialism or National Socialism (a/k/a Nazism/Facism), what it all boils down to is this, these political ideologies all took away their citizens' guns.

NOW, IN THE GOOD OLD USA, *THEY WANT OUR GUNS!*

I'm announcing that they can't have them!

This sicko pale excuse for a law, the McAlister Bill, deserves a quick death. Put a stake in its heart. Bury it under ten feet of concrete. Never let it rise again. Confinement in federal prison for owning what has been legal in this country for over 300 years? Even the Brits, when they owned us, allowed us simple folks out in the Colonies to own guns, don't 'ya know. Now this liberal, lefto, pinko, yes, Nazi, Administration wants to ban the right to own firearms. I say that we ban this President from coming in to any State where more than 10% of the population own guns!

Might not be safe for him, don't 'ya know!

Needless to say, James Elizas Brown, widely followed by his readers across the country, was not very popular with the White House, which asked the FBI to locate the man behind the pen name. Brown's/Samuel's suggestion that the President not visit certain states because he wouldn't be safe from gun violence earned him a referral by the Secret Service to the Department of Justice. The fact that he had several guns stashed under the back floor board of his well-used Jeep Wagoneer, which the arresting agents quickly located, added to his value as a target defendant.

When Brown/Samuel was perp walked, his hands cuffed behind his back, into the James A. Byrne Federal Courthouse in Philadelphia, the alerted media dutifully recorded the event. Ironically, Brown's/Samuel's public humiliation was near the Liberty Bell Center, also on Market Street. His website was shut down the same day, on petition by the DOJ which alleged that the website was in violation of the Patriot Act. He was also charged with negative attacks on a public official under the McAlister Act. The DOJ Deputy in charge of responding to media inquiries said that Brown's/Samuel's case may not come to trial for some time, due to "national security concerns."

Dan Mitchell sold guns for a living. He sold more guns than any other gun dealer in the Midwest. His was a familiar face to television viewers, as he would appear on screen, standing in front of hundreds of guns for sale in his gun store in Iowa. His sandy hair and wide smile were his trademarks, along with his famous television ads. Each ad always ended with Dan looking into the camera and saying, *"I don't care about making a profit, folks....I just live.... to sell guns"*.

During the national debate over the McAlister Bill, and before Congress made the Bill into a law, Dan Mitchell was a significant public participant in what the *Des Moines Register* called 'the Iowa Gun Fight'. The newspaper didn't much like Mitchell, and would frequently parody his ads by calling them *'Dan's Hate Weapon Promos'*. The problem for the newspaper was that Dan Mitchell became the major spokesperson in the State against the McAlister Bill, so the paper was forced to quote his colorful attacks, though it would have rather have just ignored him completely.

Possibly Dan's most memorable statement opposing the anti-gun Bill was when he called for armed resistance by Iowans should the McAlister Bill become law. He told a gun owners rally in Council Bluffs, "Mark my words. If the Congress passes this wicked Bill, we will see *blood run in the streets of the cities of Iowa*. No way Iowans will allow the President to take away our guns, no possible way. We will *shoot* anyone who tries to do it. Mark my words. And this is not about my ability to sell guns, 'cause you all know I don't care about making a profit, folks, *I just live to sell guns."*

ATF agents later denied rumors that a blown up picture of Dan Mitchell was taped to the wall of the ATF offices in the Field Division office in Kansas City, which had jurisdiction over Iowa. They also denied that someone had written across Mitchell's face – PUBLIC ENEMY #1. Whether true or not, once the U.S. Supreme Court affirmed McAlister as the law of the land, agents lost no time in obtaining a search warrant for Mitchell's home and rural farm buildings. Dan Mitchell had earlier locked the doors of his mega gun store the day after the President signed the McAlister Act in the Rose Garden. He did so surrounded by guns rights advocates carrying protest signs, and well covered by regional media. He cursed the President and the Congress for the new Law, and for its forcing him to close the business he had lived to enjoy for over thirty years. Dan told the media that, "I don't have to keep selling guns, folks. I'll survive just fine, but what won't survive is *the freedom to own a gun. That freedom died* in the Rose Garden, killed dead by this idiot President and idiot Congress of ours."

Mitchell's incendiary words on the evening news were watched carefully at the Kansas City ATF office. An internal memo was sent to the Des Moines Field Office advising the office to obtain a search warrant to attempt to locate any illegal firearms in the possession of Dan Mitchell. The memo, it was said, had been taped to the picture of Mitchell that was officially not taped to the wall of ATF offices.

The Des Moines Field Office lost no time, once the Supreme Court upheld McAlister, in asking the presiding District Court Judge to issue a sealed search warrant. Sealed, because they did not want to alert Mitchell, before they showed up to search his house and out buildings. But, it wasn't as if Dan Mitchell didn't expect them. He knew he had made himself a giant target. He even had a local t-shirt shop make him a shirt with concentric red rings on the back. He liked wearing it when he went into to town to have coffee at Nellie's Pastry Shop and Deli. He'd tell anyone who asked, "Since I know they're coming for me, I don't want them to miss and just *maim me*, I want to help them get a *good clear shot.*" No one, of course, planned to shoot Dan Mitchell, that was bit of exaggeration on his part, but he was after all, a

244

consummate show man. He was correct, though, that he was a target. He had made himself one by his own words. He had to be brought down....and shut up.

When Dan saw where the fight over gun rights was headed, he gave serious thought to leaving the country. In his research he learned that there were still several nations that allowed private gun ownership. His final first choice was New Zealand, where over 200,000 gun owners own over a million guns, which are licensed, but not registered. Gun shops in New Zealand are legal, a fact which appealed to Dan's desire to stay in business. But, Dan frittered and fretted, and couldn't bring himself to pack up and move, somewhat like the Jewish families in Europe seeing the danger from Hitler's Brown Shirts coming, but failing to escape while they still could. He later wondered how he could have been so stupid, but by then it was too late.

When the agents arrived at Dan Mitchells' farm they served their warrant, then went immediately to work. They did not expect to find any firearms in the sprawling house, but they searched it anyway. They then turned to the several out buildings. Armed with sensitive metal detectors, agents eventually uncovered a serious cache of firearms under a metal plate in the back of a straw covered horse stall in a long abandoned farm building, on the backside of the 180 acre Mitchell farm property. Over one hundred weapons of various types. Caught.

Dan Mitchell could afford a good criminal defense lawyer. His good criminal defense lawyer advised Dan Mitchell to shut his mouth, and keep it shut, with no comments, no fighting words, no nothing. He told Dan to just do the perp walk. No smiles. No frowns. Hold up your head, as much as you can, with your hands cuffed behind you. Dan argued that he was too well known for being a fighter to not fight, or at least verbally fire back, when they hauled him into the federal building on Walnut Street in Des

Moines. Dan's good criminal defense lawyer responded that if he mouthed off, each word could cost him years of incarceration or thousands of dollars in fines. Dan Mitchell got the message, and was uncharacteristically subdued when he was perp walked along Walnut Street in front of his 'friends' in the media. Several of the agents who had been less than amused by Dan's harsh words in years past gathered later at Java Joe's Coffeehouse to commemorate his arrest. One said, toasting the event with his coffee cup, "Here's to Dan. You shoulda obeyed the law, Dan. Now, you'll get to spend a lot more time with your former customers."

Results of Perp Walks

Within a week after the highly publicized perp walks, and several others that followed around the country, the various Redemption Centers reported tens of thousands of firearms brought in by obviously concerned owner

The re-writing of the Constitution was a natural outcome of years of discussions between the President, before he achieved public office, and a close friend whose background included bombing a police station as a 60's radical. Both had served on left-leaning not-for-profit boards of directors. The President's first meeting of supporters for his initial run for office took place in his friend's living room. His friend was now an outside advisor who was frequently called on by the President for his creative public policy ideas. His friend had often speculated as to how the U.S. government might one day be taken over by people who thought like they thought. He advised the President that his study of history confirmed that once a person in authority gets away with operating outside of the traditional restraints of the rule of law, the next similar act becomes even easier, as the fear factor increases. The success of McAlister fueled their determination to further radically alter America in the days ahead.

THIRTY-NINE

Asheville, NC

The Asheville Regional Airport is small as American airports go. Local leaders have for years asked for a longer and wider landing strip. Only 40,000 passengers a month flow through its gates. Thus, when the massive Air Force One Presidential aircraft landed at Asheville the plane dwarfed the modest terminal. A Presidential visit was literally a huge event for this mountainous artsy community. In planning for the major address that the President would deliver, White House planners selected a rural location as a quiet, peaceable backdrop for a speech that they knew would be anything but.

A bunting-draped platform had been erected on the airfield side of the terminal. A large red, white and blue banner welcomed the President to North Carolina. Thousands of sympathetic North and South Carolinians had been bussed in to swell the enthusiastic ranks greeting their nation's CEO, each given a small American flag to wave. The visit had been promoted by the White House Press Office as a major address, a policy-setting speech that would be long remembered. The Press Office, at least in this instance, didn't exaggerate.

The Governor of North Carolina was given an allotted ten minutes. He welcomed the President for honoring their State, thanked the hard-working event committee for their untiring efforts, thanked the assembled area high school bands for providing the best of John Phillip Sousa's patriotic marches, thanked the employees of the State for providing great government for their State, thanked the many hundreds of volunteers who made the event possible, thanked everyone else he could possibly thank. He then said that the President needed no introduction, and after nearly twenty-five minutes of political-speak, exceeding his allotment, he gave him the shortest of introductions.

"And now it is my distinct pleasure to give to you the Pres...i...dent...of...the...U...nited...States...of...Amer...ica."

After Hail to Chief was played through three times, accompanied by the cheers of the flag-waving crowd, the President, held up his arms for quiet, then looking at the nearest Tele-Prompter, plunged into his address. Notably, though he initially flashed his well-known smile, by the time he began to read his speech, his face and demeanor was clearly somber.

"My fellow Americans. We are gathered today to discuss a subject of great urgency to America, that is, if America is itself to survive as a free people. I don't say those words lightly. No nation in history has survived when its people have torn each other apart, internally inside their nation. That is exactly what we have been doing as a nation now for several years, tearing each other apart....with the hate speech of hateful people....aimed at hurting other Americans. I'm here today to announce, yes, even to proclaim as your President, that the days of open and unrestricted hate speech are over. Done. Finished.

"We all know that recently the Congress of these United States of America, elected by we the people, adopted the Lawrence McAlister Hate Speech and Hate Weapon Elimination Act. I was most proud as your President to sign the McAlister Act into law. As we all also know, the McAlister Act is now the law of the land. With a few notable exceptions, being violation of the new law by a handful of gun-loving radicals, the hate weapons part of the McAlister Act is being implemented. We will soon be a hate weapons free nation. Thank you, Congress. Thank you, ATF. Thank you, peace-loving Americans.

The cheers, routinely expected at Presidential events after a speaking point, were noticeably less than enthusiastic. The President's mention of the McAlister Act, while quite popular with most of his public employee and labor union audience, lacked support among many in this mountainous part of the country. Some in the crowd had been hunters or sports shooters, but because of McAlister, were now unarmed. The President's planners knew, of course, that the location for the speech could be somewhat dicey, but concluded that what the President would announce in his speech would win over even some of the disgruntled previous gun owners, particularly if they were unemployed.

"Getting rid of hate weapons is the good news. But, anybody who watches television, listens to talk radio or visits the internet knows that the bad news is that the hate speech portion of the McAlister Act is a very long way from being implemented. Hate speech is destroying America. Let me repeat. As President, I am proclaiming that hate speech is destroying America. It is today's enemy number one. Too many Americans are abusing their so-called First Amendment rights by using hate speech to attack other Americans, and doing it hatefully.

"A moment ago I mentioned that the McAlister Act was enacted into law by the elected representatives of the people. In addition, the McAlister Act has been confirmed as fully consistent with the Constitution of the United States of America by our nation's highest Court, the Supreme Court of the United States. Lest anyone incorrectly charge that what I am announcing today violates their First Amendment rights of free speech and free expression, I would remind them that we are a nation of law, and that our Supreme Court has ruled that the McAlister Act does not violate our Constitution, in any way. Hate speech regulation is now legal, and this Administration is committed to implementing hate speech regulation, under the law.

"How will we fight this scourge? What can we do to stop the hateful use of words to attack our public officials and our minorities? As a student of American history it seemed to me that we should reach back in our nation's proud past and revive a program that was more than successful in helping to cure our nation's ills. I am referring to the Civilian Conservation Corps, known as the CCC, created by my predecessor, President Franklin Delano Roosevelt, under his Executive Order Number 6101. When President Roosevelt was faced with tough economic times he initiated the CCC and, over time, from 1933 to 1942, he hired three million Americans to help build our nation. Today, we don't have quite the same need as in the 30's to build physical infrastructure, national parks, roads, and such. But we do have the need to re-build the moral foundations of our land, by ridding our nation of hate speech. Even Republicans should be in favor of that goal.

"Therefore, I am announcing today that I am signing Executive Order Number 13627, re-creating the Civilian Conservation Corps. Its task will be to hire as many American men and women, and young people, as apply and are qualified, to help conserve our land, as its name implies. How will these modern CCC Conservators, as they will be known, work to conserve our nation? They will be trained to help our Administration implement the McAlister Act, by locating hate speech and identifying hate speakers. Once the Conservators have succeeded in doing so, the hate speakers will be charged by the Department of Justice, through our local District Attorneys, with violating the McAlister Act. Just as the CCC rooted out unneeded trees and vegetation that stood in the path of progress in the 30's, today's CCC will root out unneeded hate and bigotry that threaten to destroy our nation today. I will shortly send a request to the Congress for legislation that will fund the new CCC. The new CCC will be administered by and under authority of the Department of Homeland Security, and will be trained by its TSA, which now numbers over 50,000 federal employees, working every day to protect traveling Americans.

Several persons in the crowd were seen high-fiving each other, as they realized that they were hearing the President say they could get a job, soon hopefully, and a federal job at that.

"I can already hear the partisan critics of this Administration. They can be expected to object to this plan to employ unemployed Americans. They will say that these newly created jobs are not real jobs, that they don't involve any meaningful work. Nothing could be further from the truth, as each CCC Conservator will be hard at work in two areas. First, Conservators will help implement the McAlister Act by monitoring the many thousands of public meetings that take place in this country, every morning, daytime and night of every day of the week. As friendly faces, they will attend these public meetings, listening respectfully, making notes on what is said and reporting any overheard hate speech to their superiors for any needed legal action. This will be the 'Oversight' aspect of their jobs. Obviously, many hours per week will be required of the Conservators to fulfill this critical aspect of their work.

"Secondly, each Conservator will be trained to train others on proper and civil speech, and how to avoid violating the McAlister Act. I hasten to point out that not every hate speaker will be charged with a felony, especially on their first violation. Identified hate speakers will generally be assigned a CCC Conservator who will work with them to show them how to avoid hate speaking in the future. They will be taught how to refer respectfully to public officials, without verbal attacks. They will receive instruction from their assigned Conservator on how to respect all persons, no matter their race, their sexual orientation or their other differences. This aspect of the job of each CCC Conservator will also obviously require many long hours, fully justifying our nation's expenditure in their training and wages. Every corps functions best when uniformed, just look at the military and the TSA. Accordingly, each Conservator will be provided with attractive forest green colored uniforms, proudly bearing the official seal of the CCC. The chosen color also bears witness to our Administration's commitment to a green economy and preserving our environment.

"Lastly, let me just say that I see a bright future for America under the guidance of the new CCC, just as the CCC helped this nation exit the difficult economic times of the Great Depression. Many Americans of note originally worked for the CCC, including Admiral Rickover, pilot Chuck Yeager, actors Robert Mitchum and Walter Matthau and baseball player Stan Musial. The newly re-created CCC should likewise raise up and mentor future Americans of great note and worth to our nation. I fully expect that the CCC will help usher our nation into a joyful, civil and hate-free future. Once the CCC is established, I am sure that there will be many Americans blessed by the program and there will be other important assignments for the many competent and skilled men, women and young people hired by our nation, which only time will reveal the nature of those assignments as we move forward. Moving forward is what this is all about, which is why I am so proud of the Americans who will work together to bless our nation. God bless them and God bless America. Thanks, Asheville. Thanks, North Carolina."

The combined Asheville area high school bands were cued to launch into Sousa's Stars and Stripes Forever, which they did with a crashing flurry, accompanied by the cheers of the assembled thousands, many of whom had just caught a vision for a new job, as a CCC Conservator. It was certainly something for them to cheer about, with real unemployment in their area hovering just over 16%.

FORTY

Washington, DC – Israeli Embassy

With the adoption of the McAlister Act behind him, the President's agenda began to turn from a focus on domestic issues to the President's role in international affairs. From the outset of his Presidency, he had preferred the adulation from overflowing crowds he received whenever he spoke overseas. Having received several peace commendations and awards, the only major international prize yet unclaimed was peace in the Middle East. None of his predecessors in the White House had managed to broker a true peace in an area riven by division for millennia. True, President Carter had arranged a peace accord between Israel and Egypt, but only after he signed a written commitment pledging that America would militarily defend Israel were it ever to be attacked. Now that the United States Supreme Court had upheld the McAlister Act as Constitutional, the President turned his hand to squeezing the residents of the Middle East to do his bidding. The participants had been summoned to Washington, DC, to prepare to be squeezed.

The Prime Minister of Israel was venting in the offices of the Israeli Ambassador to the United States located in the Israeli Embassy on International Drive in northwest Washington, DC. The Prime Minister was not pleased, and for a very good reason. The Israeli Ambassador had just informed him that the President had cancelled their luncheon appointment at the White House. That's twice, the Prime Minister thought. He stood me up for dinner in his first term, now he's purposely snubbing me again in his newly commenced second term. No, he concluded, he's not insulting me, he's going out of his way to offend the nation and the people of Israel. He can do anything to me he thinks he can get away with, but when he shows disrespect to Israel's elected leader, he hurts Israel's standing in the world, which has taken quite a battering of late, in any case.

As his anger increased, the Prime Minister slowly recalled the other offenses that he had suffered at the hands of this President in his first four years in office. How could there be such a significant difference between two men who were both elected President of the same country? The Prime Minister had been widely viewed as a favorite of one of the President's predecessors in office, with frequent friendly visits to the White House, and six trips to Israel during his time in office by the former President. How could the Prime Minister forget the off the record comments by this President during a meeting with a European leader, when they didn't know the microphones in the room where they were speaking were hot. The President revealed in his conversation his true disdain for Israel's Prime Minister, using language best kept for a private conversation.

You would think, the Prime Minister concluded, that this President would be doing back flips after Israel reluctantly caved in during the President's first term. The President had exerted maximum pressure, diplomatically, financially and militarily on the Prime Minister to get Israel to agree to the general concept of a "Two State Solution". The Prime Minister had himself campaigned for office in Israel as strongly opposed to giving up any of Israel's land to the Palestinians. In spite of his campaign pledge, under intense US, UN and world pressure, he finally conceded that Israel would eventually agree to divide the land. The Prime Minister was well aware, as he was frequently lectured by his orthodox political opponents, of the verses in the Torah instructing Israel not to give up the land, and other verses warning other nations not to divide Israel's land. Nevertheless, the Prime Minister ultimately gave in, particularly as America, Israel's major supporting allied nation in the world, was leading the parade to force Israel to agree to Two States.

Everyone involved soon learned that agreeing to the general concept of dividing the land, and then signing an agreement that actually did, were two distinctly different matters. Every time the US thought that it had the outline of a land swap plan upon which all parties could agree, something always seemed to come up. The Prime Minister was embarrassed at one point when local government leaders in Jerusalem approved the building of 2,000 new housing units in an area that the Palestinians hoped to obtain under the much-discussed, but not yet agreed to, peace agreement implementing the Two State Solution. The announcement derailed peace treaty discussions for over a year. Saying that they had run out of patience, the Palestinians pushed the United Nations for full admission as a member State, which would give the newly recognized nation international legal standing to further assail Israel.

As the Prime Minister began to regain his composure, trying to decide how to respond to the media, and whether he should leave DC for Israel before nightfall, he recalled the intense global efforts to push through the Palestinians' petition for UN recognized statehood, and how close they came. If it hadn't been for the upset victory in a special Congressional election in New York State, the UN petition would have passed. The seat had been held by a Democrat for decades. When the Republican won, with a campaign assailing the President for failing to support Israel, the UN petition was dead, at least for a while. The fact that the voter demographics in the New York Congressional District were heavily Jewish was all it took to derail the Palestinians' efforts at the UN. The President wanted re-election more than he wanted a long-sought after "peace" in the Middle East. To calm irate Palestinians, the President assured them that if he were to win re-election to a second term, then he would insure that they would be successful at the UN. He didn't need Jewish voters, or any voters for that matter, once he was safely returned to office.

Israel's Prime Minister was a veteran politician. He sensed that there was more to the President's cancelling today's luncheon than at first appeared. With the President's success in passing the McAlister Act, he was in a good position to force through a new peace agreement between Israel and its neighbors, the most important since Jimmy Carter's Camp David Peace Accords brokered in 1978. Neither the Congress nor the mainstream media would likely oppose his pressure on Israel to force it to give in and give up part of its land. The White House luncheon had been planned, according to leaks, as a strategy planning session between two allies, America and Israel. The White House Press Office followed the leaks by letting it be known that the President and the Prime Minister were expected at the luncheon to agree to final steps before negotiating sessions convened at Colonial Williamsburg, Virginia.

So, the Prime Minister wondered, since the American tenderizing process of the Prime Minister was supposed to start at lunch today, why was it cancelled? Something's up, he suspected, and he doubted that it would be favorable for Israel. He was right.

FORTY-ONE

Springfield, Missouri

When Brock Simpson decided in 1979 where to locate the home office of his newly launched trucking company, he picked Springfield, Missouri. It was about half way between St. Louis and Oklahoma City, so it was perfect, he concluded, for basing his semis. When he made the decision he only had one semi-truck and trailer, but since then had grown to over four hundred and fifty. Simpson Interstate, as he eventually named it, had become a good-sized freight hauling company, with annual gross income that he never would have believed possible back in 1979. Another thing he would not have conceived of when he formed his company was that a government employee could attend a meeting of his company's Board of Directors.

The green shirted CCC Conservator had arrived at Simpson Interstate's corporate offices at 8:00 AM. He identified himself to the receptionist. He asked to speak with Brock Simpson prior to the Board meeting to convene at 10 AM, "so that I can let Mr. Simpson know why I'm attending today's meeting of his Board." Needless to say, his initial few words created quite a stir at Simpson Interstate, mostly behind closed doors. Brock Simpson's first reaction was to call in the company's in house counsel and ask him, "Who the world does this guy think he is? Look on the security monitor. He's in his nice little green CCC shirt, leafing through our lobby magazines like he has a right to be here. Attend our Board meeting? Is he nuts? This is a private company. We don't have outside stockholders. I know, I know, I reluctantly took your advice and added some outside Directors, besides the wife and our two sons, but surely that doesn't open us up to....to....what? I don't even know what to call this? Governmental inspections, without an appointment? Sticking their nose in our internal management of the...."

"Brock, if you'll slow up for a minute....and I understand why you're upset...."

"*Upset? Upset?* I'm not just upset, I'm flamin' ticked off. I'm not gonna let this CCC jerk in my Board meeting and that's that. He can set in the lobby all day as far as I'm concerned."

"Brock, I'm not arguing with you at this point. That may be what we do. But first, I'm going out and talk to this guy and see what he's got loaded in his barrel. If its spit wads, that's one thing. We tell him to pound sand. On the other hand, if it's a 10 gauge magnum shell, well....we'll just have to see. I'll be right back after I find out what we're up against."

Brock's Counsel returned from the lobby within seconds bearing a document that neither one of them wanted to read. It was a letter addressed to CEO Brock Simpson of Simpson Interstate, dated yesterday and signed by a Deputy Attorney General of the United States of America, whose office was in Washington, DC. The letter advised CEO Simpson that the bearer of the letter was none other than a duly authorized Conservator attached to the Civilian Conservation Corps who had been tasked by his office to pay a visit to his company and to set in on his Company's Board meeting, which he understood was being held on that day. That was the good part of the letter. The ominous words were found in its second paragraph which read:

260

The above designated CCC Conservator is specifically instructed at said meeting of your company's Board of Directors to record the proceedings, make notes and to obtain copies of all documents considered or reviewed by the Board at said meeting. This is all by way of further advising this office as to the legal basis for its bringing any appropriate charges against the company. Those charges, by way of explanation, but not limitation, could arise from observed violations by your company of the Lawrence McAlister Hate Speech and Hate Weapons Elimination Act. Placement of printed negative attacks against public officials on your company's over the road vehicles may constitute violation of said Act, and you are advised accordingly. If any effort should be made to prevent or impede attendance at your Board meeting by the designated CCC Conservator, this office is prepared to immediately take the appropriate legal steps to require compliance with this demand. You are so advised.

The rough and tumble trucking industry was well suited for the likes of Brock Simpson. He didn't get to where he was in the trucking business by being a wuss. Brock Simpson lacked formal education beyond high school, but had acquired more street smarts than the average business executive. At six foot and just over two hundred and sixty pounds he would, without too much provocation, yank off his jacket, roll up his sleeves and prepare to duke it out, if necessary. Even though in his sixties, he still didn't shy away from a fight. On the other hand, his in-house counsel, who was also his favorite nephew, generally could get his attention when it came to legal matters. He could instill a calming influence, largely because he had been right so often in the past and saved Brock Simpson many thousands of dollars over the years. A calming influence, however, was not what his counsel/nephew was having on Brock Simpson at this point in time.

"I don't care what the Attorney General, or his Deputy, or any other of his lackeys threaten me with....I'm *not* gonna do it. They can throw me in jail....I'm not letting this green-shirted government snoop attend my Board meeting. Not....happening. Got it? Go back out and tell him it will take more than an eight and a half by eleven inch white sheet of paper to get him or any other government goon into my company's Board meetings. That's settled."

After trying to reason with his uncle/client/employer, Brock Simpson's nephew/counsel/employee had not changed his mind. He realized he needed to bring in additional firepower, so he convinced his client to speak with the Washington, DC law firm the company used on occasion on federal regulatory issues. That conversation only took twenty minutes, during which Brock Simpson was convinced that he had no choice, he had to allow his uninvited visitor to attend today's Board meeting. He didn't like it, but he liked the possible penalties and repercussions even less.

Because of all that had taken place, the Meeting of the nine members of the Board of Directors of Simpson Interstate convened late. Brock Simpson called the meeting to order. "OK, we're convened for our monthly Board meeting. Uh....I think....uh....by now....you've probably all been told that we have an uninvited visitor here today from the CCC. I've been told to make no comments about this matter.... to just allow him to set in and record the meeting if he wants....."

"Mr. Simpson," the CCC Conservator interrupted, "I *am* recording this meeting....every.... word....spoken....Thank you."

Brock Simpson's face flushed as he fought down the impulse to throw his government visitor through the plate glass window that looked out over the company parking lot. His nephew seated next to him gently squeezed his uncle's arm. He leaned over and whispered, "Brock, don't let him get you mad, that's apparently what he wants. He's probably been told you have a short fuse."

Brock Simpson waited until he could calm down. He was on medication to control his occasional heart arrhythmia, but he knew that stress like this meeting could cause erratic heart pulse, in spite of his meds. He told himself that this was not worth a stroke or a heart attack. Just as quickly, he thought that if defending everything he'd fought for years isn't worth blowing out a heart valve, what is? Nevertheless, after swallowing most of a 16 ounce bottle of water, he moved on.

"Let's look at this month's agenda that Judy put together for us. Thanks, Judy, you always do a great job. The first item on the agenda is a review of last month's gross billings, returns and gross expen...."

"Excuse me, Mr. Simpson. Don't mean to interrupt....but....We have an item that we have been asked to bring up at today's Board meeting that appears to take precedence over the items listed on your agenda."

"Stop....STOP.... First of all, who is the *'we'* that you speak of? Secondly, what makes you think that *you* can control what we do as a Board at *our* meeting? Thirdly, what makes you think you can decide what takes....what was your word....*precedence?* Over *our* agenda items? I've just about had enough of this...."

"If I may respond, Mr. Simpson. The 'we' you asked about is the government of the United States of America, for whom I work. The importance of what I have been asked to raise at today's Board meeting is simply this. This company has a pattern and practice of displaying words, slogans, catchy phrases, if you will, on the rear-end of its many semi trailers. Those words are seen by potentially millions of Americans as they drive our nation's highways."

"So? Now you're gonna tell us what we can paint on our own trucks? Is that this is all about? A few funny phrases that your bosses in DC may not like? This is flat ridicu...."

"Many motorists, Mr. Simpson, have been offended by your latest 'funny phrase', as you put it. How does it go? Oh, wait, I can read it on the back of that semi trailer parked out there in the lot, WHAT DO THE PRESIDENT AND KARL MARX HAVE IN COMMON? You think that's a 'funny phrase' Mr. Simpson? Members of the Board?

"And what about the 'funny phrases' used in the Presidential election? IF WE GIVE HIM A SECOND TERM, AMERICA WON'T HAVE A SECOND CHANCE. Or, JANUARY 20 - THE END OF AN ERROR. Or, ONE AND DONE. Or what about the phrase you used earlier in the midst of the stimulus fight, DON'T TELL THE PRESIDENT WHAT'S AFTER A TRILLION. Care to justify any of these? Anyone?"

Brock Simpson's wife, Delilah, had labored along with her husband in building their company. Though short in

264

stature, she was not known to be a quiet or reserved person. She couldn't restrain herself and jumped in, "Mister whatever your name is....let me tell you this....this is *our* company. We will put what we want to on *our* trucks, as long as it's not profanity, of course. So you can *just....*"

"Mrs. Simpson, not to interrupt, but that's the whole point of the McAlister Act. You can't negatively attack public officials. That's a use of hate words. If hate words are used, the government can levy substantial fines, or as you may know, criminal charges can be filed. What this company appears to have done is use hate words on its trucks, in violation of the law."

The company's counsel interjected, "We don't agree that they're hate words or that they are illegal in any way, but McAlister wasn't effective in earlier years, nor in the recent election cycle. So there could be *no* liability for...."

"We'll let the Department of Justice lawyers figure all that out, counsel. But, there's no question, in our opinion, that the words I am reading on your truck as we sit in this conference room today are hate words, they violate the McAlister Act and your company should be fined in a large enough amount to make you stop violating the law. If that won't work, then stiffer penalties can be filed, as we all know. I don't have anything else really to say, except that I see looking down to item six on your agenda that there is this entry, DISCUSSION OF IDIOTIC TRUCKING REGULATORY CHANGES PROPOSED BY THE WHITE HOUSE.

"That could easily be construed to be hate words, calling the nations' CEO an idiot, and also in violation of the McAlister Act. You can be sure I'll include that in my report and recommendations to the DOJ....I'm done. I just hope this company, after it is penalized, sees the light and decides to comply with today's laws. It's not 1979 anymore folks. This is a new era."

After the CCC Conservator left the room, Brock Simpson said, "I think what he should have said is that we're living in a new *error*. Who would have ever thought it would come to this? God have mercy on us."

FORTY-TWO

CIVILIAN CONSERVATION CORPS

CONFIDENTIAL MEMORANDUM

FROM: CCC CONSERVATOR DON OWEN
      Badge Number CCC-45683

SUBJECT: Surveillance of SIMPSON INTERSTATE, INC.
         and Recommendations for Fines/Charges

Summary of Surveillance - This Conservator was tasked by directive of DAG Scott to attend a monthly Board of Directors meeting of SIMPSON INTERSTATE, INC. based in Springfield, Mo. See the corporate jacket for details concerning this mid-sized interstate freight hauling company.

Upon my appearance at the corporate offices, without advance notice, of course, I was initially rebuffed by employees of the company. Once I presented the directive letter from our DAG, I was eventually allowed to attend the Board meeting. It started late. Present were all nine Directors, which includes the founder and CEO, Brock Simpson, his wife Delilah, and two sons.

To say that the meeting was contentious would be an understatement. Things did not go well as soon as I raised issues with slogans and phrases placed on Simpson trucks over the last three years. They don't have even an elementary understanding of the McAlister Act's restrictions on negative attacks on public officials, in my opinion. If not significantly fined, or worse, I don't think the company will ever come into compliance with McAlister. The company's CEO, Brock Simpson, and his wife, Delilah, were both in my face and refused to take instruction on how to meet the requirements of the law. They also had an agenda item that referred to the President as an "idiot", or words to that effect.

Recommendations - Accordingly, I would recommend as follows:

A. Levy a maximum fine on the company for its current violation of the hate speech law based on words currently being carried on some of their trucks (see transcript of surveillance meeting for details). I would suggest fining them $250,000 per day of violation, or $50,000 per truck, whichever is determined to be greater. The company will hire DC counsel, of course, to fight the fines, but legal fees alone will quickly run them over $500,000. That should shut down any more anti-administration slogans on their trucks. Brock and Delilah, you should have listened.

B. Speaking of the two principals of SIMPSON INTERSTATE, INC., if they decide to make a public fight over the fines, which they may well do, based on what I witnessed, I would strongly suggest sending a referral for criminal charges for violation of McAlister to the DOJ for both Simpsons, and maybe the entire Board, though I know that if more people are indicted that raises some enhanced proof of involvement issues. If Mrs. Simpson is facing charges, I suspect that Mr. Simpson will fold his tent, and do anything he can to protect his wife. Charges should only be filed if they decide to take us on, but if they do, we should not hesitate to end the fight quickly by filing criminal charges. Word of the Simpson Interstate fines will spread fast and shut up the other companies that like to use their trucks as traveling billboards for anti-Administration diatribes. It's time to get this done.

FORTY-THREE

East of Billings, Montana

"What kind of name is *Gunning*?" How many times had Gunning Bedford, Jr. heard this question, as a child, even as an adult? What made the name even more unique was the well-known fact in Montana that Gunning Bedford, Jr. was the organizer and President of Montana Gun Owners for the Second Amendment, Inc. 'What a great name for a gun supporter', Gunning had often heard. But, of course, he didn't select his name. His father had been named Gunning Bedford by his father, because as a student of American history, and a conservative, he admired Gunning Bedford, Jr., a Delaware Delegate to the Constitutional Convention of 1787, where he was an advocate of small states and limited federal government power. Gunning's dad, unable to think of a better name, bestowed the name of Gunning Bedford, Jr. on his son.

That son just couldn't get over his President desecrating, in his view, an iconic American patriot monument at Old North Bridge in Concord, Massachusetts. He had been wrestling for several months, since the McAlister anti-gun bill had been submitted in Congress, with what he should do as a leader in the Montana gun rights movement. Montana had two U.S. Senators, of course, and only one Member of the U.S. House of Representatives. All three, as would be expected, were adamantly against the McAlister Bill, and had given numerous speeches across the State rallying voters. So, there was little more politically they could do in Montana. Gunning had an internal 'itching', he later called it, to do something more, anything, to try and stop Congress from passing the McAlister Bill. But, what to do? He had spent hours patiently enduring long meetings, and then more hours of late night meetings with what he affectionately called his 'posse', the fellow members of his Montana gun rights organization. They saw the danger coming, they followed the news every day, they knew they could lose their right to keep and bear arms, no matter what the Second Amendment to the Constitution said, but they didn't know what else they could do.

Some argued for armed resistance. Others cited the Biblical admonition to submit to earthly authorities. Some said that Congress would never pass the bill because the White House didn't have the votes. No conclusion was ever reached. That is, until Gunning Bedford, Jr. saw his President desecrate the Minuteman monument at Old North Bridge in Concord, while celebrating the end of the Redemption Period under the anti-gun law. Gunning thought that the official Presidential ceremony at that particular sacred location went too far in rubbing the nose of gun owners in what the government had done to their right to own firearms. Since he couldn't get it off his mind, he knew he had to assemble his posse of friends and supporters to talk about it.

The posse's planning meeting took place in the basement of a small church several miles east of Billings. It was chosen for security reasons, as some in the group felt that the ATF had been watching the group's leaders' movements, especially after the McAlister Bill had been adopted by Congress. Only twelve of the several hundred in the pro-firearms association were invited. Each had been known by Gunning for at least twenty years. The last thing he wanted was a leak of any sort, in that what they were going to discuss had law violation implications.

After the eleven men and one woman had assembled at the church, Gunning prayed for wisdom and direction. Gunning was the natural leader for the meeting and of his gun owner association. He was widely admired by gun owners in Montana. Not just because he looked so much like Gary Cooper, tall and lanky, with leathery skin and studious eyes, but also because anybody who had ever spent any time with Gunning knew that he was a man of character. He obviously was an American who believed in bedrock principles. Some thought those principles were dead and gone, but not Gunning, and not his posse. He started the meeting by asking, "Did anyone else throw up when they saw the President and ATF Director at the Old North Bridge?"

Mark Cimarron, the most vocal member of the assembled group, readily agreed. "I fully expected the bronze Minuteman to prime and load the musket he's been holding for two hundred years."

"How many of the colonials are turning in their graves over what we've become as a nation?"

Doug Sanchez, probably the most excitable member of the association, agreed. "I didn't throw up, Gunning, but I did get sick at my stomach. The gall of those guys…it was…it was like thumbing their noses, not just at gun owners, but at anyone since 1776 that has possessed a firearm. I don't think we can let it pass, I really don't. If you guys don't want to do something, something meaningful, than *I will*, on my own." Doug had long ago shaved his head to a shiny baldness, which he kept that way, because he liked the effect it had on others. He didn't much care what anybody else thought of him. He liked to say, "It's the principle of mind over matter. I don't mind, so it doesn't matter".

Gunning knew that his posse wouldn't like how the Administration celebrated the end of the Redemption Period. What he didn't know was what they would want to do about it, and how serious that action might be. He did know them well enough, and for long enough, to know that they would want to take some form of action. What action was the question?

Doug continued, "Look, we've got to do something, we need to take some action, something that will capture people's attention, to show that we don't agree with what's happened to our gun ownership rights. As of today, we're all *felons*, along with several, I hope, million more American patriots who didn't kiss the boot by giving up their guns. Felons, who, if we're caught and convicted, will spend the next ten years in the hoosegow. So, how could it get much worse than that, no matter what we do?"

Betty Jean was the sole female gun owner present. She represented many of her gender who valued the right to protect themselves with a firearm. Betty Jean had lived a tough life, losing a husband she dearly loved, but moving on with her life, always willing to help out another Montanan in need. Though short in stature, she was seen by most as a typical cute western cowgirl. She was usually seen in boots, jeans and a buckskin vest, because that was her approach to life, nothing fancy, just western to her core. Betty Jean jumped into the discussion. "I agree with Doug. The end result of such a lengthy sentence is that it encourages unlawful behavior, because, by contrast, prison terms for civil disobedience or public disorder type crimes can't be very long. Certainly not several years."

Doug responded, "Betty Jean, I'm not restricting what I want to do to just some 'public disorder'."

"Oh....well, Doug, I won't be part of violence or....taking any lives."

"I'm not necessarily talking about that. I just think we need to send the strongest message we can, without any deaths or injuries, to the federal government, that we're not going to take it. We need to forcefully communicate that we still have our firearms, and we're going to keep them."

Gunning was skeptical, "Like what kind of message?"

Mark didn't immediately reply. He looked away, then said, "I've been thinking for some time, once Congress passed and the President signed the McAlister Bill into law, about what we should do. I'd considered disappearing into the wilderness for as long as I could survive. Eventually, I decided that I shouldn't have to run and hide, in my own country. Then, I started thinking about taking a stand against the new anti-gun law in such a public way that the country might wake up, and....and...that's where I always stalled. So what if we captured the attention of the nation, or even of the world? Finally, I realized that I can't control the outcome, how people react. All I can affect is what we do to show that America, or at least many Americans, aren't going to just roll over and voluntarily give up our guns, to show that we won't willingly surrender our rights. They can pass laws, but we can prove that there are still Americans with some guts."

Gunning suspected that Mark was about to lay out a plan. So, he nudged him. "What's the plan, Mark?"

"It's really quite simple. We take over the Montana State House in Billings, using our now illegal firearms."

"What?" Betty Jean thought she hadn't heard him accurately. "Take over the Montana State House? Isn't that...like...armed rebellion?"

"The occupation of the State House will be symbolic. The State House is the visible, physical symbol of the power and authority of the people of the great State of Montana. It will mean something, believe me, it will mean a lot more than just something. We've all watched on television those Occupy folks, all over the country, as they took over parks....and streets, even Wall Street....and buildings. They received a lot of attention, and they didn't really have a message, not one that most of us could understand. We've *got* a message."

Gunning wanted to know what the others thought of Mark's proposal, the idea of which didn't really surprise him, because he had actually had a similar idea a few months back as he watched televised coverage of Occupy groups in New York and other cities. "So what do you guys think?"

A member from Bozeman was less than excited by Mark's plan. "I get the symbolism, but I don't get how it ends. We surrender? We go to jail? We escape after we make our statement?"

"All three."

"What does that mean, all three?"

"Fifteen or so of us take over the State House, probably on Saturday, when the only person there is a guard who's probably on Medicare. We make our statement over the weekend, then, late Sunday night, most of us will adios, leaving 3-4 of us who are willing to take the fall, plead guilty and spend some time in the slammer, where we get even more media attention. Prisoners of conscience for the

274

Constitution. The sentences shouldn't be too long for civil disobedience. I read that most of those Occupy people that were arrested didn't even spend a night in jail. Maybe we'll get a fair jury or an impartial judge. Most everybody around here is really upset by this law, and furious about by the way it was passed and confirmed."

Betty Jean was beginning to warm to the plan. "So, what will make it work is that at first no one will know whether we intend to continue the occupation? They won't know if we will we continue holding the State House? It's the uncertainty that will drive the story. Do these gun patriots intend to take over the *actual government* of the State, not just its main government building? Are they trying to replace the government? It's the uncertainty."

Mark now had at least one convert to his plan who could see the value of the State House seizure. "Yeah, that's pretty much it. I know it's as strong as a garlic malt, but anything else that I've thought about just seems wimpy in comparison. Some of us will be gone for a while, after it's over, but what's freedom worth? Look at what happened to the guys who signed the Declaration of Independence. Most of them lost their families, their careers and their assets. But look what we got as a result? A free country. Maybe we can repeat that....or not....This isn't a foolproof plan, obviously. Lots of things can go wrong."

Gunning had to agree. "I'll say. For example, the most obvious problem is how do those who are vamoosing get out of a building that will obviously be surrounded as soon as they know what we've done?"

Mark hesitated in his answer, thinking how he should respond. "OK.....let me just say....that there is a way to do it.

Even though I obviously trust all you guys, and Betty Jean, of course, I....would rather....let's just say I know of a way out that hardly anybody knows about. If we decide to do this, I'll get into the details then."

"Mark, you can't just ask people to take over a government building, promising them they can escape, without telling them how."

"True that....but I want to know we are going to do this first, OK?"

Gunning, sensing that Mark needed some support, said, "Mark, I agree that something this sensitive can wait, for a little while, but the members who agree to go in will have to be fully briefed and give their consent, once they know the details."

"Of course, no problem."

Doug had been fidgeting in his chair throughout the discussion. He was well aware that everyone else attending the meeting saw him as a bomb thrower, the most violence minded in the organization. He suspected he had been invited to the planning session to represent the members of the gun owners association who felt strongly about going to arms to protest attempts to take away those arms. Unable to keep quiet, Doug jumped in the discussion, "So, are we going to do it, or are we just going to blather on and on about doing it? Are we going to seize control of our State's Capitol? My vote is yes....double, triple yes. Frankly, I'd go a lot further than Mark in making our point about this unconstitutional, evil anti-gun law, but I'm willing to give it a try. If those radicals in DC want my guns, they can come out to Montana and take them from my cold dead hands, in the Rotunda of the State House. *I'll never turn them in.*"

Betty Jean realized that Doug was saying he would be taken with his guns, which meant a felony charge, plus a sentence for occupying a government building. "Doug, hold on. I thought we were just talking about maybe thirty days, up to a year max, for a public disorder type charge. I can live with that. But, I'm definitely not too excited about ten years for illegal gun possession. I've got two grandkids."

"I understand. I'm willing to be the only weapon bearing occupant, if it comes to that. Look, we can't just do a 60's style sit in, arms linked, singing *We Can Overcome*. This fight is about firearms, and its firearms we have to carry into the Capitol to make our point. Several of us could carry weapons into the State House, letting them be seen through the windows, so that it's known this is an armed occupation. Or we could broadcast it on YouTube. Then, except for me, everyone can dump their weapons on top of a *Don't Tread on Me* flag in the Governor's office, or the Rotunda, or wherever. Alternatively, 'cause I know you don't want to give up your guns, so take them with you when you adios. Any of this make sense? Who here still has some guts?"

There was an extended silence as the gun owners who were gathered in the basement of a small Montana church chewed on what had been said. Every person in the room, all veterans of the fight to keep their gun rights for most of their adult lives, knew the stakes of what they were discussing.

Gunning spoke up first, "While everybody's thinking, there's one other subject we have stepped around. What happens if it turns into a gun battle, if we're fired on? Do we return fire? Do we really want to go down that road?"

The silence this time was even more extended. No one really wanted to consider this question. As owners of firearms they had a high regard for how they can be used, for good or ill, depending on the user's intentions. For a while it seemed that no one was going to speak.

Finally, Doug spoke up, clearing his throat, looking each person in the eye, "I don't want to hurt anyone, nor will I. We're not going there to initiate a fire fight, so we don't even have to consider that. But, as for Gunning's question about returning fire if we're fired on first, that's a significant question....I mean....oh, crud, guys, you all know what would happen if somebody tries to kill you. Self-defense is the most basic human right, so I....."

Betty Jean interrupted, "Apparently not a right at all any more in this country, since we can't legally carry to defend ourselves. So, even though I agree that we should be able to defend ourselves, if we do so using an illegally owned firearm, we'll be dead meat, d....e....a....d."

Mark, the dutiful husband he was, raised the question of what their spouses might think. "Gunning, we're all going to need some time to think and pray about all this, obviously. There's a lot at stake and we want to minimize mistakes. Some of us have spouses we need to talk to about the possible outcome of occupying the State House. This is something that will require at least their consent."

Not able to reach a consensus, Gunning adjourned the meeting, promising to meet in a different location, for security reasons, the following week. The members of the Montana gun rights association left the church each bearing a significantly bigger burden than when they arrived.

FORTY-FOUR

Denver, Colorado

The ATF is not many Americans' favorite federal government agency, particularly of those who own firearms. In 1862 Congress created an Office of Internal Revenue in the Department of the Treasury to collect taxes on spirituous beverages and authorized the hiring of three detectives to pursue tax evaders. The successor Agency has grown considerably through the years, now with 25 field division offices scattered across the country. In 2003 the Homeland Security Act transferred the law enforcement functions of the ATF from the Treasury Department to the Department of Justice. The role of the agency has greatly expanded through the years, most notably after 9/11.

The ATF Denver Field Division is responsible for Colorado, Utah, Wyoming and Montana. The number of agents at the Field Division office is not a matter of public disclosure. The ATF Special Agent in Charge (SAC) of the Denver Field Division was Rodney Stinson, a 23 year veteran of the agency, with numerous service citations and agency awards. Stinson was known in the agency as a no nonsense agent, committed to enforcing firearms laws and cutting no slack if even a margin of doubt existed. That was the likely reason that he was affectionately known, behind his back, as Iron Rod. Mindful of his nickname, Stinson carried his tall lean frame rigidly, never suffering gladly any fools, and rarely smiling. Iron Rod had an image to maintain.

The report from an undercover agent in Billings that Doug Cimarron was seen arriving at his house just past midnight the night before raised Stinson's eyebrows.

"What the heck was Cimarron doing out that late? He doesn't drink, so he wouldn't have been at the bars in Billings. He doesn't have a family, his ex lives in California and they never had any kids. No known relatives to invite him over for an extended evening. So, what's going on? Send Pete up to Billings, tell him to be prepared to stay at least a week. I want Cimarron, and Bedford and the other top gunners in town watched, and watched closely. Look for evidence of meetings, especially if they seem to be concealing the fact that they are meeting. I'm not worried about three guys having coffee at the drugstore. But, in light of McAlister, I've been expecting something from these anti-government types. They've been too quiet in my view. I want regular reports. We could have a problem."

SAC Stinson usually had an accurate sixth sense about trouble, so when he was worried, the stress level in the Denver ATF offices climbed dramatically. All the ATF offices had been on a high alert status since the McAlister Bill was first filed by Senator Blevins. There had been an increase in the number of anonymous telephone threats, more bags of excrement left at ATF doorsteps than normal and two credible leads to possible shooters, bragging to buddies that they would take out an ATF agent to show DC what they thought of the anti-gun bill. Both leads were quickly followed. One proved to be 'all blow and no go', as an internal ATF Memo phrased it, and once confronted, quickly recanted any real intentions, vowing to never mention the agency, or the gun issue again. On the other hand, the second lead did develop into charges quietly being filed, the suspect incarcerated and the danger averted. All with no media attention, as the agency didn't want to encourage any copycat acts. It also preferred, following White House direction, to foster the public perception that Americans generally supported the McAlister Act. Any events of public resistance were to be marginalized as outside the mainstream and perpetrated by radical extremists.

Iron Rod Stinson had prepared his agency's regional office to be ready for an organized effort to show opposition to the McAlister Act. In doing so, it quickly became apparent that his agents would be overwhelmed if the protestors were even minimally organized and armed. There were myriads more fervent gun rights supporters in his region than ATF agents. He knew that even if he added regional FBI agents and employees of federal and state agencies with some level of law enforcement authority, his team could still be out-gunned, and almost assuredly would be. Based on that determination, SAC Stinson asked for a face to face meeting in Washington with Director Humless, to present the Director with what would turn out to be a more than a controversial idea.

99 New York Avenue in the nation's Capitol is the headquarters of the ATF. The Director's spacious offices were familiar to Stinson, as he had attended several Field Division SAC meetings in this room. Nevertheless, he always considered it an honor to be physically present at the center of power of one of the nation's most powerful agencies.

"Special Agent Stinson, I continue to hear good things out of Denver. Your monthly numbers have been quite good. Now, to what do I owe this visit to Washington, the universal font of wisdom and knowledge?" Director Humless was known for his cynical attitude towards the DC culture, even though he was an integral part of it.

"Director Humless, this is a touchy subject, but the agency needs to be ready for what I think may soon develop in some of the more gun militant states."

"And what would that be?"

"Organized resistance, Director."

"We don't have anything on that, anything that's concrete, that is. Plenty of rumors, but whenever we run them down, it's generally been some bozo blowing off in a bar. You know the type, telling their drinking buddies, 'We're gonna take 'em down. They can't take away our guns.' Have you picked up something concrete in the Denver Field Division?"

"No, Director, nothing you could nail down, but I have a pretty accurate sixth sense, and I think we're going to have a problem in our part of the country. The reason I came to see you is simply because *if* we do have a problem, we aren't armed and staffed to respond appropriately."

"What does that mean?"

"We'd be out-gunned. We could lose some good agents, if we aren't prepared. And, frankly, that's why I asked for a private session."

"OK, go on."

"We've got to find a way to get around the posse comitatus statute."

"What? Rodney, is the air that thin in the mile high city? You know that the armed forces can't be used for domestic law enforcement. That law goes back to after the Civil War, it was part of the political deal to get federal troops out of the southern states. There's no way that the President can authorize federal troops to be used, no matter how serious the domestic insurrection."

"Director, I knew what you would have to say. I've had the same response myself when I've been asked. But....and this is a big but....we really need to be able to use the nation's military to nip this domestic insurrection thing in the bud, before an initial success leads similar groups across the country to do likewise. I don't want to over emphasize this, but what we are hearing from our undercover agents is that the anger and pressure are building and could easily lead to something this nation hasn't seen since the Civil War, when people shot other people because they disagreed with the government."

"I may grant you that the need for the use of the military may be upon us soon. I'm fully aware that most of the field division Directors are unofficially concerned that local and State law enforcement won't be willing to oppose their neighbors, if trouble starts. I'm getting somewhat frightening reports from almost every field division. But, we still have the insurmountable problem of the posse comitatus law that's still on the books."

"With all due respect, the Second Amendment is still on the books, and that didn't seem to stop this Administration. But, without getting into all that, I think I've come up with a way around the posse comitatus problem."

"Oh? I'm open to suggestions. I don't want to be part of a government that gets overthrown by gun-wielding zealots."

"It's simple, really. The actual text of the posse comitatus statute only prohibits the use of Army and Air

Force troops, believe it or not. Read the statute. The Navy and Marines are only restricted by a Department of Defense directive issued in January 1989. The Coast Guard is exempt. It would only take the signature of the Secretary of Defense to allow the use of U.S. Marines to oppose a domestic insurrection. There would be *a lot* of screaming, but once the Marines put down the rebellion, that should dry up all the other gunners that are out there right now, hatching their plots. Who wants to argue with a leatherneck, or worse yet, a bunch of leathernecks? We've got to be proactive to avoid any unopposed uprising from spreading across the country."

Director Humless and Division Special Agent in Charge Stinson probed how the lifting of the restriction on the use of U.S. troops would work, what the pitfalls might be and how feasible Stinson's plan was politically in this President's second term. Finally, Stinson asked, "Director, are you willing to raise this with the White House?"

"Rodney, let's just say that your proposal to deal with insurrection will be considered at the highest levels of our government. I think your plan might possibly get approval, especially after what you and other SACs are picking up out in the boondocks. But, if it doesn't come to anything, we *never* had this discussion."

"*What discussion?* Thank you, Director Humless, for your time."

FORTY-FIVE

INTERNAL MEMO
SIMPSON INTERSTATE, INC.

TO: VALUED EMPLOYEES-SIMPSON INTERSTATE, INC.
FROM: BROCK SIMPSON
SUBJECT: CORPORATE CHANGES — OWNERSHIP & MANAGEMENT

As many of know, we have been visited recently by an agent of the federal government. We didn't invite him. He just showed up. Why was he here? Not for what you might think. It is well known in the trucking industry that our government, federal, state and local, highly regulates what we do and how we do it. Drivers, vehicles, hours of operation, charges, weights, use of electronic devices, hazardous materials, intermodal equipment, logbooks, visor cards, emissions, etc., etc., etc.

I'm become somewhat accustomed to federal regulations, however, but what I will never get used to is the government telling me what I can paint on my trucks. As long, as it's not obscene, what right does the government have to tell Brock Simpson what I can place on Simpson Interstate trucks? Well, that's the unanswered question after we were visited by a "CCC Conservator" a couple-three weeks ago. You know these green-shirted guys and gals, you've seen them on the streets and in the malls, I hear they're even in our churches. Now they even come to private companies' board meetings.

They think they can enforce that new so-called anti-hate speech and so-called anti-hate weapon bill, by just their word alone. If they don't like my words, or the words on my company's trucks, they supposedly can just tell me and I've got to do what they say. If they don't like my words they can fine me and my company a gazillion dollars. If I fight the fines, well, that will cost me another gazillion dollars paid to my lawyers. Great system, hunh?

What if my independent American spirit tells me that I won't do it? What if I tell them to get lost, I'm not paying their exorbitant fines and I'm not changing my words on my trucks? That's where it gets really frightening. If I don't pay, and I fight them, they can file criminal charges and try to imprison me, or my board members (including my dear wife and sons). All just because they don't like what they call "negative attacks on public officials". What a load of baloney (my wife cleaned this part of my memo up).

So, why I am I writing you, the employees who have made this company a success through the years? You deserve to know that I just signed a Letter of Intent to sell Simpson Interstate to a Minnesota freight company that's slightly bigger than we are. I asked for job security, as much as one can expect in today's market, for those of you who have been with me for five years or more. The final contract will spell it all out, but it looks like that part of the deal will be included. I'm telling you this now because word of this sale will leak, it always does, and I don't want our best people jumping ship. It looks like most of you will be OK with the new owners, and not too much should change.

One quite obvious change, of course, will be that the Simpson family will no longer be running the store. We'll miss you all, and we'll never forget how hard you all worked to put us where we are today. Do I have to sell? No. I could stay and fight. I thought long and hard about doing just that. Most of you know I hate to lose and I don't give up. Like Churchill said, right? "Never, never, never give up."

But, Winston, sometimes you gotta decide what's most important in life. When my attorney told me that my wife, Delilah, who is a company officer and director as you may know, could be charged with crimes for what I put on my trucks, I knew I could never live with myself if I let that happen. So, Mr. President and your fellow bureaucrats, you win. No more words you don't like on our trucks, which will now belong to a company that fully understands what they won't be allowed to do, after our experience.

What are we going to do now? I've located a medium sized trucking company in New Zealand for sale at a decent price. I understand that they speak a form of the English language there, that the people are great and that the nation believes in free enterprise. I'm looking forward to it. Come visit us and the Kiwis. See ya all down the road! Brock (and Delilah)

FORTY-SIX

Journal Entry / Letter from Jail - November 12th

To know Ralph Snyder is to love him. Sort of. I think.

Why the ambivalence you might ask? Good question.

Ralph is now one of my best friends, but it wasn't always that way. As I mentioned earlier, as you know, journal (they say you've been in stir too long when you start conversing with inanimate objects, like diaries and journals), I met Ralph at that Rotary meeting where I met Fred Rose, who wasted no time introducing me to the Lord. Fred invited me to his Bible Study and Ralph asked me to attend an organizing event, the same week, for a new political organization in east Texas. I'd never heard of a tea party, except the obvious ones, like tea and crumpets with the Queen, or with the Mad Hatter in Alice in Wonderland.

I soon found out at the meeting held at the American Legion Hall that crumpets were not what they had in mind. No, but they were interested in hot water. But not for brewing anything, except exit parties for the politicians who were increasingly getting our country into the soup. How's that, journal, for a mangled mixed metaphor? (Another sign of slammer fatigue is laughing at your own pitiful jokes.) Well, you get the idea. There were about twenty or so east Texans there and I can quite honestly say these folks were the most serious people I had met in a long time. I don't mean that in a negative way. They had a sense of humor, they recognized what they were up against, but they were obviously willing to sacrifice, really sacrifice, their own time and treasure to try and rescue the nation before it was destroyed by people without any apparent self-control when it came to sound fiscal public policy. Serious folks.

Ralph, as it turned out, was the main instigator of that organizational meeting. He called the meeting to order and simply stated that America was on an unsustainable path to destruction of its currency, its economy and our way of life. He said that since the dollar is no longer the world's reserve currency, the price of about everything has shot up. He told us that China owned the U.S., because it was buying billions of dollars of our debt. He said that almost 40% of what Americans spent every year in goods and services is subsidized by other nations picking up our debt instruments. He asked what will happen when they open the bond window some day at the U.S. Treasury and no nation wants to buy any American debt?

Others added additional horror stories of excessive federal debt and spending on all manner of wasteful and frivolous projects. One lady said she didn't think being in debt 15 trillion dollars plus is what any of the founders of America conceivably thought the central government would ever be doing, even adjusted for inflation. Which is another point someone made. He said that since the time that Congress created the Federal Reserve System, which is owned by private banks, and allowed it to issue the official U.S. currency, the value of that currency, due to inflation, has fallen by 95%. Not a very good record of accomplishment, we all agreed.

Once we had gotten our concerns off our chests, Ralph asked who was willing to actually do something about it. Everybody there raised their hands and the Tea Party movement in east Texas was born. I guess I may have mouthed off more than my share, because when it came time to organize formally, I got elected President of our east Texas group. Well, it didn't take long for other Tea Party organizations to spring up across the State of Texas. Then, Ralph coordinated a meeting in Austin of the leaders of the various local Tea Party groups.

By the end of the week end we had a full-fledged state-wide Tea Party organization. Yup, journal, you guessed it, yours truly running my mouth again, I ended up as Co-Chairman of the State Tea Party group. I wouldn't be using a stainless steel toilet today if I had managed to miss that Austin organizational meeting, which eventually led to my October 22nd political speech, oops, wrong title evidently, as the President and half of DC call it my Austin Hate Speech.

But that speech was no such thing. I still marvel at how I can be an enemy of the state for engaging in political dialogue about issues of the day. But, of course, almost all political prisoners could say the same thing, whether they are imprisoned in China or Cuba or the Sudan or any number of nations that allow speech suppression. We all got this elevated status by saying what we think, when what we think wasn't acceptable to the powers that be.

So, how did I get here? Whenever Ralph visits me, which is as often as he is able with his busy schedule, I remind him that I'm here because of him. We both get a good chuckle out of it. We like to spend time trading jail house humor. Ralph told me once he had seen a sign on a bail bond agency on the way to my prison that said, "We'll Get You Out of Jail, If It Takes Twenty Years". One of my favorites was about the dad who wrote his inmate son and said he didn't have anyone to till the garden now that his son was in jail. His son wrote back and said 'don't do that dad, that's where I buried the bodies'. The prison censors read the letter and alerted the local police who dug up the garden trying to find the bodies, which didn't exist. His son then wrote his dad, and said, 'that's the best I could do from here, Dad, enjoy your garden.'

Most prison humor, I'm sorry to say, isn't that clean. Things can get out of hand in a setting like this, and this is one of the better federal prisons.

So, if you go to a Rotary meeting and meet two guys for the first time, one may lead you to the gates of heaven, but one may lead you to the gates of the slammer. You just never know. Any way, if you get to read this someday, Fred and Ralph, love you both. You're my buddies, you're my pals.

FORTY-SEVEN

West of Billings, Montana

Gunning's second planning meeting was held at his hunting cabin high in the Beartooth Mountains west of Billings. Access was along a rock-strewn trail up a heavily wooded ravine. The cabin had no electricity, so the late afternoon to evening meeting was eventually illuminated by kerosene lanterns, giving the meeting a spectral character in keeping with the subject being discussed. The ten who gathered returned to the subject that had originally brought them together, without any preliminaries nor light-hearted banter. Gunning kicked it off.

"OK, we've had a week to talk to our spouses, pray and agonize. We've lost two of us who both told me that their wives put the kibosh on their joining us. I'm assuming the rest of us have spousal consent?"

No one spoke up. Gunning waited an extra few seconds just to be sure.

Betty Jean finally spoke up. "Look guys, as you know, Bill's gone, so I don't need any spousal approval. But, I do want to throw in our discussion some things I've been thinking about since we last met. Then, we can get on with our vote, that is....Gunning....if you're taking a vote. We need to decide on our plan, if we decide to do this thing."

"Sure, Betty Jean, what have you been thinking about? You're not getting cold feet, are you?"

"Hardly. I'm more convinced tonight than when we met last week. Let me tell you why. I've been doing a lot of thinking about this goofy gun law that they rammed down our throats, by one vote in the Congress and one vote in the Supreme Court. The only reason that we're having this discussion, the only reason that we're planning civil disobedience that might land us in jail, is the shooting last October of the three federal officials, including, of course, the President. It's now been several months. How many arrests have there been since October last year of the shooters?......That's right.....Exactly none. How could that be? The Director of the ATF gets popped, a Senator shot, an attempted assassination of the President, and NO arrests? We have the best FBI money can buy, tens of thousands of federal law enforcement agents in government agencies all over the country, and not one person, of the three or more shooters, has been arrested, indicted, named, hinted at, suspected? Come on."

"What're getting at, Betty Jean?"

"Isn't it obvious? I'm not a big conspiracy theory person, but anyone can see that they haven't arrested anyone because they either don't want to arrest anyone, for political reasons, or because it was an inside job, and the shooters are being protected."

"Awh, now, Betty Jean, isn't that kind of a stretch? There's been no hint in the media of any anything remotely like it, no reported conspiracy, no one even speculating like that."

"You expect the media to even speculate on the possibility of a put up job? I'm not saying the White House, or that blow hard Blevins, had anything to do with the shootings, but who knows who might be have been working behind the scenes and who wanted to change the outcome of the election? They were losing, you know. My history teacher told me that Jack Kennedy was behind in the polls in 1963 when he was shot, and then LBJ swamped the GOP in the following elections, it was a total wipe-out. I'm just saying stranger things have happened."

"OK, so what's your point? Are you in or out?"

"I thought it was obvious. Of course, I'm in. I don't think we should lose our right to keep and bear arms just because some group of schemers may have pulled off a history-changing shooting, and then we lose our guns because of it. One nut job overseas pops a few dozen folks, as tragic as that was, and everybody in the whole country loses their right to defend themselves? After I've thought it all through, I'm more convinced than ever that we have to make our statement at the State House. Let's do it!"

Sounding out his words slowly, very much like his look-alike, Gary Cooper, Gunning said, "Has....anyone....had any....further thoughts....about the plan? Anything we should....change, or....improve?"

Betty Jean immediately asked, "Are we sure that we want to carry firearms into the State House? We can make our point by just being there, and by what we say....why endanger ourselves....and maybe others, by being armed?"

Doug, irritation obvious in his voice, was having none of it. "*Look*, Betty Jean, the only reason I'm doing this is to show we're *serious* about not giving up our weapons. If we don't take our weapons in with us, we might as well just throw a donuts and coffee reception for the media and tell them how really, truly upset we are. That would get *zero*, *nada*, coverage. Only our guns will make our point obvious to everybody who hears about our occupation."

Gunning, seeking to defuse the emerging argument, jumped in and asked, "Wait a minute....by a show of hands....how many say we carry in our weapons?" Everybody present held up their hand, except for Betty Jean, who after thinking about it for a moment, said, "I still think it's a bad idea, but I won't stand in the way. It's okay with me. We can't get in much more trouble than those Occupy people, who apparently didn't get in much trouble for what they've been doing all over the country, including shutting down parts of cities."

"Alright.....So, then we have an agreement to adopt Mark's plan, that is, to occupy the Montana State House in Helena?" No one spoke up.

"Well, then next, we all need to know who is going to stay and face arrest and prison, and who plans to adios late Sunday night?"

Two held up their hands, Mark and Doug. Doug spoke up, "It will actually be three of us. My son is going in with us. He's going to stay with his dad, and he's willing to go to jail to protest our anti-gun government."

"How old is your son?"

"He's twenty. He's been back from Afghanistan for two months."

"His tour of duty is over? He's a civilian now?"

"Yup. He told me that he didn't go to Afghanistan to fight for America to stay free, only to come home and see those freedoms taken away. He's a good kid. Solid. Steady. He'll be a big asset in our occupying group."

Gunning asked, "Anybody object to Doug's son going in with us?" No one did.

"So, ten will enter and occupy the building. Three will stay in the State House, armed, while seven of us make our point and then we depart the building Sunday night. Mark, last week you assured us that you had a foolproof exit strategy. For those of us who plan to exit, it would sure be nice to know the details. Otherwise to be frank, we don't have an agreement."

"You're right, Gunning. Here's the plan. Here's how you get out of the State House Sunday night undetected." After hearing Mark's plan to escape the occupied State House, each agreed to civilly disobey the law by temporarily occupying the State House of the Great State of Montana.

FORTY-EIGHT

Helena, Montana – Montana State House

His somewhat worn and tarnished badge said MONTANA STATE HOUSE SECURITY. His hair was white and his shoulders were slightly sloped. His uniform appeared to have been originally purchased for a larger man. Once he reached retirement age, he had been assigned the weekend shift so he could supplement his social security income. The elderly guard preferred the weekend shift because his childhood sweetheart bride had passed on, which left his Saturdays and Sundays empty and lonely. The weekend shift this time of year was notorious for inducing sleep, as the legislature wasn't meeting and State employed bureaucrats didn't generally work outside of Monday through Friday. He was armed, but he had not been to a firing range for several years.

There are several entry doors to the Montana State House. After 9/11 it was decided that foot traffic into the building should be limited to two doors, one for the general public, with metal detectors, and one coming from the closest parking lot limited to government officials and employees, with appropriate ID. On the weekend, the general access door was padlocked. Anyone wishing to enter the State House had to access the building through the officials' door, showing their ID to the aged security guard. The guard was well known to anyone with an ID, and he was always good for a friendly welcome to the Capitol building.

Gunning Bedford, Jr. had earlier confirmed State House weekend security details with a member of his association who was employed in the Montana State Treasurer's office. He knew that the occupation would be opposed by a single aged security guard. What to do with the guard during their building occupation was a question that occupied no small amount of planning. Eventually, they decided to place the guard in a room with a member assigned who would keep watch on him and provide food during the occupation. Their plans for the guard were based on the assumption that he wouldn't have a heart attack when he first realized what was happening.

Doug and his son had volunteered to enter the State House and disable the guard. At 9 PM on Friday night Doug and his son, wearing a small back pack, both dressed in plaid shirts and blue jeans, walked up the steps of the entry limited to employees. They slowly pushed open the large carved wooden door. They were greeted by the smiling elderly guard who said, "Howdy, gents, what brings you to the State House this late on a Friday night?"

The visitors to the State House smiled back and Doug said, "Well, ol' partner, we're actually here about the anti-gun bill, don't ya know."

"Wrong place gents, you need to go a little east of here, over to DC and talk to those boy geniuses. Nobody in this building, far as I can tell, supports taking away your guns."

As Doug was talking with the guard, his son slowly edged to his right side, then with a swift move placed one hand on the guard's holstered gun, and his other hand on the guard's arm.

The move took the veteran security employee by surprise, "Whoa, watcha doing there, son?"

Doug moved to the guard's other side, securing his left arm. "Sorry, ol' partner, but we're going to have to ask you to relax and enjoy the next few hours. We're here to make a statement against taking away our guns, not to do you any harm. You'll be fine. We have some food for you and we'll find an office here with a TV, and maybe a coach, so you can be as comfortable as possible. I'm going to put these zip cuffs on you, with your hands in front, real loose, so you'll be comfortable and can even feed yourself."

"Well, boys, I sure hope you know whatcha doin'. You might have a good message, can't say I disagree with ya, but you'll go to jail, sure as shootin'."

Doug pushed the send button on his cell phone, signaling his compatriots that it was safe to follow their path into the building. They were quick to respond and pushed through the now cleared entry door, carrying several containers with firearms, food and communication devices. Within minutes the guard, with his new guard, were secured in a room off of the legislative chambers. The others decided to scout out the Rotunda and halls of the building to determine the best location for their media event, the areas that might be breached if an assault were to occur and the area from which seven of them planned to escape late Sunday night.

After some deliberation, Gunning made the final decision that the media event would take place in the Rotunda, the circular area in the middle of the State House, supporting the Capitol dome. They opened the communication case and proceeded to hook up a television camera that would broadcast their occupation message to the world via You-Tube. A large yellow *Don't Tread on Me* flag was unfurled and secured to the wall in the Rotunda. The flag, which portrayed a coiled rattle snake, was the first flag carried into battle by the Continental Marines in the

Revolutionary War. Mark and Doug, along with Doug's son, planned to stand, with their firearms, in front of the historical flag, and deliver their attention-grabbing message. The other seven occupiers would only show their backs to the camera, as they would stand between the flag and the speakers, with firearms up on their shoulders. The total picture would show a not insignificant number of Montanans willing to risk their freedom to stand up for the freedom to keep and bear arms. The stage would soon be set.

FORTY-NINE

Helena, Montana – Montana State House

"The best laid plans of mice and men oft times go astray." (Robert Burns)

"No OPLAN ever survives initial contact." (Murphy's Law on Military   Action)

Friday night at the Montana State House was quiet. Gunning's posse bedded down in various rooms, so as not to all be in one vulnerable location. They didn't think there was much of a chance that anyone would want to visit the State House on Friday night, and that assumption proved to be correct. Saturday came early. Betty Jean had prepared java and her famous breakfast sandwiches. Using the Governor's private galley to prepare the food was a special treat for her. The group's plan was to send an e-blast notice of their occupation of the State House to media in Helena and other Montana cities at 8 AM. At the same time they planned to e-blast all of the national networks, cable outlets, the large metropolitan newspapers that were still in business and the Associated Press. The text of the e-blast would read:

URGENT NOTICE TO MEDIA – A newly organized association of American gun owners opposed to the new federal anti-gun law has today occupied the Montana State House. Mark Cimarron, a leader of the group, announced that several owners of firearms, all residents of Montana, peacefully entered the State House on Friday night. No one in security was injured and are being well cared for during the occupation. The Montanans in the State House are all armed as a visible demonstration of their strong opposition to the federal law which prohibits private ownership of firearms. The occupiers of the Montana State House assure all law enforcement authorities that they will not use their firearms, as their occupation of the government building is a peaceful protest. A video statement by leaders of the occupying group of gun owners will be made available on YouTube at 10 AM this day – click on Montana State House Occupation.

At 9:30 AM, Mark, Doug and Doug's son recorded their statement for posting and viewing at 10 AM. As planned, they stood in front of the historic Colonial military flag, facing the camera, with their compatriots behind them, their backs turned to the camera, and with firearms visible. Mark spoke first.

"After the United States Constitution was approved, Samuel Adams said 'The Constitution shall never be construed to authorize Congress to prevent the people of the United States, who are peaceable citizens, from keeping their own arms.' What America has witnessed since October 26th of last year is a panicked seizure of our Constitutional right to keep and bear arms. This Congress has proven Samuel Adams to be wrong – this Congress *has* construed our Constitution to prevent the people from keeping their own arms. Hundreds of thousands of Americans have bowed to our tyrannical government and given up their arms. But, they didn't do so voluntarily. Our fellow Americans only gave up their arms under the ominous threat of prison. No free nation should so threaten its own people. Another Founding Father, George Mason, said, 'To disarm the people is the best and most effectual way to enslave them'. As free American citizens, peaceable American citizens, we are serving notice today that *we will not be enslaved.*"

Doug spoke next. His comments were video recorded immediately after Mark's. He had been warned by those who

304

knew him and who knew that he could sometimes lose his self-control to watch his words. He silently told himself to be calm and to not lose his easily lost temper. His son placed his arm on his dad's shoulder, as a comfort, and so he could exert some unseen pressure if his dad lost control.

"I'm carrying my firearm today in this official building as an uninvited visitor for just one reason. We are occupying this State House this weekend to demonstrate to those Americans who may think that we are no longer the home of the brave, that *there are still* Americans who are willing to risk jail, or worse, to advance freedom. If the federal government wants to take my firearm away from me, let them come here to the Rotunda of this building, and pry it away from my cold, dead fingers. I will *never willingly surrender my weapon* with which I can defend my family. If necessary, I'll use my fire....". Doug's son thought he knew what was coming next, a threat by his dad to use his gun, so he gently squeezed his shoulder. Doug got it, so he wrapped up his statement, "....uh, that is, nobody wants to use their firearm, unless we have to. What needs to be done? We strongly urge the Congress that just barely passed the McAlister Anti-Gun Law, to *repeal the law,* and restore freedom in this nation. That's all I've got to say, though what I just said probably violates the anti-free speech part of the new law. So be it, I'm still a free man, freely speaking my mind. God bless America."

Doug's son, still bearing his military close shaven haircut, and by far the youngest of the occupiers, was brief, "I agree with my dad, and Mark and the other brave men and women who are standing up for our Second Amendment rights. I didn't fight in Afghanistan to preserve American freedoms, just to come back home and witness those rights being taken away from us. That's it."

The camera was turned off. The recorded segment was uploaded just before 10 AM as a YouTube segment. Over the next few weeks, the segment became the website's most viewed, as millions clicked in to see the historic video.

The group's two hour advance notice to the media, was a wise move, as most media do not staff heavily on Saturdays or Sundays. Two hours was enough time to call in the major network and cable talking heads, and many prime time commentators. When the video went up on YouTube, America's media was ready. Within a short time, the various media outlets had aired and re-aired the recorded video from Helena, each overlaid with varying news story headlines:

CBS NEWS

MONTANA REBELLION

NBC NEWS

MOUNTAIN INSURRECTION

CNN

RADICAL GUNNERS IN THE CROSSHAIRS

FOX

MODERN DAY PATRIOTS FIGHT BACK

New York Times

Gun Rights Leaders Grab Control
Of Montana State House in Helena

Federal Troops Called up by White House

FIFTY

Helena, Montana – State Capitol Grounds

Colonel Carlos Jimenez was not happy about his unit's call up to Helena. As a Marine Corps officer, of course, he did was he was ordered to do, but that didn't mean that he had to like it. When he was handed his squad's mobilization order his first question to his CO was what the blank were the Marines doing involved in a domestic disturbance? Didn't the Montana State Police know how to handle trouble makers in their State? How about the Helena Police Department? And above all these issues, what about posse comitatus? His questions were ignored. Why are we here, Colonel Jimenez asked himself? Why are we entrenched in front of the Montana State House? As a military man, he found it very difficult to support the concept of taking away firearms from civilians. Worse yet, if his command structure wanted his unit to actually take down the occupiers of the Montana State House, *that* was a problem. His stated Rules of Engagement, which he was assured came from the highest levels of command and control, were to shoot to kill, if necessary. He knew what he was being ordered to do, but he wrestled with the idea of firing on his fellow Americans, especially, he thought, when you agree with their cause.

As Saturday dawned, Gunning's group quickly became aware that the building was now surrounded, not by State Troopers, but by federal troops. And not just federal troops. U.S. Marines. Gunning called his posse together and gave them the bad news.

"I'm not going to try and dress this up in any way. We have a *significant* problem. Believe it or not, we've got a front plaza full of U.S. Marines. Semper Fi. They didn't come here

307

to congratulate us on our protest. Looks like the Administration has decided to nip protests like ours in the bud. Even if they might side with us, they've got to do what the command and control structure tells them to do, including taking us all out. We are in deep doo-doo, to put it mildly.

"I'm open to ideas, but this changes our plans. When we thought we might be faced with some Montana State Troopers, most of whom are with us, many of whom we would probably know, that was an acceptable confrontation. But, *Marines*? Hello. Whose brilliant idea was it to call up the Marines, for just a simple civil protest?"

Betty Jean was known for being practical and hard-headed. She had managed dozens of Forest Rangers through the years, a group known for their independent approach to life. She had been the member of the occupying group who was most concerned about their exit strategy, worrying that if anything could go wrong, it would. She differed with Gunning's description of what they were doing as a simple civil protest.

"Look, Gunning, you know I love you to death, but this is *not* simple, it's really *not* very civil, since we're armed, and it's certainly *a cut above* a protest. A protest is marching with a sign on the sidewalk outside an abortion clinic, which many of us have done at one time or another. What we are doing here is seizing the seat of the government of our State. I'm not shocked that the White House rolled out the leathernecks. They've got to stop gun owning America from anything else even remotely like what we're doing. If we succeed in what we are trying to do, there will be copy-cat actions all over the country. They don't have a choice. Stop the gun owners in Helena or face them in Nashville and

Phoenix and Baton Rouge and maybe even at Concord Bridge, again.

"What we've got to decide, and I mean decide *now*, is whether we fold up this little weekend outing, turn in our guns, say we're sorry, we was just a funnin', or, stick with the plan, make our point, then most of us adios, except for Mark, Doug and his son, who will be left to take the heat."

Doug jumped in with both feet, "What? What are you *saying*, Betty Jean? Are you seriously suggesting that we just *give up* and turn in our guns? I'll *never*, under *any* circum...."

"Stop, Doug, stop. I'm just saying that the game has changed. We're not up against Trooper Barney Fife and his buddies, guys who would treat us decent. We're lookin' down the gun barrels of people who are trained to kill. These guys aren't here to make nice. I'm frankly surprised that they haven't breached the entrance doors already. There's nothing stopping them, and when they do, we're toast."

Mark had been listening with increasing anxiety. He didn't mind a stretch in jail, but he hadn't bargained for an armed assault on their position by the nation's best. He said, "Look, we've got to compress our plan, and do it right now. We can't wait until Sunday night for you guys to leave the State House. We may not have an hour, let alone a full day or more. I suggest that Doug, his son and I go out on that balcony or parapet, whatever it's called, now, like we talked before, and essentially give you cover, while you are exiting the way we had planned. We'll say some appropriate words, read some freedom quotes and attract the attention of the media and the Marines. You make your way out the horse tunnel that Doug knew about. After a decent interval, we'll

309

lay down our guns on the *Don't Tread on Me* flag, surrender and face the inevitable music."

Mark's reference was to a planned escape route which was constructed when the State House was initially built in the late 1800s. It was a sloping ramp that became a short tunnel leading to the basement of the State House. In the years before automobiles, Montana officials would ride their horses, or their horse drawn carriages, into the basement of the building, which was the location of their official offices, where the horses were tended and fed, until their owners were ready to leave at the end of the day. The tunnel had long ago been closed, with two large metal doors sealing off the entrance installed at an almost horizontal angle near to ground level, and in an unused portion of the State House parking lot. The doors, Doug had discovered, were chained shut from the bottom side, preventing access from the parking lot.

Upon entering the State House on Friday night the occupying group first went to the basement and located the area in which the horses had been kept a century before. The large room still showed evidence of the original stable walls. It was now used to store pallets of copy paper. They then snapped the chains with the heavy duty wire cutters they had brought with them for the task. The last thing to do was to insure that the doors could actually be opened, with three of them standing under the nearly horizontal doors and pushing together. Once access to exit the building was confirmed, those who were planning to use the exit breathed a large sigh of relief. The three who were not leaving were almost as pleased, knowing that their plan would most likely succeed.

Gunning called for a vote on Doug's suggestion to provide them cover for their exit. "If you agree with Doug that the three amigos give us cover from the little balcony thing, I don't even know what a parapet is, while we exit through the horse tunnel and across the parking lot, hold up your hand."

Betty Jean, ever the practical one, stopped the vote. "Before we vote, I've been thinking. I'm good with the balcony speech distraction to cover us, but I think we have to wait a bit. Why? When we pop up from the forgotten horse tunnel doors at the far edge of the parking lot, and try and slip away across the street, I'd like to do it so with some additional cover. I've been watching the crowds grow outside, and I think we could slip out without being seen if a handful of our buddies were standing around the area of those doors, to sort of screen us when we pop out. We can call Tom on his cell. I saw him, and some of his guys, out the window, a few minutes ago."

"Makes sense to me," Gunning replied, "Everybody agree? We call Tom, tell him to get positioned in the next ten minutes, and you three guys get ready to talk to the world from the balcony. Right after you walk out on it, we head out the tunnel. Sounds like a plan, even though it's very much a changed plan. Anybody disagree? None heard. OK. To quote an America hero, 'Let's roll'."

The balcony was on the third floor of the Romanesque building, under the Capitol dome, facing Lockey Avenue. It was mounted so that the columns on the front of the building partially shielded the parapet and the overhang of the entrance structure shadowed it so that it was not well illuminated by normal daylight. It had only been used infrequently, almost always for a swearing in, usually of the Governor of Montana, if the weather allowed. Mark, Doug

311

and his son decided that to maximize the cover they would send an e-blast message advising the media that they were about to make a public statement, and designating the exterior parapet as the location. Just before they opened the glass and walnut doors to the balcony, they could tell that the digital heads-up had worked, as the area at the base of the building was filled with cameras and reporters. They also noticed that the Marines had moved their emplacements to within about a hundred feet from the building.

The three's only disagreement, right before they walked onto the building's balcony, was whether they should bear arms, showing that they were still carrying their firearms. Mark was concerned, suggesting that they leave their arms inside, since the video already showed that they were carrying arms. Doug disagreed, and disagreed strongly enough, that Mark gave in. They then walked out on the balcony, each carrying their own rifle. Mark carried his Winchester 30-30 lever action rifle vertically, with the barrel lying up against his right shoulder. Doug carried his Marlin Model 3630 with both hands, the barrel pointed straight forward. Doug's son carried his Smith & Wesson M&P15T rifle pointed straight down, as he had been trained in the military.

Mark clicked the cell phone in his pocket, alerting Gunning and those with him that they were in position to provide cover, so that the escape from the State House could proceed. On their way to the tunnel they had placed their firearms on the *Don't Treat on Me* flag laid in the middle of the State House's Rotunda. Gunning, feeling his cell vibrate, stepped forward, into the short tunnel. As they came to the metal doors, Gunning and two of the stronger protestors stood under the right hand door, braced themselves and attempted to push the door open. Unlike Friday night, the metal door wouldn't budge. They pushed again, even harder, with no results.

"What the....the chains are cut. The stupid door won't move....not even a little. Let's try the left door...........Shoot....try again....what's going on? We can't open either door."

Betty Jean suggested, "Call Tom's cell, he's right near the doors. Ask him what's happening out there."

Gunning, with a rising sense of fear, keyed his cell. "Tom....Tom....are you near the tunnel doors? You are? Say again....I didn't get....oh, my....oh boy...we're cooked....you can't....no, of course you can't....You'd better get out of....Tom....are you there?..............They just grabbed Tom....they're Mirandizing him....crud....this is going downhill fast."

"What did he say? What's happening up there?"

"It's not good....not good....There are two Marine armed vehicles parked on top of the doors. They just arrested Tom. He thinks they were tipped to the doors when we called him to provide cover in that area. Why didn't we think of that? Of course, they would track all calls around here....and our call to Tom was all they needed to stop our escape. We're toast, gang. We've got to walk out, unarmed and face the music. But, at this point, we're still in the civil disturbance category of criminal charges, so we've made our point, and the punishment shouldn't be too severe."

What Gunning couldn't have known was what was happening at the same time on the exterior balcony of the

Montana State House. After Mark, Doug and his son, all armed, walked onto the parapet, Mark began to speak.

"As we said in our video, we are here today to protest the federal government's attempt to take away our right to own firearms to protect ourselves. Thomas Jefferson once made a statement...."

Colonel Jimenez interrupted with a barked command on his bullhorn, which echoed off of the limestone building, "Lay down your weapons. *Now.* Lay down your weapons, or we will be forced to...."

Mark, ignoring the warnings, plunged ahead with his statement, referring to his notes, "As I said, Thomas Jefferson once made a statement about firearms that directly applies to our protest today at the Montana State Capitol. Jefferson said, 'The strongest reason for the people to retain the right to keep and bear arms is, *as a last resort,* to protect themselves against *tyranny in government'.*" Our protest at the State House today is truly *a last resort*, and it's a protest, in fact, against *a tyrannical government* that has passed laws to take our firearms away from us, even though our Constitution *prohibits* the government from doing so."

Marine Colonel Jimenez, following standard firefight protocol when faced with an armed potential adversary, snapped out on his command com system to his squad, "Weapons up....Acquire targets....Hold....Hold....Hold"

Later video showed that Mark's rifle fell forward at that point, into a firing position. It was unclear whether it slipped forward and he grabbed it, resulting in it being in a firing position, or he intentionally moved it. No one will ever know, as the moment two of the protestors had Marines in their firing zone, Colonel Carlos Jimenez gave an order that he felt he had to give, though his guts wrenched as he did so, *"Take your shots....Confirmed....Take your shots....Ahw, doggone it."* Mark and Doug entered eternity due to clean mid head shots. As Doug fell, his weapon discharged, whether intentionally or not, also never to be known, sending a bullet through the upper arm of a Marine private who was at the farthest edge of their emplacement. Doug's son dropped his weapon and fell to the balcony floor for cover. As he dived for cover, a bullet shattered part of his lower jaw. Gunning and the others with him, not yet knowing the fate of their three friends, surrendered by holding their arms above their heads and slowly walked out the 6th Avenue Capitol exit doors, on the opposite side of the building. They did not yet know that they would each soon be charged with conspiracy to commit murder of a federal employee, assault on a federal employee and threatening a federal employee with a firearm. What CNBC called 'The Montana Armed Insurrection' was over.

FIFTY-ONE

Letter from Prison - Journal Entry - November 12th

I've learned in the slammer that news among inmates travels at warp speed, particularly if it involves criminal acts on the outside. Professional curiosity, perhaps? Thus it didn't take long after the Montana Standoff, as I preferred to call it, ended in a blaze of gunfire, that we all heard about it through the prison grapevine. Normally, we didn't have daytime access to a television in my wing of the federal prison, but for some reason, the word was passed down, and the guards let us go to the rec room to watch the coverage. Once I saw what happened at Helena, I figured they were eager to have us watch, particularly me, I think, as a political prisoner. They wanted me to see that resistance to the federal government was futile. That the feds would always win, always.

I don't know Gunning Bedford, Jr., nor any of the other occupiers of the Montana State House. Never met any of them, but I certainly admired their guts for being willing to make a statement. Should they have carried guns with them out on the balcony? Undoubtedly, no. That was a tactical error that cost two of them their lives. The media reports on the recently retired soldier who was shot in the jaw weren't very good, though he will live, they said. Hindsight is always really good, so we all know that they should have released their video, left their guns on the Colonial flag in the building, and turned themselves in for short stints in the vertical bars Hilton.

My heart sunk when I watched, and re-watched, the video of three brave men paying a very high price to assert their American right to keep and bear arms. The media were apparently prevented from interviewing the Marines, but the video clip showing a Marine Colonel throwing up behind his transport vehicle told me all I needed to know about his view of what he felt he was ordered to do.

Except for Fox News, I didn't see any other media question the use of the military in a domestic peacekeeping capacity. Fox's White House guy, whom I think is smart and also tough, insisted at the White House media briefing that the President's Press Secretary answer his question on what looked like a violation of the posse comitatus statute. The President's press guy hemmed and hawed, then, looking at his briefing notes, referred the media to an Order signed by the Secretary of Defense, supposedly several days ago. The Fox guy said, well, that's nice, but what does it say? Again, he answered with his nose buried in his notes, like he didn't want to look anybody in the eye. He then mumbled that the SecDef, government-speak for the Secretary of Defense, had withdrawn a prior SecDef Order that had applied the posse comitatus statute also to the Marines Corps.

I almost fell out of my metal prison folding chair. Say what? With the stroke of a pen it's okay, it's legal, to use one branch of the military in internal domestic US disturbances? The Fox guy, likewise, was visibly taken aback, and blurted out something like, "Are you serious, Mike? Are you saying that the Act of Congress in the 1800's never applied to the Marines, and now the Pentagon has withdrawn the Marines from an Order that had applied posse comitatus to the Corps? What a crock of".....or he said something like that. The President's Press guy, nodded his head, mumbled something else we couldn't quite hear, and said the news conference was over, and walked out.

Normally, that kind of performance would have guaranteed massive media reaction. But, as I wrote above, only Fox ran in a big way with the story. The lame stream media, that is the main stream media, almost totally spiked the story. Totally. It doesn't take a genius to figure out why. If the peasants and the hay shakers out in the boondocks figure out that this White House is abusing its power, they might pick up their pitch forks (they don't have any guns anymore, right?) and march on Washington. Can't have that, so they try to make it "legal" (I write the word in this letter/journal in quotes) for the military to be used against American citizens.

Who will oppose it, even if they know about it? The military won't object, they are under command and control from the Commander In Chief. The Department of Justice won't object, same basic reason, it's what the boss wants. Any private citizen would have his law suit tossed by the federal district court judge who would rule that the citizen lacks what the lawyers call 'standing', that is, no basis to be in court. Congress could expand the statute to include the Marines, but that's not going to happen, with control of both Houses by the President's party. So, my fellow American citizens (I write hoping that some will eventually read these words) you are no longer living in the land of the free. Your duly elected government has decided that if you get out of line (and they decide where the line is) you are looking at the barrel of a military gun that you bought and paid for originally to keep you free from foreign aggressors. Now, it's domestic aggressors (and even peaceful protestors) who are the new target of our military. Americans under siege in their own land. How does this differ from what Soviet citizens faced? What a frightening situation. Sorry, journal, sorry, outside reader, but I'm really, truly upset, and I think for good reason.

How did it come to this? What could we have done to prevent the wholesale destruction of our rights? Oh yeah, I know. We could have denied the President a second term. That would have done it. I tried, I certainly tried, and look where that got me. Depending on how the trial goes, I could be a free man, or, alternatively, if the White House, and its Department of Justice, and the federal judiciary (based on past court rulings in my case) have their way, I'll become a long term guest of the federal government.

One side note to anyone who may read my letter from jail.

The prison grapevine says that Gunning Bedford, Jr. is being transferred to this prison, with his case venued to the same judge who has my case. Things may be looking up, after all. Gunning and I might get along quite well.

FIFTY-TWO

Washington, DC – Cannon House Office Building

Offices of Congressman Adam Nation

Offices furnished to freshmen Congressmen are notoriously small and inconveniently located. Offices are selected based on seniority and freshmen don't have any. Among the incoming class a random drawing determines who picks in what order from the remaining bad offices. Newly seated Congressman Adam Nation had the misfortune of picking the equivalent of number 433 of 435 positions. When he finally selected his office, it was in what was originally the attic level of the aged Cannon Office Building, proven by the fact that the elevators didn't go to his level. Visitors from his Congressional District in Ohio had to be told to take the elevator to the top floor, exit, take the nearest stairwell, turn right, and look for the first office on the left. Welcome, Congressman Nation, to the U.S. House of Representatives.

The Congressman's official office was the largest room in the suite, which in total contained fewer square feet than a good-sized mobile home. When the Congressman met with his fourteen employees, there was barely enough room, but, the rent was free, the mailing address was impressive and the chances for advancement to a nicer suite of offices were high, for those who won re-election, of course. Congressman Nation had convened today's staff meeting for what he considered to be a critical purpose. How should he respond to the seizure of the Montana State House by gun rights supporters? As a leader of the Tea Party Caucus he would be asked by reporters at their afternoon news briefing, and he needed to be ready with his official position for the media.

"OK, folks, we've all heard the news from Helena," the Congressman said. "You know they'll pound those of us on the right to try and get us at the afternoon news conference to disavow the protestors who took over the State House. Mark it down."

The Congressman's Chief of Staff, who had worked for five prior members of the House, immediately chimed in, "Well, duh, of course, you have to not only disavow the protestors, you have to make it really clear that you are concerned about the questionable tactics of the pro-gun people who are opposed to the McAlister Act." His Legislative Director agreed. "Right on, you can't be seen as being on the side of the gun nuts. The media'll crucify you. Standing up for the Second Amendment is one thing, but supporting violence is another."

The Congressman listened carefully as he heard his two top staff members recommend that he attack the Montana protestors at the news conference. He was most interested, though, in hearing his District Director's views, as she was closer to his District's voters than the members of his DC-based staff. The District Director had been asked to fly to DC for this meeting. She wasn't hesitant to disclose her views.

"Look Mark, you're thinking like a voter in the District of Columbia, all wobbly-kneed over the cowboys in Montana opposing the gun bill by shaking their rifles. Out in our District people are still very upset about losing their rights to own guns and their right to criticize government officials. I understand that the Congressman's gonna' get pummeled by the mainstream media if he doesn't attack the protestors, but so what? The Montana group had the right to express their opposition to this insane bill. Maybe they could have been a bit more subtle, but it worked, we're talkin' about what they did, aren't we? If they had invited the media to join them for jelly doughnuts and conversation at a coffee shop in Billings, who would have shown up? Nobody. The media cover news. These guys made news.

"The shootings are another matter, of course. Nobody wants to see deaths in political controversies, but more and more people are seeing the shootings as either an accident or, more likely, an over-reaction by the government. Kinda like Waco, where they brought in tanks. I think the Congressman should just come out and support what they did in Helena."

The Chief of Staff left his chair, confronting the District Director by leaning over and positioning his face in front of hers, placing both hands on her shoulders, "Allie, have you totally lost your political senses? They'll label him as America's newest nut job. Time magazine will front cover him as America's latest political walnut, or worse. Our only choice is to distance ourselves from these gun rights supporters."

"I agree, the Legislative Director added. "We have to be consistent and do the same thing in the future with every protest that captures media attention". Other staff members added their thoughts, no one agreeing with the District Director's advice to support the Montana protestors.

After extended discussion, silence took over, the staff members turning to their boss, as they realized that he was no longer engaged in the debate. It was obvious that Congressman Nation was deep in thought. He was considering several ideas, many at variance with his other thoughts. If he dissed the Montana protestors, he knew he would appear to be more moderate than many in the media may have previously thought. That would score him points. If he attacked the protestors it would raise his standing with some of the more liberal members of the House Republican Caucus. If he ever wanted to rise in leadership in the House, he would need their votes.

By attacking the protestors he could probably pick up some advantage with the White House, and maybe get a push from the President for the federal highway grant for the eastern part of his District that needed infrastructure improvement. He had been told by a former Senator, he recalled as he was considering what to do, that if you don't bring home the bacon, in federal grant money, the voters will find a new 'sugar daddy' who will. That remembered thought from a former member of Congress, though, reminded him of the advice that he had received from the Congressman who came to see him after his election. What had he told Adam? He had seen many members of Congress stray, not all from their spouses, many had strayed from their core principles?

Congressman Nation had made up his mind. Now it was time to tell his staff what he would say at the afternoon news event, "Look, I'm not going to attack or even mildly criticize any American who protests the McAlister Bill, even if they used poor judgment in how they protested. There are plenty of libs, public service union guys and federal government employees to do that, let alone all the non-stop media coverage."

"But, Congressman, with all due respect, this could cost you re-election. Won't you re-consider? There's a lot riding on how you handle this."

"Yes, I know that, which is why I'm not going to cave on one of the first big decisions I am faced with making as a Member of Congress. I didn't come here to impress anybody. I'm never going to be a darling of the media. I don't care if I get re-elected. I don't care if I'm never a leader in the GOP House Caucus. I will support the protestors because they had the guts to lay it all on the line to save their rights under the Constitution. Could they have done it better, in a more acceptable manner? Of course. But since they've done what they've done, millions of Americans are beginning to see just a little bit of what it took for the guys who started this country to make it happen. It took guts. It took a personal willingness to lose it all, which many did. Attack the Montana protestors? Never. If I lose this over-exalted job because I praise Americans who took a stand to protect their Constitutional rights, so be it."

By now his Chief of Staff, believing that he was about to count six former Congressmen as his past employers, was beside himself, "But, Congressman, you just can't do that. That's not how things are done here. You have to go along to get along. I couldn't work for a Member of Congress who actually supported such hooliganism, and I think...."

"Well, Mark, I accept your resignation. You can clean out your desk. Mary, get him a bankers box for his stuff."

"But....but....I didn't mean to...."

"That's okay, your time in this office is over, and our meeting is concluded, also. Mary, stay with your notepad. I need to dictate what I'm going to say in a couple hours to the media. And let me give you the phone number of a former Congressman I want to call and thank for the best advice I've had since I was elected."

FIFTY-THREE

Colonial Williamsburg, Virginia

The large number of satellite trucks alone would have been an indication that big news was being made in this historic American village. The news trucks were clustered around the Governor's Palace, in the original structure of which a critical vote was taken for America's independence from Great Britain. The opulent building had been selected as the primary site for negotiations for peace in the Middle East, not only because of its historic setting, but because the 300 acre village could be secured from potential protestors, let alone terrorists.

The President officially convened what the White House had labeled as 'The Path to Peace Conference' with a short media statement. "In my time as President, I've been able to achieve numerous successes, but none will be as memorable as obtaining an agreement between the ancient adversaries in the Middle East. Many have tried, sometimes in good faith, to make it happen, but I'm committed to staying here in historic Williamsburg until we get the job done. We'll keep you updated as we make progress along the Path to Peace. Thank you."

Israel's Prime Minister was advised before the President's statement to the media that he would not be accorded time for a similar statement. White House staffers had concluded that if the Prime Minister spoke to the media before the negotiations began that he might lock himself into an intractable position, because of what he said to reporters. They needn't have worried, as the Prime Minister had no desire to talk to reporters. His mood was such that he didn't much care if he spoke to anyone, that is, except for the

327

President. He really wanted to talk with the President, privately. Among his listed topics to discuss was item number one. What was the real reason for cancelling last month's White House luncheon and embarrassing him with his political and governmental supporters, let alone Israel's enemies? More important than the 'Sandwich Snub', as the media had labeled it, was his high level of interest in knowing what Israel would get from the Path to Peace agreement? How would Israel's security be enhanced? What about Iran's nukes? Most critically, what could Israel expect from the US should its new treaty partners renege on the new peace agreement, and attack Israel in the future?

The Prime Minister was well aware that the eyes of the world were focused on him. He had been portrayed by US mainstream media as 'The Obstacle to Peace' and by Israeli media as 'Israel's Sell Out Chief'. He knew, though, as soon as the results came in on America's Presidential election night, what Israel would have to do. With the President safely elected to his second term, Israel would either bend to his will, or walk away from its only remaining national friend on the globe. Once his remaining questions were answered by the President, he would do what he had to do to try and protect his tiny nation from almost sure extinction at the hands of the one hundred and fifty million who surrounded Israel. He knew he would now have to sign a peace agreement, so the only question was how strong would the assurances of Israel's survival be in the agreement?

Coming off of a strong re-election vote and success in pushing through the McAlister Act, the President was sailing high. He had never been so confident in his ability to get his will, on whatever topic or issue he might choose. He wasn't seen as arrogant, his staff told him, but nightly polls did pick up a growing number of Americans who thought he was becoming proud in his mannerisms and speeches. His Chief of Staff, being a decades long friend, was selected by the White House staff as the one who could get away with advising him to tone it down a bit. Sure, things are going well now, but anything could happen in the future, the President was told. He responded that he wasn't about to take any guff from Israel's Prime Minister, whom he didn't like personally, as he had famously let the world know over an open microphone.

Though many participants were in Williamsburg for the peace talks, everyone who had followed the lead up to the event knew that it would come down to what three leaders would agree to sign. The Palestinians had privately assured the White House, in advance, that, unlike past peace efforts, they would agree to any reasonable proposal that the President could work out with Israel. They knew from his past pronouncements that the President would obtain the best agreement that they would likely ever obtain through negotiations. They knew that no other US President would do more for their cause than the current occupant of the Oval Office.

With what amounted to a blank check from the Palestinians, the President walked into his private conference with Israel's Prime Minister assured that he was about to make peace, and world headlines. The two person meeting was held in the ornate Governor's Office in Williamsburg's Governor's Palace, rebuilt in 1934 after it burned in 1781. The paneled walls featured crossed muskets and swords from America's early history.

The President greeted his guest, "Mr. Prime Minister, this has been a long time coming, for both of us, for both of our countries."

The Prime Minister was ready for almost anything that would come out of the President's mouth, so he wasted no time in getting to the core issues facing Israel, "Mr. President, thanks for hosting. Let's just get to it. I'm way over the 'Sandwich Snub', as your media called. I concluded that you were...."

"Let me just say, Mr. Prime Minister, that we have a lot more important things to talk about than who ate lunch at the White House, or didn't, as the case may be....much more important issues to discuss."

With this response, and the notable lack of even a hint of an apology, the Prime Minister immediately knew that the public cancellation of his meeting with the President, just like the prior dinner cancellation, had been calculated to embarrass and denigrate him. Not a good sign for today's negotiations he quickly concluded. "Agreed, Mr. President. So let's get on with it. How are you going to assure Israel that if we give up part of our land, we'll be secure in what remains? We haven't witnessed good results in the past after we made peace. Take Gaza, for example. We reluctantly gave up Gaza and we've had nothing but grief, and missiles and bombs, ever since. We give up land and we get bombs in return."

"Well, I'm not unmindful of your argument on this point....We can...."

"With all due respect, Mr. President, it's not an argument, it's a fact. Why should we sign, why should *I* sign, any document unless we know, with assurance, that we can live in peace and security? We all want peace, but you'll have to admit that the past behavior of our adversaries is not comforting on this critical issue for Israel."

"Mr. Prime Minister, I hear similar arguments from your adversaries, as you call them. They say that Israel just keeps building housing settlements, and expanding your presence in the land. So, both sides have....".

"Now, let's not try and compare, *again*, I might add, killing innocent civilians with building apartments, on land that we own, I might add. You can't...."

"Own? *Own*, Mr. Prime Minister? Or land that you *occupy*?"

"I wouldn't go there, Mr. President. How much of the land America owns did it 'occupy' from native Americans? Do you really...."

"We've had this argument before. We're not getting anywhere....Let me just cut to the chase....America is prepared to recommend to the parties the following. In exchange for Israel surrendering control of the designated and agreed land areas in the West Bank and Jerusalem, the Palestinian Authority and Hamas will agree that Israel has the right to exist, and that they will act to prevent any persons under their control from taking any action, of any nature, to harm any resident of Israel....that's what you've been asking for. I think we can get it done."

"Well....umh....you're *sure* the Palestinians will agree that Israel has the right to exist? That's not been their position in the past....In fact, they have specifically...."

331

"Just trust me on this. They don't want to make that concession, but I can make it happen."

"That capitulation would be, as you know, Mr. President, a significant breakthrough. But, of course, it's one thing to recognize that a nation can exist, and quite another to agree not to ever attack it or try and annihilate it in the future. What assurances, what teeth in the agreement can we expect to...."

"Let me work on that. I'm not concerned that we can make it happen. I am concerned though, that Israel may stumble over the details of the land swap we're going to put on the table later today."

As excited as the Prime Minister had felt upon hearing, for the first time, that Israel's right to exist and assurances of its security would be offered, his stomach took an instant turn upon the President raising problems Israel would likely have over what land it would have to give up. If the President suspected that Israel would have issues with the land swap proposal, the Prime Minister knew Israel certainly would object.

"What....details....are....we....talking....about? Can I just see the maps now? No surprises, Mr. President?"

"No. I've decided against either side seeing the maps early. You all get to see them at the same time. It's only fair that...."

"Whoa! Hold on, sir. If our roles were reversed and I were telling you that I wouldn't show you a map of what I was taking away from your country, say part of California or New York, wouldn't you demand the right to at least see the maps before you're asked to agree to the land being taken away?"

"Let's get this straight. America isn't up for grabs. Israel is. We're all going to agree to take away some of the land that you occupied in 1987 when Israel was invaded. What land? Why should you care, really? Land is land. You give up some dirt, and you get everyone's promises that you can live in peace on the dirt you don't give up. Simple as that."

"Simple as that, hunh? Mr. President, it's not simple. And it's not just dirt, its people's lives. People who have lived for decades on the land, and now you want to just rip them out of their homes. We could never agree...."

"*Never agree*? I told you that I would cut to the chase, so here it is. Plain and simple. Iran has nukes. Your Mossad confirmed that last year. You can't take them out, the whole world has warned you not to even think about it. We won't allow it, and you're not going to do it. Your only defense against those nukes now is that America let it be known what we will do if Iran ever uses its nukes. Israel is now as the US and the old USSR used to be, MAD, Mutual Assured Destruction, since you now both have nukes. So, Mr. Prime Minister, Israel *will sign* the Path to Peace Agreement. You *get* the right to exist, you *give up* the land we've decided you have to give up to make this deal work and you get *guarantees of security*. No more bombs, no more missiles and no more suicide bombers. Peace. Peace in our times. Finally."

In his heart the Prime Minister wasn't really surprised by what he had just heard. He knew it would come to this when he first heard ABC call the election for the President early in the morning following the closing of the California polls. The best he could hope for was to salvage something in the peace agreement being forced down Israel's throat that would assure Israel that it would truly live in peace.

"Let me go to the bottom line, also, with all due respect, Mr. President. Maybe we're not in a good position to argue about specific areas of the land that we're being forced to give up....to abandon...., but I will *never* sign a document that leaves us at risk of further attacks, more killings, more blood."

"You're wrong, Mr. Prime Minister. You *will* sign the agreement. The reason you will sign is that if you don't sign, the following three bad things for Israel will soon follow your refusal to sign. First, the UN *will* admit the newly created State of Palestine, with the rights that follow. Second, the new Budget Bill will not include any, that's *any*, US foreign aid for Israel. That's over three billion dollars this year, and every year thereafter. Third, I'll publically announce that the Jimmy Carter Memorandum of Agreement that was signed with the Camp David Peace Accords in March, 1979 is *null and void.*"

"What? Null and void? America promised Israel in writing in that document that you would come to our military assistance if we were to be attacked. I thought this issue might come up, so I brought along a copy of the Memorandum of Agreement. In paragraph 3 your country guaranteed Israel that if there is *'an armed attack against Israel, the United States will be prepared to consider, on an urgent basis, such measures as the strengthening of the United States presence in the area, the providing of emergency supplies to Israel, and the exercise of maritime rights in order to put an end to the violation'.* So, how does the United

States just walk away from this guarantee to protect what the document calls the security interests of Israel? Are America's promises, in writing, worth nothing?"

"Mr. Prime Minister, please....please....please. We're neither one virgins in these international treaty matters. If America decides it won't support what a prior President put in writing, then we can come up with dozens of reasons why it's no longer *operative*, as they say in diplomatic language. I'm simply saying that if you don't sign this Path to Peace agreement, this week, then they'll be a new UN created nation on your doorsteps, you'll be cut off from US foreign aid and we will specifically disavow the Carter Agreed Memorandum."

"You realize, of course, Mr. President, that should you....what was your word....*disavow*....the US commitment to militarily defend Israel, that....that, would be equivalent to an *invitation* to the Palestinians and the jihadists of the region to invade us, to try and push us into the sea, as they have promised to do. We'd be under attack within hours of such an announcement, undoubtedly nuked by Iran. Unbelievable."

"It's very believable, Mr. Prime Minister. I don't want to have to revoke the Memorandum....but....I've got to do what I've got to do. My advisers, my State Department, are all in agreement, having studied you for years, that if I don't make it clear, shall we say, what we will do if you don't sign, that you will never sign. It's time to sign, Mr. Prime Minister, it's time to sign."

The Williamsburg peace negotiations went on for most of the week, but by noon on Friday, the media were alerted to breaking news. A peace agreement had been reached, with details to be announced shortly by the President. The history-making agreement to be signed the following week on the lawn of the White House, the same site as the Camp David Peace Accords in 1979. A Middle East Peace Agreement had been agreed to by ancient enemies. Peace. Peace in our times.

FIFTY-FOUR

Office of the Director of the CCC

Every government agency includes at least a few employees who are disgruntled about some aspect of how their agency treats them. Given the right circumstances, some will even leak internal documents intended to place their place of work in an unfavorable light with the tax-paying public. Thus, it was by an internally-leaked memo that the world came to know how the Director of the relatively newly created Civilian Conservation Corps had internally suggested arrest powers for his department's employees, well before the White House Press Office eventually made the announcement.

FOR INTERNAL USE ONLY-CONFIDENTIAL-NOT FOR DISTRIBUTION

TO: Section Commanders - CCC

From: Director Alcorn

Subject: Law Enforcement Functions - Conservators - IM#1037

I don't need to dwell on the unpleasant reaction that our new agency has experienced from many on the right wing, religious activists and former gun owners. Even though the McAlister Act clearly gives the federal government an oversight role to prevent hate speech, there appear to be increasing numbers of hate speakers who are not willing to obey the law. The shrill and vitriolic words coming from these folks poses a danger to the nation, as the President noted when he formally announced our agency in Asheville. In

337

fact, I have just received a report showing that there have actually been more hate filled attacks on the President and the Congress since the establishment of the CCC than in the three months immediately preceding its creation.

Obviously, this situation cannot be allowed to continue.

The President and I were both given assurances by White House staff who worked on setting up the CCC that by placing our agency's Conservators in public meetings, including church services, lodges, veterans' meetings, etc., hate speech would be severely curtailed. Unfortunately, the presence of our trained CCC Conservators has had the opposite effect. Referrals for criminal prosecution by the CCC to the Department of Justice were supposed to have the added effect of drying up hate speech. That also has not happened.

Therefore, CCC Conservators, with White House approval and upon official Presidential announcement, will have arrest powers, similar to any other law enforcement agency. Each will be given a numbered agency badge and will be given training in providing Miranda warnings, in appropriate cuffing techniques and in booking procedures. Each of you will shortly receive a draft training manual for your review and input.

I want to emphasize that we are not implementing this program until the WH announces that the CCC Conservators will be granted arrest powers. It's critical that this matter be kept on an internal confidential basis until the WH goes public. Any premature leak could be quite harmful to the future of the agency. There are still several in Congress, primarily in the minority, naturally, who oppose our goals and who would use knowledge of this new arrest authority to attempt to thwart our efforts going forward.

Watch your incoming for the draft of the arrest training manual. I want responses to the draft within three days of receipt of this non-existent memo. I have the impression we have very little time to get ready. Critical concerns or questions? Call me. (Don't e-mail for obvious reasons).

FIFTY-FIVE

Sheridan, Oregon

Sheridan Federal Correctional Institution is located in northwest Oregon, almost to the Pacific coast. It's about as far from Tyler, in east Texas, as one can get, still be in the U.S. and also be a medium security federal prison. With the intervening mountain ranges, ground travel from Tyler to Sheridan is a 2,100 mile, thirty-four hour, multi-day effort. The federal government's decision to transfer John Madison to the Oregon federal prison was thought by many to be punitive, to separate him from his family and supporters. That theory, however, changed somewhat when Gunning Bedford, Jr. was transferred to the same federal prison, the week before Thanksgiving. Once it became known that both would be inmates at the Sheridan federal prison, their counsel searched for any other reason why the two prisoners would be in the same facility. Chuck Webster told Bedford's attorney that in his opinion a major part of the decision was based on the federal judge in Oregon who would be presiding over the trials of both men. U.S. District Judge Hiram 'Hanging Judge' McDermott did not come by his nickname by accident. He worked at it. He held the record among federal district court judges for sentencing criminal defendants convicted in his Court to maximum terms, with a particular emphasis on sentencing to full terms on each count brought against defendants charged with firearms violations.

John Madison's attorney had filed preliminary motions with Judge McDermott to transfer his client back to a location closer to his home in Texas; to require the Department of Justice to pay for expenses of their witnesses and others forced to come to Sheridan; and to extend the time before the trial to allow for added preparation time due to the increased distance. Judge McDermott denied all three motions, all without a hearing to consider oral argument of counsel. The Judge routinely used a large two inch by five inch rubber stamp which simply said DENIED. He would stamp it on motions, with red ink, to clearly convey what he thought of motions that didn't meet his favor. John Madison's attorney knew that he not only had his work cut out for him, he was facing possibly the most anti-defendant judge in the federal system. It appeared to Counsel that his assignment to preside over the case was no accident.

Everybody in Sheridan prison, inmates and guards, knew when Gunning Bedford, Jr. arrived at the facility. As the inmates had a high regard for John Madison, they likewise were looking forward to meeting Bedford, who was now at least as prominent a federal prisoner as John Madison. His assigned cell was at opposite ends of the prison from Madison's cell, by choice of a Deputy Attorney General monitoring the case. What the suits in DC could not control, however, was what the guards did inside the Oregon prison to allow their two high-profile prisoners to interact. All but two of the guards had been gun owners, and were not at all pleased with the McAlister Act, which took away their right, as individuals to own guns. They had discussed the irony that they could carry inside the prison, but it was a felony outside. Consequently, the guards arranged morning personal, recreational and free time to allow maximum interchange opportunities between Madison and Bedford, who were more than appreciative.

John Madison was slightly apprehensive as he waited in the recreation room for his first time meeting with Gunning Bedford, Jr. Like the rest of America, he knew that

Bedford was charged with a long list of serious federal crimes. That, of course, did not cause him to be wary of Bedford, after all, he himself was likely to be charged with violating the federal criminal code, eventually. As he understood what happened at the Montana State House, Bedford was a leader in the occupation, but he had no connection with the one shot that was fired, many thought, by accident. He had concluded that Bedford was a civil protestor in a demonstration that went bad, mostly because of over-reaction by the feds, such as happened at Waco or Ruby Ridge. He was anxious to meet him and see if his initial conclusion was correct, or if alternatively, that Bedford was what the feds and the mainstream media said he was. It didn't take him long to learn who Gunning Bedford, Jr. really was.

A friendly Sheridan guard brought Bedford into the recreation room, introducing his two famous guests. "Mr. Madison, meet Mr. Bedford."

Madison stood and grabbed Bedford's rather large, leathery hand. "Name's John Madison, Mr. Bedford, nice to meet 'ya."

"Same here, but it's not Mister. Just Gunning."

"What kind of a name is Gunning? Just kidding, you must get that a lot."

With a big smile, Bedford replied, "Yep, I do. If I can call you John, let me ask you how are you doin'? Lots of rumors about you. They say you're America's number one political prisoner. What's it like here?"

"Well, like the comedian W.C. Fields once said, 'On the whole, I'd rather be in Philadelphia."

"Didn't he also say, 'there comes a time in the affairs of man when he must grab the bull by the tail and face the situation'? So how are you facing *your* situation?"

"The inmates here, Gunning, will treat you respectfully. They know why you're here. Most, but not all, of the guards will do the same. It's pretty obvious the prison administration and the Bureau of Prisons are under a lot of pressure from the Administration in DC. So you'll get little breaks like this meeting, but on things that show up in the official records, like outside visitors, you won't get any breaks. None. We each get 12 visitor points a month. A weekend visitor costs you two points, so you can expect that you won't see a lot of family or friends. Won't happen."

"I can get used to all that, I think. At least, eventually. I'm mainly worried about my wife. How do you handle being away from your spouse?"

"Not easy. She's up here this week, still trying to find a job that will pay enough to justify moving to Oregon through the trial. We don't have a trial date yet. How about your wife? Is she interested in moving to Oregon?"

"Her parents are both ailing, plus our two kids are trying to finish college, in Montana. It doesn't look good for a move out here. We've talked about it. She'll get here probably twice a month, but Billings is a lot closer than Tyler. What happened to your income? Weren't you in the insurance biz?"

"Yeah. That's all gone. My boss was supportive, but his boss got some heat from some place, who knows where? Insurance regulators? Anyway, they let me go, not long after

I was arrested by the feds. Gave me six months severance, which helped, but you can't live forever on it."

"Well. Let me ask you, on a different subject...."

"How's the food?" Madison asked with a smile.

"No. I don't expect a gourmet five star establishment. My question is what are you hearing about our Judge, you know, the 'Hanging Judge'?"

"Big problem. Besides distance from home, the major reason we're in Oregon. Pro-government in his rulings from the bench. Occasionally overruled when he's gone too far, but generally seen, my attorney tells me, by the DOJ as a fairly reliable judge for the DOJ, as well as a good court to try a high profile case. Judge McDermott isn't shy when it comes to being in the public spotlight with a case that the government really wants to win."

"Like our two cases?"

"Yeah, like our two cases. What I hear, again from my attorney, since the DOJ doesn't call me, is that the government wants to convict us in order to shut up verbal protestors, like me, and, to shut down demonstrations, like yours. A loss of either case would be seen by the Administration as a real set back. If they're going make McAlister stick, they need to scare Americans who upset about the gun law. Their goal appears to be to create a state of fear....the fear of speaking up as well as the fear of protesting."

"Un-hunh, the way any government in history has grabbed and kept control – scare its citizens into sheep-like compliance. There's nothing new under the sun, as Solomon once said. I just wish I was from Texas, the only State in the Union that, by law, can withdraw from the Union. It's actually a Republic, as it was an independent nation for ten years before it joined the Union. If you ever get out of here, you should help lead Texas out of the Union."

"Sure, that's what I need, more trouble, to be a bigger target. I'll pass....for now." But, despite John Madison's protestations, a seed had been planted.

"Gunning, do you mind if I ask you what really went down in Helena at your protest?"

"I don't mind at all, if you'll then share with me the background of your speech in Austin that got you in so much trouble."

"Deal. You go first."

"No matter what you've read or heard, we didn't take over the State House to start a fire fight. Except for the three guys that were shot by government troops, one who's still alive, as you probably know, but not in very good shape, the rest of us were going to exit the State House late Sunday night. We just wanted to make our point against the government trying to cancel our right to own firearms, and then we would just fade away. But, it all went south on us. The three guys who volunteered to be arrested and jailed shouldn't have carried their firearms with them for their speech out on the balcony. That cost two of them their lives, as it turned out. Actually, we should have all left our firearms at home. Then, our escape route was blocked. The rest is history."

"And now you're here."

"Yup", he chuckled, "But I get to meet a nice class of people, including the famous rabble rouser John Madison, high on the President's enemies list."

"The truth is there are things about the President that I like. He works on spending time with his family, for instance. It's just that almost every position he takes on a public issue, I disagree with him. His handling of the economy is clearly wrong-headed. If we had a President who understood business and how jobs are actually created, those millions of Americans who are unemployed would be back to work. It wouldn't take too many Presidential speeches and DC policy changes to convince the small business owners of the country that they could start expanding their businesses again."

"John, do you buy the theory that he's trying to bring down the financial system, because at heart he detests capitalism?

"I don't know if I do or not. What I do know is that this President's background and training, and his growing-up friends and associates, could lead you to that conclusion. Now, what about your speech in Austin?"

John Madison related to his new prison friend the details of his speech four days before the October 26th shootings warning that the President, if re-elected would try and take away Americans' right to keep and bear arms. He shared his belief as to why he was targeted, among the many others who were giving similar warnings, and why what he said publicly led him to become an inmate at a medium security federal correctional institution in Oregon.

To an observer it would seem that Madison and Bedford were having a confidential conversation. But, things are not always what they seem, especially in a federal prison. The sealed playing card box on the middle of their table in the recreation room at Sheridan federal prison was a sophisticated microphone and transmission device. Every word spoken by the prison's two leading inmates was being recorded and simultaneously transmitted to the Deputy Attorney General at the DOJ in charge of prosecuting Madison and Bedford. Though the Deputy AJ didn't learn anything of note in this initial meeting, he was convinced that future such meetings between the two inmates at Sheridan would yield information that would implicate others in the government's efforts to mold the First and Second Amendments more to the Administration's liking.

FIFTY-SIX

Denver, Colorado & Washington, DC

Violence begets violence. There is something in the human psyche that raises the blood level and the propensity for violent behavior when one witnesses violence, particularly when coupled with perceived injustice. When television newscasts showed Rodney King being assaulted by police officers, widespread violence by others soon followed. Likewise, when Americans who still possessed guns saw the shootings by the American military of three gun rights protestors at the Montana State House, the fuse was lit for more violence yet to come.

Three days after the Saturday shootings in Helena a powerful bomb blew apart the front two-thirds of the ATF field division offices in Denver. The bomb went off at one in the morning. If it had ignited during working hours it was estimated that over four hundred would have died, counting those in adjoining offices. Two days later a similar device exploded, demolishing the ATF offices in Little Rock. This time, the bomb, which ignited at just after 9 PM, killed two persons passing by the offices. One day later, the Portland, Oregon ATF field division offices were decimated, but the bomb went off at just after 6 PM, killing three late workers and five in an adjoining office's conference room.

The next morning the President summoned the national media to the White House to issue a statement. As he approached the podium his expression could only be described as one of fury, absolute rage. He seemed to almost spit out the few words of his brief statement which he uncharacteristically made without a Tele-Prompter.

"I have a statement to make. These bombings of federal offices are an unacceptable atrocity. America is under a domestic terror siege. I am calling up and I am field assigning our military to protect and defend our government from these....these....haters. Deprived of their gun hate weapons, they have now turned to more serious and violent means of hate. I have just signed an Order providing arrest powers to members of the CCC. Any criminal act, in word or deed, witnessed by a Conservator can now be the basis for immediate arrest. If necessary, I will declare martial law....The haters are warned."

The President turned, abruptly exiting the White House Press Room, followed by numerous shouted questions, the loudest of which was, "Mr. President, do we have any evidence who planted these bombs? Could they have been by outside terrorists, or someone not part of the right wing? Do we know anyth.....". The President stopped short and turned, glaring at the reporter, whose well known voice he instantly recognized. Ignoring his Press Secretary's advice not to take any questions, he shot back in response, "Ed, are you implying that someone in the government bombed our own offices? Is that your question? That's reprehensible, even for Fox News. There's no Reichstag fire here. The bombings were by the crazies, the radical right wing that just can't get used to losing their hate weapons."

Not to be outdone, the reporter shouted to the retreating back of the President, now almost out of the Press Room, "Mr. President....how can you be so sure this close to the bombings? How can you know these bombs weren't planted by your supporters, or by.....". By now he was only talking to the press corps, most of whom looked at him with disdain.

FIFTY-SEVEN

Indianapolis, Indiana

Ideas have consequences. Likewise, big ideas can often have outsized results. When John Madison and his pro-gun rights friends met in Chicago to write *Plan X*, they could have had no concept as to the far-reaching results of their wintry day meeting. They learned *some* of the consequences of their meeting within hours, of course, because they were all arrested. Things would have been different had Alex McDaniel not crashed in his Cessna leaving the Chicago meeting. They wouldn't have been so quickly arrested if the Administration hadn't been provided the notes and text of *Plan X* from McDaniel's briefcase discovered by the NTSB at the site of the crashed plane. The drafters of *Plan X* had concluded that if they could keep the plan secret for even a short time, maybe a couple of weeks, they could have quietly lined up support for *Plan X* across the country, from all manner of groups and associations, and maybe leak it to the media, scaring the White House into withdrawing McAlister before it passed. If that had happened, which, of course, it didn't, the Administration, sensing public support for calling a Constitutional Convention to change the nation's broken federal government, might have buckled and withdrawn the McAlister Bill. Woulda, coulda, shoulda, as they say.

Because of the plane crash, and because the organizers behind *Plan X* were sequestered in federal prison, details of the plan had not become known to the American public. That is, until one of the NTSB investigators who had made a copy of *Plan X*, contrary to agency rules, shared it with his nephew in law school. He asked his relative what he thought of the ideas in the plan, and specifically he wanted to know if it was legal to make so many major changes in the

351

how the federal government operates in a Constitutional Convention. The investigator had a low opinion of the Congress, and wanted to know if there was any possibility of limiting its Members to how many years they could serve and making their laws apply to Members, as well as to all other Americans.

The investigator's nephew was not really sure of the answer himself, as he had not yet taken his law school's course on Constitutional Law. He took the copy of *Plan X* given to him by his uncle to the professor who taught the course, who just happened to be a conservative, rare in most American institutions of higher learning. His professor immediately understood the implications of the document. He scanned it and circulated it to the leaders of the Kincaid Street Gang, a coalition of conservative national organizations, which met monthly in Washington, DC. The leaders of the member groups upon receiving the document, in turn, realized its importance. They also now understood why John Madison and his compatriots were in prison. The administration had claimed that they were being held as threats to national security, which, of course, was the official cover reason for their continued retention in prison, with Madison still not formally charged with any crime. It was also the excuse for why they were not allowed any significant direct contact with the media, or anyone else, except immediate family.

The text of *Plan X* was soon featured on NewsMax, World News Daily, National Review, Fox News and almost all of the other conservative news sources in the nation. Conservative bloggers spread it even further, suggesting that America give serious thought to calling a Constitutional Convention. To many it seemed like *Plan X* was like a match tossed into a lake of gasoline. The fire of real governmental reform began to spread across the country. Tea Party activists, gun rights groups, home schoolers, evangelicals, economic conservatives, Republican Party leaders in the southern and western states and Americans generally who were worried about the survival of their country, began to meet and talk about joining together to lobby their legislatures to petition for a Constitutional Convention.

An organization meeting was called for mid-January in Indianapolis, the crossroads of America, as the city best located for a meeting of leaders from every State of the nation. Over 2,700 angry, yet hopeful, political activists gathered for a three day meeting to develop strategy at the Indianapolis Convention Center. Of the people present, more than a hand full were federal employees, who had become involved undercover in various conservative activist organizations.

By late afternoon Saturday those assembled had voted, by a lop-sided margin in favor, to organize as *Americans for a New Constitution*, with leaders named in all fifty states. They adopted proposed Constitutional amendments and highlighted them on their advertising literature, bumper stickers, posters, and hopefully, if the funds allowed, in television ads. The reform planks they chose were condensed to simple, but powerful, slogans:

TERM LIMIT CONGRESS

NO MORE FEDERAL DEBT

DEMAND A CONSTITUTIONAL CONVENTION – NOW!

What the movement soon learned was that these promises struck a raw nerve in the American electorate. Fed up with empty promises by politicians, they saw the movement to call a Constitutional Convention as the *only* way to save their country from utter destruction. Volunteers and dollars poured in. The White House was more than mindful of what was beginning to grow and stir among the nation's citizens, taxpayers and voters. The President's Chief of Staff, Bill O'Dayson, a former public official himself, convened the President's brain trust to develop a strategy to stop the movement to convene a Constitutional Convention.

O'Dayson called the meeting for the Cabinet Room, not only to add some additional prestige to the meeting itself, but also to accommodate his brain trust, many of whom worked for him when he ran one of the nation's largest cities, as its tough-as-nails, take-no-prisoners Mayor.

"OK, we all know why we're here," O'Dayson said as he convened the meeting, sitting in the middle chair of the long Cabinet Room conference table, a position of prominence normally occupied by the President. "What we are *not* here for is to develop happy, clappy talking points for the media. That won't get it. This thing has the potential to develop into a full-fledged movement to call a Constitutional Convention and it's serious, people. We thought we had it under control, with John Madison and his conspirators in federal pens. But someone leaked it and it's taken on a life of its own."

"But, Bill, isn't this just a bunch of the Tea Party nuts, trying to stir up trouble, to try and make points for the next election?"

"I wish. Two problems. Our overnight polling, which is usually very accurate, shows a solid majority of the voters supporting the idea of amending the Constitution and term-limiting Congress, among other major changes. Over 68%

support a debt elimination amendment, with similar numbers term limiting judges. Second problem, which is why we are here, is that these guys are actually on to something. They only need 34 State legislatures to adopt a simple resolution calling for a Constitutional Convention."

"But, what about Congress. We control both Houses. They'll never get Congress to go along, and so their...."

"Read your Constitution. Article Five. There are two ways to call a Constitutional Convention. One requires that Congress convene it, by super majorities of both Houses. As you pointed out, that's never going to happen, not in our lifetime. However, there's another way that the old guys who wrote it provided for calling a Constitutional Convention....by a resolution adopted by the legislatures of two-thirds of the states, that is 34 states. Once that happens, it's mandatory that Congress call the Convention to consider amendments. Once a Convention, which, by the way, has never been called or convened, meets and passes amendments, three fourths of the states then must adopt the amendments."

"Three fourths of the legislatures?"

"Actually, either three fourths of the legislatures, which would be 38 states, or, alternatively Congress, could require that ratification of the newly proposed amendments be by three fourths of special conventions called in each State. That's only happened once, when they ratified the 21st Amendment, so Americans could legally drink again. They thought it would be 'quicker to the liquor', so to speak, to go the State convention route, since many legislatures didn't meet every year back then."

"Bill, this is a fascinating history lesson, but what are we going to do to stop this speeding train?"

"We really only have one good option. We have to make sure that at least 17 states refuse to adopt a resolution calling for a Constitutional Convention. If 17 states say 'no way Jose', 'keep your cotton pickin' hands off our sacred Constitution', then we win."

"Wait a momento, Bill. You just referred to the Constitution as 'sacred', that's not what we've been saying in our talking points, and blogs....plus Congress just ripped the guts out of both the First and the Second Amendments with the McAlister Act. Sacred? Are we changing our tune?"

"Yep, we sure are. The best talking point, the best TV ads, will be based on not messing with such an important, yes, sacred, document. We're doing an about face in order to beat back this movement out there to change our government. If they actually got a convention called, Congress will be toast. Congress's support level is below Adolph Hitler, or close, anyway. So we have to scare people. We have to convince enough people in at least seventeen states that if their legislature resolves to call a Constitutional Convention, that the Convention could take away *all* of their rights."

"As opposed to just taking away their rights to speak and own a gun?"

"Precisely. You got it. The bigger danger theory. We won't waste our efforts, and money, in most of the states, let them do what they want. I've got a list here of 21 key states. We'll pour all of our people and bucks into those states. We just need 17 of them to stop a Constitutional Convention. In reality, we only need 17 of the *separate* legislative bodies in each State, whether the House or the Senate, to say no. Since it takes both chambers in a State to pass the resolution, our blocking efforts in a single State can be focused on the chamber we decide, after we count likely votes, would be most likely to say no."

"I know where we're going to get our volunteers, from the usual supporters of the Administration, the labor unions, especially the public employee unions, etc. But, where's the money coming from?"

"Let me handle that. We'll be more than well-funded. Don't forget that we're in office. We control the giving of grants and the awarding of contracts for the largest enterprise in the world, the US government. We can raise all the money we need to raise. No problem with enough dinero. Any questions before we discuss each of your assignments?"

Thus, the Administration launched its plan to stop Americans from changing their government as set forth in their Constitution.

FIFTY-EIGHT

White House Oval Office

Washington, DC

"General, don't you get it? Hunh? Are you deaf?

"Do....you....not....understand....the....words....that....are....coming....out....of....my....mouth?"

"Oh, I understand, Mr. President, what you are asking the United States Department of Justice to do. I....understand....the....words....that....are....coming...."

"Alright, no need to be sarcastic. Sorry for my anger, but you just don't seem to get what I want you, as Attorney General, and your DOJ, to do."

The President and his Attorney General had known each other since they organized voter drives together, before either one of them had any hope of serving in high public office. That long-time friendship, however, didn't prevent them from frequent verbal clashes. The AG was a loyal soldier, a fact which he found he had to on occasion remind the occupant of the White House. The President had never practiced law, though he had a law degree, which hindered him in his ability to understand why his choice for the nation's top lawyer wouldn't always do what he wanted him to do.

"Mr. President, I've told you this before, and once again, it bears repeating. If I file some goofy pleading, or bring ridiculous charges against Madison, that not only hurts my credibility, and that of the Department of Justice, it back-splashes on you, and hurts your image."

"Image? I don't care about that now, Erik, I won. Remember that? I'm in my second term. This is the 'big things finally get done term'....Image?....Who gives a rip about my image? They're never gonna' carve my face on Mount Rushmore, let alone print my charming smile on our currency. Image?"

"You misunderstood what I meant. I also don't give a fig for what the voters tell pollsters. Voters? Who are they? After the election they lost their standing. What I was *trying* to say was that if we operate the DOJ like we don't know what we're doing, and go off half-cocked, we'll be held in low esteem, to say the least, by the Judges we have to deal with every day. Need I remind you, since you used to teach this stuff, that there is a supposedly co-equal branch of government in this country called the judiciary. You know, the guys that throw out acts of Congress and rule that you exceeded your legal authority? We don't want those guys and gals in black robes coming to the conclusion that this Administration is incompetent. I can live with them thinking you're a radical leftist, because a lot of them are too, but if they conclude that we're totally inept, then that will hurt us with their future rulings."

"But, Erik, how many of these Judges were appointed by Clinton, or Carter, or by O...., or by us?"

"I don't know the current breakdown, but over half are our party's appointments."

"So, if I file, excuse me, if you file, the DOJ or the District Attorney, or whomever, files a hate crimes charge against this Texas televangelist, are you telling me that some federal judge is just gonna' throw it out? How do you know that?"

360

"Mr. President, let me go over this again. You are very close to the line on the free speech issue. The First Amendment says....you remember that one. It's right before the Second Amendment. The two we modified in the McAlister Act."

"One of the highlights of *both* of our lives, I might add."

"Yes, but back to my point. The media helped us mightily on getting rid of the right to keep and bear arms, but it won't be so easy to modify the First Amendment. It provides for protections for the media that they jealousy guard."

"Why can't we just focus on the free exercise of religion part, and stay away from the free speech and press part? Am I missing something here?"

"Kind of, you are. This young pastor, the son of your least favorite Texan, who is, I might add, still in the federal pen awaiting trial, will launch his much-announced sermons on what 'the Bible says about perverted behavior' next month. The fact that his dad has been labeled by Fox as America's number one political prisoner will add considerably to his viewership. Assume he says what we think he's going to say. We can have several CCC Conservators in the congregation to witness his words. We can bring hate crime charges for violating the federal hate crime statute, besides, of course, charges for violating McAlister. We'll emphasize that he is abusing the free exercise of religion clause, trying to jam his religion down folks' throats, using the public airwaves and thus violating the separation between church and state, etc., etc. That we can do. Unfortunately, by presenting his hate speeches verbally, and on television, his lawyers will claim it's all protected speech. First Amendment protected speech. See the problem? It's a fine line, like I said."

"I get it. I get it. I didn't practice law, but I understand the problem of losing the media. Can't we come up with something that we can add to the charges that will kind of....you know.... cover over the free speech issues and highlight the violation of the separation of church and state part?"

"We're working on it as we speak. We'll be ready. He's doing a series, so we can send in the CCC Conservators for the first sermon, nail down his hate words, then, maybe we'll arrest this guy as he's giving his next sermon right on the stage of his Dallas church. He threw down the gauntlet with those billboards and promo ads in large letters saying, What Does the Bible Teach on Perversion? He's just asking for trouble from us."

"I was told that he didn't agree with his dad. That he thought John Madison was wrong to take me on so viciously in the campaign?"

"I don't know. I just know he's inviting scrutiny of his words. Don't forget that Pastor Jack Madison's words will be spoken *after* the McAlister Act. His dad's speech was *before* McAlister, which makes convicting his dad much harder than convicting his son. But, I actually think it helps that he's John Madison's son, sort of makes it look like he's thumbing his nose at the Administration, even though it's on a different topic than the one on which his dad campaigned. He knows that we have to strictly enforce McAlister. We can't have televised hate speech like what he promises to talk about. What do you think?"

362

"Back to what I said when you first got here. Send in the Conservators and nail down his hate words. Then prepare the charges and go after him as soon as he's finished his next hate sermon. Let's hope that there's some red meat in his first sermon, some references to Sodom and Gomorrah, that kind of thing. I hear they go after pastors in Canada and Sweden all the time, so why can't we? These guys on the religious right want to send us a message. I'll send them a message, one they won't soon forget."

"All right. You're the boss. In any case, we'll be ready for Pastor Jack Madison. I just want you to know what can happen if we're not careful. Let's hope our Judge agrees."

FIFTY-NINE

Louisville, Kentucky
Editorial Offices – Louisville Colonel-Journal

Gordon Ziegner had been the Editor of the Louisville Colonel-Journal, the State's oldest daily newspaper, for over twenty seven years. He thought he had seen it all, reported it all and printed it all during those years. He was wrong. The official-looking Department of Justice letter lying on his keyboard grabbed his attention, as his assistant knew it would. She knew that if she placed it on his paper-strewn desk it might never be seen. As a trained editor, he read it all in one swift top to bottom scan, but, unlike most reads, this writing required a more intensive analysis.

Editor Ziegner was officially informed in the letter by a Deputy Attorney General named Roger F. Scott that his newspaper was about to receive a visitor from the government. Upon re-reading, he saw that the visit would be that afternoon. Not much notice, he thought, but not a big problem, I can make time before the Editorial Board meeting. But, hunh? As he read it again, he saw that the visitor, a Conservator with the Civilian Conservation Corps, was coming not to see Editor Ziegner, but to meet with Editor Ziegner and his newspaper's full Editorial Board. Now, that's strange, he thought. Don't think we've ever had someone invite themselves to a meeting of the Editorial Board.

The Editorial Board of the Colonel-Journal, consisted of five editors or associate editors of the paper. It met every afternoon to discuss the next day's editorials to be published, which guest columns to select for publication and how to prioritize the stories on the paper's front page and the first page of the metro section. When elections came around, the Board would invite in candidates and interview them for potential endorsements. Service on the Editorial Board, inside the newspaper, was considered the top of the newspaper food chain, a position to be coveted.

Editor Ziegner read the DAG/DOJ letter the third time, and then the fourth. He then scanned it and e-mailed it to the other four Board members, asking for their comments. As it was a quiet news day, his e-mail and the accompanying letter stirred up a storm of comments. The City Editor wrote him back, "WHAT? This guy or gal from some federal agency is going to attend our Editorial Board meeting? WHAT EVER FOR? Tell them to forget it, we've got a newspaper to publish!!! (Yes, Gordon, I used three emphasis marks plus three words in caps, so mark me up, already!)"

The newspaper's lead editorial writer, Tim Matheson, a strong supporter of the President, who had written both editorials endorsing him in his two runs for the White House, took a slightly less adversarial approach in his comments, "OK. I don't see any BIG problem here. A bit unusual, but maybe this agency has some good ideas they can share with us. We might develop several future editorials based on what we learn from this CCC person this afternoon. See everybody then. Cheers."

As was the norm, the Editorial Board convened at 3 PM to shape tomorrow's news, in print form. None were shocked that their visitor wore an official CCC green shirt, as there were many federal employees now who wore that official uniform. None were surprised that their visitor actually showed up as announced in the letter from the DOJ, as they had all read it in advance. But all were flabbergasted when they looked up to see that their guest was Jim Mooney, a former reporter from the paper, who had been laid off over a year ago, in a newspaper staff downsizing, caused by lower newspaper revenues. Mooney had been rumored to be having trouble finding a job. Obviously, though, he was now employed, and by the United States federal government. He was accompanied by an armed TSA Agent.

"Well, Jim, it's great to see you again," Editor Ziegner said warmly. He had liked Mooney as a reporter, whose beat had been to cover the Kentucky State House in Frankfort for the Colonel-Journal. He regretted the owners' decision to let him go. He knew when Mooney was let go that coverage of what went on in State government would suffer, and that state employees who were tempted to cross the ethical line were encouraged by seeing a reporter watch dog like Mooney move on.

Jim Mooney appeared to be happy to see his former comrades in publishing. He brought with him a digital recorder, a large expandable file folder and a reporter's note book, which he opened once he and his TSA companion were asked to sit at the conference table.

"Jim, we've all read the letter from the Deputy AG from Washington. You're an old pro at this stuff, so what gives? The letter didn't say why you're visiting us, only that a CCC Conservator would be stopping in to visit. Congratulations, by the way, on your new employment."

Jim Mooney hesitated, coughed once, looked down and then said, "Thanks, Gordon. Here's the deal guys....there's a new sheriff in town. I've been deputized to help him out. With the new McAlister anti-hate speech law now in place, things are changing and changing fast. The old days of throwing around any old words we wanted to throw around are over."

"What the heck does that mean, Jim? We don't use hate words here, never have. We're really careful about what we write. You know that. You, of all peop...."

"I don't think you get it. Most people don't get it....yet, that is, though they will soon enough. This new law, which as you well know has been upheld by the Supreme Court, allows the government to eliminate hate speech. Hate speech is defined in the McAlister Act as speech that negatively attacks a public official. All of us here would agree that's a bunch of baloney....off the record....that is. Just because I criticize a public official, that shouldn't get me in any trouble, right? Well, that was then, and this is now. Negative public official attacks are a thing of the past. Everybody still employed in the news editorial biz is going to just have to get used to it. Television stations don't usually run editorials anymore, so they're not an issue. Once the newspapers are brought in line, that just leaves talk radio and Fox, and I hear there are big plans by the White House for both."

Ziegner responded, "Jim, I'm not horribly shocked that the government wants to shut down criticism, that's been the case since government started. Dictators usually have no sense of humor when it comes to persons who oppose them. Lest we forget, it wasn't too many years ago that negatively criticizing public officials in Europe could get you imprisoned or shot."

Mooney quickly said, "Gordon, let me just give you a little tip here. That comment, implying that the McAlister Act, or the federal government, or the President, or the Congress, whatever, whomever, are in any way like Nazi Germany or Fascist Italy, could get you charged with a Hate Speech Act violation. So, be very careful. I'm just warning you."

368

A distinct chill could be felt across the room. No one wanted to say what they were really thinking about the threat made by the federal employee in their presence. The chilly silence was finally broken by the City Editor who perceptively asked, "Jim, you're here for more than just a warning to us to watch our spoken words, aren't you?"

Mooney opened up his large expandable filing folder and withdrew several pages. "Afraid I am. I've been given the assignment by DC of going through all the major editorials in this paper for the last several months. My job is to highlight negative attacks on public officials. At first, I thought that meant just federal officials, but they interpret that part of McAlister to include *all* public officials. So, this print-out is a listing of all of the paper's attacks, on all public officials, arranged by date."

"Does it include the two editorials in which we endorsed your boss, the current occupant of the White House? Were those considered negative attacks, hunh, Jim?"

"No reason to get snippy. There are parts of this I don't much like either."

Ziegner was becoming less and less comfortable not only with what Mooney was saying, but also with even remaining in the room for such a discussion, "Jim. Hold up a minute, buddy. Don't you....didn't you....see any First Amendment problems with going through our editorials, as a federal employee, and picking out what the government may not like that we printed. And then, much worse than that, coming in here to the newspaper and telling us what you....what the government....doesn't like. Talk about chilling our First Amendment rights. Are you going to tell us next what we can print in the future? Are you going to be our newspaper's government paid censor?"

"Umh, guys, look....I told you there's a new sheriff in town. The Sheriff's not allowing anyone to violate the law which prohibits folks from speaking ill about him. If you don't like it, run for office and repeal McAlister. In the meantime, get used to obeying the law. As for censorship, we all got a memo directing us to never use that word. The memo said some people might think it has bad connotations. Well....I guess so. But what's going to be happening is going to feel a lot like censorship."

"Clarify please, Jim," asked Tim Matheson, the President's biggest supporter in the room. "What's going to happen? I have the distinct feeling I'm not going to like this at all."

"It's simple, really. But you're right, you're definitely not going to like it. Our office will need the draft version of the next day's editorials, by e-mail transmission, no later than two hours before your afternoon Editorial Board meeting convenes."

"*For what?*", Editor Ziegner asked, incredulously.

"As I said, it's very simple. We'll do a quick review, just to make sure that the words in the drafts comply with the law, zip you back a quick approval, or changes, as the case may be, and that's it. You go to press."

"Say *what? Changes? As the case may be?* Does that mean that you will edit our editorials? If we write that *we question whether or not the President's proposal is right for America,* you can write back and say, no, change it to *the*

370

President's proposal is right for America'? Am I getting this correctly?"

"That's pretty much it, folks. Sorry to be the bearer of bad news, but, like I said, times change, the laws change. Stuff happens. You'll still be selling newspapers, and stuffing them with Sunday's overflowing ads, it's just that your editorial page will be more people friendly."

"Don't you mean more President friendly, Jim? And, the funny thing, though it's not funny at all....the ironic thing....is that we're *usually,* though not *always,* in his corner."

"Well, that will just have to change to *always.* I'll look forward to tomorrow's editorial drafts, the new Sheriff's deputy starts work then. Have a good afternoon."

Ziegner couldn't control himself, though he sensed that he should be quiet and become a good and obedient servant to the new order. "Jim, if we tell you, your agency - the CCC, the federal government, all of you, that we're not going to comply, that we're offended by this assault on our Constitutional right to a free press, and if we lead the charge to expose all this to the public? What then? You didn't tell us what the downside is of we don't let you censor our words, though I suspect I know the answer. I want to hear you, as a former journalist, say the words. What are we threatened with for non-compliance?"

"Look, Gordon, we both used to be journalists. I'm no longer a member of the fourth estate. I'm now a part of the government. I took an oath to enforce the law. We're going to do that. Now, to answer your question. If we don't see immediate compliance, if you don't send us your drafts on a timely basis, sent every day, the newspaper will be fined a very significant monetary fine for every day of violation. The fines will vary by the size of the paper, but for a good-sized paper like the Colonel-Journal, fines could be $25,000 or even higher for each violation. The feds are very serious about this. Once fined, the burden is on the paper to show why it shouldn't have to pay. It'll cost you mucho dinero to fight the fines. If there are a series of violations, since the feds don't have a sense of humor, the next step will be to file criminal charges against the owners and, yes, the editors. The new regs will say that the paper can't pay your legal fees to defend yourself, you'll have to come out of pocket for that. Is that clear enough? Did I leave anything out?"

Jim Mooney shut off his recorder, gathered his notebook and stood to leave. The TSA Agent, who had said nothing, also stood to leave. Three of the five editors were staring at their guests with their mouths still open in unbelief. Another had his head down in his hands. The fifth was wiping away a tear from his cheek. The meeting was over. Likewise, freedom of the press in America.

The next day, the newspaper sent drafts of its proposed editorials by e-mail to CCC Conservator Jim Mooney at his Regional CCC office for review. At the same time, Gordon Ziegner tendered his resignation as Editor of the Louisville Colonel-Journal. He then called his oldest son living in Panama to tell him that he had resigned from the paper and would be visiting him soon, with the high likelihood that he would be emigrating from the U.S.

SIXTY

Dallas, Texas

Pastor Jack Madison's church is located in the Park Cities suburban area of northeast Dallas. The upscale area is made up of University Park and Highland Park. Park Cities boasts several larger community and evangelical churches, some with several thousand members. Jack Madison's church was growing, had almost two thousand members, and was considered as one of the area's up and coming churches. His congregation was a diverse mixture of age groups, with many young families, but also with retired couples who enjoyed his Bible-centered teaching.

This Sunday's service was expected to be packed out, as it had been promoted with billboards and some radio advertising. Jack and his Board knew that they faced the potential of a disruptive interruption during the service, so they hired a few off duty policemen and women from their local suburban police forces. As the service started on Sunday morning all was peaceful, with no protestors outside the church. But peace was not to be.

After several minutes of spirited and worshipful singing, Pastor Madison strode briskly to his pulpit, with his Bible and his notes firmly in hand. Spiritually speaking, it was show time. He had thirty minutes, max, to make his point, repeat it and make sure everyone understood it. Tell them what you're going to tell them, tell them and then tell them what you just told them, as he had learned in seminary.

Jack laid his Bible and his notes on the pulpit, said a silent prayer and looked out over his congregation. What he saw caused him to stop. Scattered among the congregation were several, maybe as high as 20 or 30 people, all wearing identical green shirts, the uniform of the CCC. Why hadn't someone noticed this during the seating time and warned him, he wondered. Not that it was any huge deal, he thought, everyone's welcome here. Whomsover will may come, as they say. Still, he would have liked a heads up. I won't change a word of what I have planned to say, he swiftly concluded. Maybe some of these government employees will respond to the Gospel through this visit today, he comforted himself by thinking. But, he did have to admit that his stress level went up considerably, as anyone could attest whose father who had been arrested for his words. Memories of the earlier visit in his church office by two FBI agents added to his anxiety.

Pastor Madison began with his traditional greeting, "He is risen."

"He is risen, indeed", responded the congregation, using a first century greeting exchanged by Christians.

"I welcome you all to our church. We're a church that emphasizes the study of God's Word. Before we look at the Word, though I'd like to welcome our first time guests here with us today. So please stand if today is your first time to be with us, and the Deacons will give you an information packet about what we do as a church in this community and how you might fit in."

As Jack looked across the sanctuary he only saw a handful of first timers standing, scattered across the room. None of the green-shirted Conservators stood to be recognized. "Come now, I see several, maybe as many as thirty, first timers who have not yet stood, all in those sharp green uniform shirts. We welcome our friends who work for the Civilian Conservation Corps, which has a long and noble history of service in this country. One of my distant family members served in the CCC in the 30's, building national parks, so we welcome you and ask to stand and be recognized." None did. "Well, that's fine, that's OK, you're always welcome here any time. Now, let's open our Bibles and see what the Lord has to say to us today from His Word."

As he opened his Bible, Jack looked down at the two Conservators seated just to his right on the first row. He noticed that both had lapel microphones attached to their uniform collars, and both appeared to be leaning slightly forward, as if anxious to get all of his words recorded. He never had any doubts that his words could be used against him. He was more than well aware of his father's entanglement with federal authorities over his speech in Austin. In addition to which his church recorded and broadcast locally in the Dallas-Fort Worth area his morning services, including his sermons. He wasn't keeping secret his message. Which made him wonder, fleetingly, as he looked down at his notes for his next point, why the government felt it needed to record his words spoken in the sanctuary? They could just turn on the local cable channel. But, they may have worried that Jack wouldn't broadcast the words that they were most interested in. They just didn't know Jack, he smiled to himself, at his own feeble attempt at humor. Oh well, he concluded, *let's give 'em somethin' to talk about*, as the country song says.

"As many of you know from the radio spots and billboards, this month's sermon topics are centered on this question– What Does the Bible Teach on Perversion?.... Please turn your attention to the video screens."

A segment from the movie, The Princess Bride, appeared on the sanctuary's three large video screens. In the clip the movie's male and female heroes are standing at the altar in front of a challenged cleric, who says, *"Mawwaige. Mawwaige is what bwings us togwether today. Mawwaige, that bwessed awwaingement"*. The clip ended to widespread laughter. Pastor Jack followed it with, "my accent won't be as good as the cleric in one of my mom's favorite movies, but, it's true....marriage is what brings us together today. Where did the idea of marriage come from? What is marriage? Does marriage have any purpose in this modern age? Is it really a blessed arrangement? Why shouldn't anyone, or any group of someones, be allowed to marry? Is marriage in danger of extinction? These are all questions, along with others, that we will examine today and in the next three week's sermons.

"First, where did the idea of marriage come from? Who thought it up? I'm going to read to you a few sentences from a sermon given by a Swedish Pastor named Ake Green. Pay attention to what he said, because he was arrested and convicted by the Swedish judicial system for what he said. As you listen to the beginning of Pastor Green's sermon, ask yourself if you think his words are hate words. The Swedish government charged and convicted Pastor Green with a hate crime for these words. Here are Pastor Green's opening few paragraphs:

"From the beginning God created humans as man and woman. We begin in Genesis 1:27-28:

"So God created man in his own image, in the image of God created he him; male and female created he them. And God

376

blessed them, and God said unto them, Be fruitful, and multiply, and replenish the earth, and subdue it: and have dominion over the fish of the sea, and over the fowl of the air, and over every living thing that moveth upon the earth."

"Here, God's Word clearly states that you were created to be Father and Mother - as man and woman - designed for parenthood. The Lord states that very clearly here....The marriage institution is also clearly defined in Genesis 2:24, where it says:

"Therefore shall a man leave his father and his mother, and shall cleave unto his wife: and they shall be one flesh."

"Only man and wife are referred to here. It is not stated any other way; you can never imply or interpret it to mean that you can have whatever sexual partner you wish to have. ...."

"What was it that led to these cities (Sodom, mentioned 30 times in the Bible, and Gomorrah) perishing, losing their dignity, disappearing from the face of the Earth? It was because they lived in homosexuality. It will be the same on that day when the Son of Man is revealed; consequently, this is a sign of the times we are facing. As people lived in the time of Lot, so shall they live before Jesus returns. This is something we cannot deny in any way. Jesus says that the lifestyle of Sodom shall be active in the whole Earth before the coming of Jesus. The one who represents this lifestyle today goes against God's order of creation."

"Are Pastor Ake Green's words hate words? Or are they instead words of truth from God's Word? Due to a high level of international interest in Pastor's green's conviction and sentencing to jail, the Swedish Supreme Court eventually overturned his conviction, I am happy to say. I am unhappy to report, however, that in doing so, the Swedish Supreme Court ruled that his Bible-based message did, in fact, constitute hate speech. The Court said that a higher

European Court might not agree with them, so it threw out his conviction, even though they ruled that he was properly convicted as a hate speaker. Think about that for a moment. Pastor Green has been labeled by his government and his government's highest Court as a disseminator of hate speech for those Biblically-based words in his sermon, though they spared him from serving time in jail.

"Could that same thing happen in America? Many of you know that my father, a resident of Tyler, was charged by the federal government with various crimes, all arising from his use of words in a speech in the election campaign that he delivered in Austin to a political meeting. Many of you may also know that I didn't agree at the time with my dad's speech, and what I then thought was harsh rhetoric to use in describing the President of the United States. I used, ok, maybe, misused, the verse about rendering unto Caesar that which is Caesar's.

"I love my father, John Madison, but we didn't see eye-to-eye on this subject, and frankly, it put a strain on our normally very warm father-son relationship. On more than one occasion, usually when I was visiting him in prison, I asked my dad if he knew what he was doing? Was it worth it to lose his insurance executive job and spend time in federal prison, away from mom and his family, just because of words? Dad loves me, as I do him, so he would always gently reply that he was right, and that I would eventually see that he was right.

"Last week I was able to tell my dad that he was right in two ways. First, I told him that I now agreed that he was right to do what he did in opposing an administration that has frequently acted contrary to the best interests of the people of this nation. Secondly, I told him that he was correct when he said that I would one day see that he was right in his actions that led to his arrest and imprisonment. It was a sweet moment, my friends, to be able to be re-united not only in our love for each other, as dad and son, but also

378

united in our belief that standing up for what you believe in is worth the cost, whatever that may be. Words do matter. I'm here today, using words from God's Word, for which I may be, like Pastor Green, charged with criminal acts. I can't control what those in authority may choose to do to me for using God's Word, in their view, in a politically incorrect manner, in their view. I can only control what I say.

"I said to John Madison, my dad, last week, a man I consider to be a true American hero, 'Dad, you stood up when others, including me, should have spoken up before the second term happened. If more Americans had stood up and raised our voices, as you did, we would still have our First and Second Amendment rights today. Please forgive me.' And, congregation, please forgive me for not leading you to stand up and speak up when we still had the chance to do so. Because of my lack of leadership, and the lack of leadership by many other pastors and priests, we now live in a different nation than we did before the last election. We can't go back now and change that, but we can admit we were wrong and speak up now. Will that mean we will be charged with violating the McAlister Hate Speech and Hate Weapon Elimination Act? Only time will tell, but as for me and my house, we will serve the Lord."

All of the CCC Conservators present that Sunday morning had been carefully trained to avoid any controversy. They were to attend, act respectfully, observe and record what went on and what was said at the worship service and render a recommendation, in writing, after their visit. The Conservators' joint Memorandum recommending action was completed and submitted to the Regional CCC Offices in Houston by Wednesday and conveyed to national CCC headquarters by Friday.

A draft of a formal notification of the levying of significant fines to be levied on the Church and on Pastor Jack Madison and his Board members was on the desk of the Director of the CCC by the following Tuesday. On the same day a copy of the Memorandum was delivered to the Deputy Attorney General responsible for initiating criminal action. Criminal charges in several counts against Pastor Jack Madison were drafted for final review by the Attorney General. Jack Madison and his Texas church were on a collision course with the government of the United States of America.

SIXTY ONE

U.S. District Court, District of Oregon

"All rise. The United States District Court for the District of Oregon is hereby convened, the Honorable Hiram McDermott, presiding. All persons present are advised that any outburst in the Court will led to your immediate ejection, and possible incarceration. You may be seated." Thus began the trial of federal criminal defendant John Madison.

Judge McDermott called the case, "The cause before the Court today is the United States of America versus John Madison, Cause Number 13-ODC-276. The charges brought by the people of the United States against John Madison are a.) that he advocated the overthrow of the government of the United States, b.) that he conspired to advocate the overthrow of the government and c.) that he violated the federal hate crimes act. The charges will be read in full by the District Attorney shortly. You have been selected as a panel of potential jurors to hear and consider the evidence and to render a fair and impartial verdict. Anyone of you on the jury panel have a problem with doing so?....No....Okay, we'll move to the questioning of the panel. If you've been a juror in a state court trial, you'll notice that we do it differently in federal court. In this part of the trial, what's called voire dire questioning, I'll be the one who asks you questions. In state court the lawyers ask you a lot of loaded questions, all attempting to try their case before it actually starts. I just need to find out who should and who should not be jurors of this important case."

Judge McDermott routinely used voire dire to quickly weed out any perceived 'anti-government types' who might be tempted to vote to set free any criminal defendant, just because the federal government, mistrusted by a juror, had filed the criminal charges. He viewed it as giving the District Attorney a 'level playing field'. Oregon defense counsel saw it as stacking the deck in favor of conviction of persons accused of crimes by the federal government.

Even with federal judges, though, things don't always go as planned. The District Attorney had read the three criminal charges against John Madison to the members of the panel, including the statutes on which the counts were based. Judge McDermott inquired as to their past jury service and anything about that duty that might affect the potential juror's ability to be objective in the people's case against John Madison. He had just started to ask the members of the jury panel if they were related in any way to the Defendant or any of the lawyers, when two panel members raised their hands, at about the same time.

"Oh....yes....potential juror...let's see... Ms. Litz, what's your question? Seeing as how I haven't even started asking my next question. ....And then, let's see....potential juror Hankins, we'll take your question next. Ms. Litz?"

Amanda Litz was a registered nurse, taken away from her ICU patients by her call to jury duty, and none too happy about it. As she listened to the charges being read against John Madison, she pondered why everybody was so upset about a mere speech, when the streets and government buildings had been full of real rebels, breaking windows, burning flags and causing havoc. Before she enrolled in nursing school she had given serious thought to a career in law, as her high school and college teachers and professors had praised her for her analytical mind, telling she 'thought like a lawyer'. Thus, it was that she addressed the Court with a question that did not please the District Attorney.

"Your honor, I don't know the procedure here, whether I can ask a question or not...." The Judge, momentarily distracted by a staff member whispering a message to him, missed his opportunity to head off the question, as panel member Amanda Litz plunged ahead, "Well....ok....it just seems to me that accusing a man of trying to overthrow the government when all he did was just give a speech, for crying out loud, and he apparently wasn't violent in any way, or he would have been charged with that, too....and the law that the DA just read said that the overthrow attempt needs to be by force or violence....I mean....your Honor....why are we here? Who would ever vote to convict another American in such a weak case...seriously....this looks like a big waste of everybody's time....including...."

Crack. Crack. CRACK. "Stop....STOP....No more...." His gavel slamming the bench, the Judge was so flustered he could barely spit out his words. He had been distracted enough by his staffer that he had only just started paying attention to Amanda Litz late in her run-on commentary on the government's case against John Madison. By then, it was too late. The jury panel had been hopelessly corrupted by her comments, as the lawyers like to describe such a case-destroying outburst.

Hoping that possibly he had not heard what he thought he heard once he paid attention, Judge McDermott tried to ignore her. "Thank you, Ms. Litz. We'll let the lawyers sort out all those issues. Mr. Hankins, what was your question? Keep it short, please, I let Ms. Litz go on way too long."

"Well, Judge, it's funny, because I was about to say the very same thing that she just said....how can we convict somebody for advocating the overthrow of the government when there's no allegation of force or viol...."

Crack. "That's quite enough, Mr. Hankins....Quite enough.... Counsel, we'll meet in chambers. This Court stands in recess." ALL RISE.

Judge McDermott held in disdain government prosecutors who had no case, but who appeared to be asking him to use the power of his bench to rescue them from imminent defeat. After listening to the digital recording of potential jurors Litz and Hankins' comments on the government's case, the Judge, his robe freshly hung up, glared at the lawyers assembled in his chambers. "All right. Blame where blame is due. I should have paid attention when that woman started going off on your case, instead of listening to my aide tell me about a decision overturning one of my cases from the 9th Circuit. But, gentlemen, you all have tongues. You could have objected, and shut her up, and got my attention before she polluted the panel.

"Now, we got ourselves a real problem. It would clearly be reversible error to let this panel decide this case after what just happened. Not going to happen, as I'm sending them home. But the government has an even bigger problem. Madame DA, you just got a mini-verdict from two random citizens of this District. They not only don't like your case, they think it's a witch hunt, far as I can tell. My suggestion? Call your Deputy AG in DC, or call the AG himself for that matter, and tell them what happened in Oregon today, in a Court that's historically not been too antagonistic to your cases.

384

"Tell them that the Judge suggested a thorough review of this case....a ....thorough....review.... of this case. Remind them that what was said today will be carried by every newspaper, TV station and radio talk show in this District, from whom the future potential jurors will be selected. That is, if there is a future panel of jurors, as I doubt seriously that this case will ever be tried. I've already denied Mr. Madison's dismissal motion, so I'm not throwing out your case....but....today you saw what will happen if you actually take this poor excuse of a case to a jury. They would likely vote to exonerate before they even have time to order pizza. Again....two words....thorough....review....Got it? Now, you all get out of here. And as for you, Counsel for the Defendant, you can wipe that smile off your face. That woman's destruction of the government's case today was only by the grace of God."

"Your honor, I couldn't agree with you more. Thank you, sir."

It was late Friday afternoon following Judge McDermott's aborted voire dire of the jury panel in the U.S. vs. Madison case. The Clerk of the U.S. District Court for the District of Oregon was preparing to close for the day, when an employee of the U.S. District Attorney, officed in the same building, walked in with a last minute filing. The pleading withdrew all charges against John Madison previously filed by the United States. No media representatives were in the Clerk's office at the time of filing. By Monday, when it became known that the charges had been dismissed, mainstream media justified not reporting the story as being "Friday's news". John Madison was informed by prison authorities in the middle of the day on Saturday that charges against him had been dismissed and that he would be released within 24 hours. John and Debbie Madison wept as they talked by telephone of the answer to their many prayers. Though their son, Jack, was equally happy at the good news, he warned his parents. "Dad and Mom, this thing's not over yet. Not nearly over. As good as this news is, I'm convinced the Madisons are not off the President's radar screen. If what I saw in the eyes of the government visitors to our church services means anything, your son, and this church, are facing significant trouble. Sooner rather than later."

Pastor Jack Madison could not have known then how right he was.

SIXTY TWO

Tyler, Texas

After what seemed like an interminable time away from home, John Madison felt strange sitting in his favorite chair in his favorite room, his comfortable family room. But, he knew he would quickly adjust to being a free man, and to being with Debbie, his wife of twenty-seven years. Surrounded by his bookshelves and able to watch whatever he wanted on his big screen TV, he was thankful for the fact that he no longer faced conviction as a federal felon. But, just as he was relaxing in his new found freedom, his world was shaken by news from Debbie.

"John, now that you've been home for a couple of days, I think I need to tell you something."

"We won the lottery?"

"Very funny, John. You know we don't gamble, though I was tempted when we were low on funds to make our mortgage payment. Praise God for friends who helped us out. My employment by your friend Ralph was a Godsend. Literally."

"I know. The guy walks his talk. So, what's your revelation?"

"Something happened the day before you came home, after it was known that your charges were dismissed and that you were being released. I decided to wait to tell you until you'd settled in and adjusted to life back in Tyler."

"Yes....Okay, so I'm relaxed, but I'm quickly unrelaxing waiting on you tell me what you're slowly leading up to. What is it? Are the kids all right?"

387

"Sure. No, if it was about the kids I would have told you that right off. No, John, this has to do with politics."

"What? Politics? That's what landed me the slammer, Debbie, lest we forget. Politics? Whatever are you talking about?"

"Well, let's start by my telling you that the day before you got home I had some visitors, here at home."

"Visitors? *Who*? *What did they want?*"

"Calm down, John. Let me tell this my way. You get impatient some times, as you may recall my telling you a few hundred times."

"Sorry. Tell it your way. Who came here to see you?"

"The Chairman and Vice Chairman of the Texas Republican Party and the Chairmen of the three largest Tea Party organizations in Texas. They had with them a person who was introduced to me as a representative of the largest financial contributors to the GOP and the Tea Party in the last election cycle."

Of all the things Debbie could have told John Madison, the identity of her visitors was the last thing he expected to hear. For a moment, he couldn't speak, as he was staring at Debbie to see if maybe an emerging smile might betray a mischievous plan to kid him by pretending to have been visited by such a high powered group. No such smile appeared. After twenty seven years of marriage John knew Debbie well, and he could tell that she was deadly serious.

Finally finding his voice, John asked, "Debbie, what could they have possibly wanted? You of all people know that we're not able to contribute any money right now until I get back on my feet, go back to work at the insurance company and make some money."

"No, silly, you think they need our paltry contribution? Even if you were employed? These folks run things in Texas on the conservative side of the political spectrum. No, they don't want your money, they want you."

"Hunh? Me? For what? To fund raise for them? I'm not very good at shaking money out of folks, Debbie. I hope you told them that."

"John, let me get my story told, okay. Patience, my dear."

"Sorry. Again. Go on."

"These men and women are convinced that bad things are going to happen in this country and they want to do something about it. They thi...."

"*Going* to happen? What about what's *already* happened? Over $16 trillion in debt we can't pay back. Historical unemployment. The McAlister Act taking away our Constitutional rights. The CCC snooping into our personal affairs. How much worse could it get, Debbie? What are they talking about?

"They mentioned those problems, but they think the US dollar is headed south, that the basic financial and governmental structures will collapse. That as things get worse, much worse, there will be anarchy in the streets and a tightening down on average citizens by the government such as we've never seen before in this country."

"So? I agree with all that. Some of that I talked about in the last campaign in my speeches that got me into so much trouble. What's their solution?"

"You, John....You."

"Help me out here, Debbie....I'm not following you too well. Maybe too many months in the joint has softened my brain. I'm the *least* of people that could help on any of this. I'm a just-released federal prisoner, with no appreciable assets, except you, my dear, and fortunately I've kept my health. Why, please tell me, did a group like that come here to Tyler....to talk to you?"

"Simple, really, John. These are smart people. They know that if the spouse isn't on board with a major political plan it probably won't happen. They wanted to gauge my reaction before meeting with you and making a formal presentation."

"You still haven't told me what they want me to do, I assume because you know I won't do it. Did you tell them thanks, but no thanks and send them on their way? Politics is what got us in so much trouble, so it's the last thing either one of us would wa...."

"Let me stop you there, John. I told them we would pray about it and get back to them shortly."

"*What?* Why didn't you just tell them we weren't interested? We gave at the office, thanks. Nothing here. Move on."

"Because I think you should seriously think about doing it, John?"

"Doing what? Finally, tell me what you are talking ab...."

"Running for Governor of Texas."

For the second time in their conversation John Madison was tongue-tied. He couldn't put together three coherent words, "Wha?.... You.... I mean.... Your.... Saying.... Governor? ....Come on....You can't....Whew...."

"John, take your time. Think it through. You are the obvious choice, really. In the upcoming election there's a vacancy in the office, so you wouldn't be running against an incumbent. Your name ID, they tell me, is higher than any other Texan, except for the retiring Governor and the state's two sitting US Senators. You're highly respected when the pollsters ask the 'do you trust them' questions. You score hig...."

"Wait. Pollsters? They've taken public opinion polls? Who's paying for all this? Don't they need my permission to ask people about me?"

"John, you're no neophyte. Anyone can take any poll they want...without permission. As for whose paying, I don't know, I didn't think to ask. I would guess the Party is. They have resources and a pretty obvious desire to grab the Governor's office. But, you haven't yet asked the right question, John."

"Alright, Debbie, what question should I be asking?"

"How could John Madison, as Governor of Texas, possibly make any difference in the national scheme of things, how could you have any impact in a nation that appears to be falling apart? I love you, John, and I personally think you would be a great Governor, but, let's face it, anybody of medium competence could fill the office and run the state, but what good would that be long term? You'd just be another politician filling a government job. Sorry."

"No need to be sorry, I agree 100%. Why would you think I would ever want to put us through all that, just to get a job that doesn't pay all that well, and could get me back in the soup again? You know this President would have a coronary if he thought I might actually get elected Governor of Texas, the state that has the second largest economy in the nation, and, I read somewhere that it's the 13th largest economy in the world. They couldn't let somebody like me get elected to run the second larges...."

"What do you think the President would think if you promised in your campaign for Governor to lead Texas out of the Union?"

John Madison normally was quick to speak, but now three times in the same day his wife had stumped him. Debbie began to smile, but John knew this was not her 'I'm just funning you smile', but instead her 'now, finally, you know what I've been holding back' smile.

"John, these folks appear to be serious about re-forming the Republic of Texas, as it was back in 1845, when Texas joined the Union. They've been watching you since you got into trouble with the powers that be in DC, and they think you could possibly be the only Texan, who is well known and respected, and who also has the guts to run on a campaign to withdraw Texas from the Union, and then actually lead the fight....once you were elected. Which, by the way, they firmly feel you would be elected, running on such a platform. Their focus groups show a margin in favor of seceding."

"Humh….Well, there was a Texas Governor not long ago who publically suggested that Texas secede from the Union. He got a lot of high level attention for even suggesting it. I'm not sure if I even favor the idea, to be candid, Debbie. I could see a good argument could be made for returning to the days when Texas was a free and independent sovereign nation, if it's even legal to do that. Didn't the Civil War settle that question? We'd need for some of the really smart people in this state to thoroughly research the legalities of reforming the Republic of Texas. And, as for the polls, I don't doubt its popularity, Debbie. Texans might vote for withdrawal, but that's not the issue. Here's the issue, plain and simple. Can you get along without me, again, if I'm thrown back in the slammer? Because I surely would make myself target one, again."

"We briefly talked about that, John. That's the main reason they came to see me first. If I had shooed them away, the trembling wife fearful of your being arrested and imprisoned, again, we would have neither one of us ever heard from them again."

"But that's not what you conveyed, I take it?"

"No, just the opposite. I told them we would certainly pray about it, but that I'm not automatically opposed to your running."

"Whew. Well, you certainly know how to get a man's attention. A week ago I was worried about whether the prison cooks would serve mystery meat again for dinner, and now I'm hearing my wife tell me she's not against my running for Governor of Texas. Honey, please know that Nelson Mandela I'm not."

"No, but you are John Madison, whom God has placed in a special position. So don't walk away from their proposal out of fear for how it would affect me. I made it through before, and if things turn bad, and they figure out how to take down a candidate for the highest office in Texas, which I seriously doubt they will do, I'll survive the next time too."

"It would be awkward for the White House to explain arresting me again, that's true." John rubbed his temples as he contemplated everything he had just heard. Then he raised his head, looked at his wife and said, "Debbie, we're forgetting one thing in all of this."

"What's that?"

"The kids. Jack and Katie, but mainly Jack, since Katie's overseas where they can't do much, if anything, to her. But Jack is already in the cross-hairs. His worship service last week was monitored by several federal employees, those CCC Conservators in the green shirts. The feds have made it clear that they're looking for cases of so-called hate speech so they can justify all those CCC Conservators running around all over the country. If it becomes known that I'm a candidate for Governor, or even thinking about it, they'll turn up the heat on Jack. Sure enough they will."

"Jack was the first person I called after my visitors dropped their bomb and left."

"Before you even talked to me?"

"Yes. You were in transit and I couldn't talk to you. I had to talk to somebody and Jack was the obvious person. Plus, once they left and I started thinking and praying about what they had said, I also realized that Jack could be directly impacted if you ran for Governor."

"Well, I understand....I think. What did he say?"

"He also wants to pray about it, but his first reaction was for you to go for it. Jack was never a fearful child. If anything, he was our biggest risk-taker. He said that if you're a candidate for Governor it might actually help him, and might scare away the feds from interfering with a pastor who is just preaching the Word, and, whose dad, by the way, is running for Governor of Texas. Jack's a smart boy, as you know, and not one to shy away from a fight."

"That's for sure, Debbie, but I'd first suggest that we go to Dallas and sit down with Jack and Debbie and talk this all through. There's a lot at stake and the four of us need to insure that we know what could happen. I'd like to know what Jack thinks about this Republic of Texas idea."

"We're going there this weekend. Arriving on Saturday for lunch. We watch the kids Saturday night so they can have a date night out, then church on Sunday. Jack's started that series on what the Bible says about perversion. We'll have plenty of time to talk this out on Saturday afternoon."

"Debbie, you never cease to amaze me. Sounds like a plan."

Thus, John and Debbie Madison took their first tentative steps down a path that could lead they knew not where, but they were willing, by faith, to step forward.

End of Book One

Watch For

THE WARNING

The Second Book in the SECOND TERM Trilogy

- Will Pastor Jack Madison be charged and convicted of hate speech law violations?

- Will talk radio and Fox be shut down?

- Will Texas secede from the Union?

- Will widespread rioting erupt in America?

- What end times prophecies will be fulfilled in America?

- Will America support Israel when it's invaded?

- Will radical Islamists use WMDs on the U.S.? How will they use them? Where?

Follow the SECOND TERM series:

www.secondtermbook.com

Sign up for the *Second Term Newsletter* and receive notification when the second book of the series is released.

See next page for Chapter One of Book Two

ONE

Dallas, Texas

Jack Madison's Senior Accountability Group had not met, due to the holidays, for the last few weeks. During that period the world had witnessed the signing of the historic Path to Peace Agreement on the front lawn of the White House. Israel, and its Arab neighbors were now at peace. Soon after the signing, Pastor Madison e-mailed the members of his men's study group to advise them that their assignment was changed. They would instead look at the 223 Daughter of Babylon/Babylon the Great verses they had been studying to see if the verses revealed anything about Israel being at peace. He told the members of the group that he looked forward to a lively and informative discussion.

As a result, no one missed the evening meeting of the group, nor was anyone late. "Men, I suggest we pray before we discuss this subject. We really need wisdom from above, though, of course, we always do....Lord, we're looking to You to give us wisdom, as You promised You would do if we asked for it. Guide us as we look into your Word. In Your name....oh....and Lord, thanks again for yesterday's good news about my dad, and his release from prison, I know many prayers were answered by what You did to get his charges dismissed. Thanks, Lord. Amen."

Jim, as was his norm, kicked off the discussion, "Whew, Pastor. Ya think we've got a few things to talk about? I about fell out of my lazyboy when I saw the President announce at Williamsburg that Israel had actually agreed to sign a peace treaty."

Max quickly followed, "Yeah, and incredibly they also agreed to give up some of their land. I couldn't believe it. Pastor, didn't you give a sermon last year quoting several verses that warned Israel *not* to give up its land?"

"Yes, Max, and I also quoted the verses that warn the nations of the world not to force Israel to divide the land."

"None of this would mean anything, we wouldn't even be talking about Israel signing a peace treaty, if God hadn't brought Israel back to its land, as He prophesied He would do, right, Pastor Jack?"

"Right. Ezekiel told Israel in chapter 37 that God would someday bring the nation back into its same land. Ever since He brought them back in 1948 Israel has been fighting just to stay alive. Egypt finally stopped kicking Israel around in 1978, but with the changes in Egyptian leadership, who knows if that'll change? With the new peace treaty, we now have a chance to see even more prophecies fulfilled in our times."

"What do you mean, Pastor? Which prophecies?"

"Max, I'm talking about Ezekiel's prophecies, in chapter 38, that Israel would sign a peace agreement and will dwell safely in what he called a land recovered from war. He even says Israel, during this time of peace, will be peaceful and unsuspecting."

"Unsuspecting of what?"

"That's where it gets very interesting. Ezekiel prophesies that when Israel is dwelling safely and unsuspecting, after it's in a peace treaty period having recovered from war, then....wham....its invaded by its treaty partners. He even lists the nations that will invade Israel. All of them are either today Muslim, interestingly enough, or, in the case of Russia, with a large Muslim population. He lists Persia in the invading force, which is today known as Iran. Iran has been working on nuclear weapons for some time. Iran's streets have been filled with Iranians crying out for DEATH TO ISRAEL and DEATH TO AMERICA. Other nations are listed that will attack Israel including Libya, which is also Muslim."

"Whoa....so Israel gets into a peace agreement, which you told us in your sermon that God always told them not to do, not to lean on other countries, then when Israel's at peace, it gets invaded? Right? Don't they ever learn?"

"Pastor, is this the same peace agreement that the Antichrist makes and then breaks?"

"No, Max, it's pretty clear that these are two different end times peace agreements. The one with the Antichrist is broken when the Antichrist commits the abomination of desolation, which we don't know exactly what that will look like, in the middle of the last seven year period. The Ezekiel peace treaty, on the other hand is breached when Russia and Iran and their Muslim buddies invade Israel. Plus it takes seven months to clean up the bodies after the Ezekiel invasion, which isn't consistent with what scripture tells us about the final battle at Armageddon."

Jim responded, "Yeah, I can see that there are two different agreements with different treaty partners and different outcomes. What happens when Russia and Iran invade? I didn't get that far in my reading."

"That's ok. What happens is what I wanted to focus on this week, especially now that the treaty's been signed, and Israel is now starting to dwell in safety."

"And unsuspecting."

"Yes. Jim asked what happens when the Russian/Arab invasion takes place? Ezekiel describes a land invasion of Israel from its north, which makes sense because Russia and Iran would both enter Israel from that direction."

"Why a land invasion? Why not just throw a nuke or two at Tel Aviv or Jerusalem?"

"Ezekiel describes a several day land invasion. Maybe it's because Israel contains several Muslim holy sites, mainly the Dome of the Rock, as you know. In any case, it gives the world some time, as it watches this unfolding major invasion of Israel, to decide how each nation will respond."

"Pastor, you said the world would be watching, but don't almost all of the nations of the world hate Israel, or could be expected to just look the other way?"

"Max, you have described the state of the globe today when it comes to Israel. God loves Israel. The world, though, generally hates Israel, maybe in part because they know that God loves Israel. Here's what I'd like us to focus on for our next study. The 223 verses we've been pursuing tell us that the Daughter of Babylon/Babylon the Great will betray Israel when it's invaded by Russia and Iran and their allies. In our study for next week we'll cover your prior assignment that I changed because of the peace treaty with Israel. Look at the 223 verses to search for prophecy clues and we'll see if any other nation besides the US could be fulfill the role of Babylon the Great/the Daughter of Babylon. Plus, men, while you're looking at the 223 verses, concentrate on the verses that tell us what happens at the *end* of the peace period that just started recently at the White House when Israel signed the Path to Peace Agreement. "

"So, Pastor, we should look for verses that reveal what will happen to Israel, and I guess also the world, when this new peace treaty gets broken when Israel is invaded by Russia and Iran and their Muslim allies, right?"

"Exactly. God gave us clues to the future for a reason. He did it for more than to just show us that He's omnipotent. He must intend for us to understand and apply what we learn. So, let's learn."

"Pastor, I hesitate to say this, but...."

"Go on, Jim....what?"

"I was really excited when I saw Israel signing the peace treaty. Now....I'm not so sure that it's going to be a big plus for Israel, or for America, for that matter. If America is the Daughter of Babylon....well...I don't even want to think about it, when I read what *prophecy says will happen* to that end times nation for betraying Israel. This is serious stuff, Pastor....Know what I mean? Am I missing something here?"

"That's the subject of next week's study. Pray, read and research. Then we'll look into the only book that can accurately tell us the future, the future of Israel, and increasingly, I believe, revealing to us America's future. See you then. In the meantime, God bless."

ABOUT THE AUTHOR

John Price was, until recently, an Indianapolis attorney who was active in political and governmental matters. He now devotes his time to writing. He and his wife live in Florida. The author may be contacted at:

john@secondtermbook.com or

john@endofamericabook.com.

For a non-fiction look at

America in prophecy:

www.endofamericabook.com

CPSIA information can be obtained at www.ICGtesting.com
Printed in the USA
LVOW061128100212

268091LV00002B/4/P